Plant Communities of New Jersey

Plant Communities of New Jersey

A Study in Landscape Diversity

Beryl Robichaud Collins and
Karl H. Anderson

Rutgers University Press
New Brunswick, New Jersey

Library of Congress Cataloging-in-Publication Data

Robichaud, Beryl.
    Plant communities of New Jersey : a study in landscape diversity /
Beryl Robichaud Collins and Karl H. Anderson.
      p.   cm.
    Rev. ed. of: Vegetation of New Jersey. 1973
    Includes bibliographical references (p.   ) and index.
    ISBN 0-8135-2070-3 (cloth) — ISBN 0-8135-2071-1 (pbk.)
      1. Plant communities—New Jersey. 2. Botany—New Jersey—
Ecology. 3. Phytogeography—New Jersey. I. Anderson, Karl,
1938–   . II. Robichaud, Beryl. Vegetation of New
Jersey. III. Title.
QK175.R63   1989
581.5′247′09749—dc20   93-36695
                                    CIP

Second paperback printing, 2000

Contents

IV   The Future

Illustrations

Tables

Preface

More than two decades have passed since the first edition of this book was published under the title *Vegetation of New Jersey*. In these years both global environmental conditions and the degree of public interest in the quality of the environment have changed dramatically. Two decades ago reports of acid rain depositions and of air pollution caused by excessive ground-level ozone were nonexistent; predictions of global warming and depletion of the protective ozone shield in the stratosphere had yet to come. Few were concerned about loss of biological diversity.

Two decades ago in New Jersey 10 percent fewer people were living in the state and far fewer automobiles traveled the highways. Superfund toxic sites were unknown, at least to the public. The state Department of Environmental Protection issued no daily air pollution health alerts, and no official record of endangered plant species existed. The leapfrogging of development into rural areas was barely underway, and more than 180,000 acres of land now covered with houses, office buildings, and shopping malls were still farmland or other open space.

This new edition gives us a snapshot of the state's landscape—its natural habitats and types of plant communities—as we approach the year 2000. The background for understanding why the vegetation of New Jersey is what it is has been updated; even ecological theory has changed in the last twenty years—biological communities are not as stable as ecologists once thought. There are changes too in the elements that influence the natural vegetation. The book contains a new soils classification map, current climatic data, and an update of the biological influences, human and other, that have an impact on the state's natural vegetation. Modifications also have been made to the classification of the state's upland forest vegetation.

From the ridgetops in the northwest to the southern coastal sand dunes, New Jersey still has an astonishing diversity of habitats and plant community types. The new edition contains added coverage of the state's plant communities, particularly those found in South Jersey. More complete descriptions of the composition of communities are also included and additional site locations identified. Also, to simplify reference for the reader, former appendix material on where to see the typical plant communities is now woven into the body of the text.

Finally, reflecting the worldwide concern about environmental deterioration, the last chapter focuses on current and foreseeable threats to the landscape of New Jersey—both those that arise within the state and those from global sources.

It is our hope that this book will further the understanding of New Jersey's natural landscape, its habitats, and its natural vegetation and, in so doing, stimulate greater concern for its future.

Acknowledgments

This book has been made possible by the accumulation of information about New Jersey's natural landscape over a long period of time. Detailed descriptions of the geology, soils, and forests of the state were recorded in bulletins and annual reports issued by the State Geologist in the years 1870 to 1917. Also available in published form are the late-nineteenth- and early-twentieth-century findings of well-known botanists, including N. L. Britton, Witmer Stone, and John W. Harshberger. Later work by field botanists such as Louis Hand and the research findings of Dr. Silas Little of the Northeastern Forest Experiment Station, a unit of the U.S. Department of Agriculture, were of great value.

The studies of many others were used as background for the book, particularly those of graduate students at Rutgers University and state colleges whose research work involved some aspect of New Jersey vegetation. The list is too long to enumerate, but to all of them the authors express appreciation for their part in the knowledge of the various aspects of New Jersey's natural landscape.

Various members of the New Jersey Department of Environmental Protection and Energy were extremely helpful in providing information for this edition. George Pierson and George Koeck of the Bureau of Forest Management updated us on the condition of New Jersey forests and provided photos. David Snyder and Robert Cartica of the Office of Natural Lands Management furnished information on endangered plants, and Robert Stokes of the Green Acres Program provided helpful background on open-space needs.

We thank Dr. David Smart, Ronnie Taylor, and Alan Albanir of the U.S. Soil Conservation Service for their cooperation in preparing for this edition a new classification map of New Jersey soils and for making their photo morgue available for our use. In addition, special thanks go to Dr. J. C. F. Tedrow for his continued interest and help in the preparation of both the first and second editions of this book.

To Judy Elchin we owe thanks for her patient and careful execution of all the charts and maps contained in the book.

Finally, we dedicate this book to the memory of the late Dr. Murray F. Buell, who encouraged the research that led to this book and who co-authored its first edition. Dr. Buell founded the study of ecology at Rutgers University, and he and his students made extensive studies of the structure and dynamics of New Jersey's vegetation. Named the country's Eminent Ecologist of 1970 by the Ecological Society of America, Dr. Buell was also a distinguished teacher. He and his wife, Dr. Helen Foot Buell, guided many students in their studies of ecology. The senior author is very grateful to have been one of these.

Plant Communities of New Jersey

Introduction

New Jersey, the fifth smallest of the fifty states of the United States, has a land area of only 7,509 square miles. Measured at its greatest length, from High Point, near the northwestern boundary, to the southeastern tip of Cape May, the state extends 166 miles. At its greatest width from east to west the state is only 57 miles wide; in midstate this distance narrows, and a line drawn from Trenton on the west to the Raritan Bay at the northeast would measure only 32 miles.

According to census figures, the 1990 population of New Jersey totaled 7,730,188, an average of 1,029 persons per square mile. This makes New Jersey the most densely populated of the fifty states. Perhaps more startling is the fact that New Jersey has more people per square mile than India, Japan, or the Netherlands, areas that are usually considered to be overcrowded.

Economically, New Jersey is highly industrialized and ranks seventh among all states in the value of gross state products. It is first in the manufacture of pharmaceuticals, its leading industry, and second in chemicals. The state's other important industrial products include electrical equipment, petroleum, and plastics. New Jersey ranks third as home to corporate headquarters, which are scattered over the landscape.

The relative importance of agriculture has been declining sharply, and New Jersey is losing its grip on its title as the Garden State, but still 18 percent of the total land is used for poultry and dairy farming or for growing vegetables, fruit, grain, hay, and ornamental plants. Of these, nursery and greenhouse products, and sod are the leading commodity groups, and in 1990 the state ranked second in blueberry and third in cranberry production. Farm stands stocked with Jersey produce like tomatoes, peaches, apples, pumpkins, and berries are popular stopping places for state residents.

Mining and quarrying operations, while less significant in the state's economy, show their imprint on the New Jersey landscape principally in the form of traprock quarries and sand and gravel pits.

To accommodate these economic activities as well as the travel needs of its population, the state has built more miles of highway per square mile than any other state. Its transportation network carries the densest flow of traffic in the world.

In spite of its relatively small land mass, its dense population, its advanced state of economic development, and its highly developed transportation facilities, New Jersey still has extensive tracts of natural vegetation. Even more surprising is the great variety in the vegetation—the landscape diversity—that now exists in the state. Although the main purpose of this book is to describe the vegetation of New Jersey in terms of its appearance and plant composition, an equally important goal is to explain why the vegetation is now what it is. The authors hope that a fuller appreciation and understanding of the present natural landscape will stimulate more interest in and concern about what we may leave for those who live after us. It is the people who have the ultimate responsibility for the use of land resources and for the selection of actions that will have a significant impact on the future landscape of the state. Thus an informed public is necessary to ensure that wise decisions are made today to preserve a legacy for future generations.

To achieve these purposes, this book provides, first, background for understanding why the vegetation of New Jersey is what it is today; second, a description of the present plant communities of the state; and finally, a look into the future of the landscape of New Jersey.

Throughout the text each plant is referred to by its common English name if one exists; Appendix III contains a two-way cross-reference between the common and scientific (Latin) names for each plant. No attempt is made to describe the botanical features of the hundreds of plants mentioned in the text. Instead, a list of references on plant identification is given in Appendix II. Included in Appendix I is a guide to locations where the vegetation types of New Jersey can be seen.

References and Source Material

New Jersey State Department of Commerce and Economic Development. 1992. *New Jersey Garden State: Facts and Fun—1992; New Jersey: You Should See Us Now, 1990–1992; New Jersey: Facts and Facets.*

New Jersey State Department of Agriculture. 1991. *New Jersey Agriculture Annual Report.*

Part I

Understanding a Natural Landscape

Chapter 1

❧ *Why the Vegetation of New Jersey Is What It Is*

This chapter sets forth definitions and fundamental concepts of vegetation as a basis for understanding what follows in the rest of the book. The basic concepts, relationships, and characteristics of vegetation described here can be applied to other parts of the earth as well as to New Jersey.

Definitions

The word "vegetation" is used to refer to the total plant cover of a region, whatever its scale. Thus, we may talk about the vegetation of 1 acre, of a whole state, or of the whole country. The term "natural vegetation" in a strict sense suggests plant cover that has never been influenced by processes other than natural ones. However, because the impact of human actions has been so all-pervasive on our landscape, the phrase "natural vegetation" is most commonly used today to refer to the plant cover that, while subject to disturbance by humans, grows and develops without their purposeful intervention.

The plant cover of any one locale comprises different types (or species) of plants that grow together. Simply described, a plant species is a particular type of plant that maintains its identity because it generally does not interbreed with other plant species. For example, a tree such as the white oak or sugar maple, a shrub such as the bayberry, and a flowering herb such as the common daisy are all examples of different plant species. Many plant species are known by a common English name, but botanists also identify each by a scientific name. The scientific label for a plant consists of two Latin words, the first classifying a plant by its genus category (like the surname of a person) and the second identifying each specific type of plant within a genus by its species name (like the first name of a person). For example, the scientific name for a common tree in New Jersey, the white oak, is *Quercus alba; Quercus* is the genus name used to identify all oak trees and *alba* is the word that designates the species of white oak, as contrasted, for example, with the red oak, which is known as *Quercus rubra*.

The word "system" has been with us for many years. However, only in recent decades has the word been widely used by biologists, who are discovering living parallels to the solar system—a system composed of the sun, nine planets, and all other celestial bodies that orbit the sun. In such terms as "biological system," "solar system," and even "stereo system," the word "system" refers to a specific group of objects related to each other by mutual interactions. For example, the planet Earth is only one of many objects in the solar system, and it interacts with the sun, and other planets and solar bodies. A speaker is just one component of a stereo system, and to serve any purpose, it must interact with other parts of the system.

An ecosystem is a particular type of biological system in which plants, animals, and environmental factors are related to each other and affected by their interactions. Thus, the vegetation of any region or area can and should be viewed as a component, and only one component, of a particular ecosystem. The word "ecosystem" is derived from "ecology," which is the study of the interconnections among living organisms and their environment.

Vegetation as Part of a System—the Ecosystem

Since life began on this planet, living organisms have constantly interacted with each other and with environmental factors. These interactions have continually caused changes to the organisms themselves as well as to elements of their environment. Ecologists usually identify five ecosystem components that have interacting relationships—geologic and soil features, climatic elements, plants, animals, and humans. The human species is distinguished from other living organisms as an ecosystem component by its unique power and disposition to alter and even to exploit the other parts of the system.

Because this book is concerned with vegetation, interactions among the five ecosystem components are viewed primarily from the standpoint of a single component—plants. But the reader should keep in mind that important and interesting interrelationships exist among other components of the system—between climatic elements and soil-forming processes and between climatic elements and humans, for example.

Relationships Among Geologic and Soil Features and Vegetation

Geologic processes of mountain building, erosion, and glaciation sculpture our landforms by carving out ridges, hills, valleys, and even basins for lakes. Relief of land has an impact on vegetation because of its influence on drainage and exposure.

Even more important to vegetation, however, are the geologic processes that, interacting with climatic elements and living organisms, produce the soil in which plants grow. Soil, which is nothing more than disintegrated rock particles modified by plants, water, and air and combined with decomposed organic material, is the medium in which plants root and obtain their nourishment.

Soils differ in their water-holding capacities, in their supplies of mineral elements, and in their properties that affect the availability of nutrients to plants. One of the soil characteristics that affect the water-holding capacity is texture, that is, the relative proportions of the sand, silt, and clay particles that make up soil. Water quickly drains through sand particles but adheres tightly to the smaller clay particles. The result is that while very sandy soils tend to be dry, those with a lot of clay often are waterlogged.

Soil substrates vary widely not only in water-holding capacity but also in the type and amount of mineral elements most needed by plants—such as nitrogen, phosphorus, calcium, magnesium, potassium, and iron. Each plant species exhibits a specific range of need and tolerance for particular nutrients as well as for other factors such as soil acidity. Thus a plant species that grows and reproduces successfully on one type of soil may not be able to exist under different conditions. With too little or too much of a specific element in the soil or too low or too high a level of acidity, as measured by a scale known as the pH scale, a plant will die.

While soil characteristics have a great impact on plants, plant cover, in turn, influences the process of soil formation. Soil organic material is derived from dead plant roots and from decomposed leaves and branches, as well as from the decayed remains of animals. In this way vegetation can significantly alter the characteristics of soil. The plants of a grassland leave a different imprint on soil than do trees of a forest, and even different forest types have distinctive impacts on soil.

Relationships Between Climatic Elements and Vegetation

Perhaps most easily understood is the impact of climatic elements on plants; even good nurseries dealing with plants for the home gardener are careful to outline the water, temperature, and exposed requirements or tolerances of particular plant species. The three most important climatic factors affecting plant growth are temperature, precipitation, and light.

To plants, as to all living organisms, temperature is important because it controls the rate of chemical reactions necessary for existence and growth. Every physiological process involves temperature limits above and below which the process ceases and an optimum temperature at which it proceeds at a maximum rate. For example, little or no plant growth may take place during a hot summer day, and each plant species has an optimum temperature for germination of its seeds. With respect to temperature and to all other climatic factors, plant species differ in their tolerance to extremes and their optimum for growth and for reproduction. Thus, while a species may flourish under the temperature, soil moisture, and other climate conditions in one geographic region or even on one site within a region, it may be unable to reproduce successfully or even to exist in another region or site having a single environmental condition outside its tolerance.

Precipitation, whether in the form of rain, snow, or atmospheric humidity, is important to vegetation because some water is needed for all plant life processes. Water is required as a medium for chemical reactions and for the transport of mineral ions, both of which take place in every green plant. Lack of water often hinders plant growth, as can be observed when houseplants wilt from lack of water. As in the case of temperature, different plant species have different requirements and tolerances for water.

The water that a plant uses comes mostly from soil moisture, which the plant absorbs through its roots. While much rainwater is lost to plants because of runoff and evaporation, precipitation provides most of the soil moisture used by natural vegetation.

The third important climatic factor affecting plants is light. Each species has an optimum light requirement, because light is essential for the process of photosynthesis, by which a plant produces the food for its existence and growth. With too little or too much light, a plant may die. The seasonal differences in length of day that vary from one latitude to another are partly responsible for some of the geographical differences in vegetation.

Wind and atmospheric composition are among the other climatic factors that have an impact on vegetation. To some plants wind serves as the most important mechanism for the carrying of pollen from flower to flower and thus for aiding plant fertilization. Wind may also carry seeds from one site to another, making possible a wider dissemination of particular plants. But excessive wind can damage and kill plant buds and stems as well as reduce the amount of soil moisture available for plant development.

Recently, attention has been focused on the effect of atmospheric pollutants on vegetation. Scientists are finding that excessive pollutants in the air weaken and even kill plants as well as humans. When a green plant takes in the carbon dioxide necessary for photosynthesis and the oxygen for its metabolic processes, it also absorbs gaseous or particulate forms of matter originating from industrial and automobile emissions and other atmospheric contaminants. These may kill or weaken leaves or other parts of sensitive plants.

In all these ways climatic factors influence vegetation, while, to a lesser degree, vegetation has an impact on climate. As an example, the temperature on hot days and nights is considerably lower in a forest than in a nearby urban area; wooded areas also act to decrease the force of heavy winds.

Relationships Between Animals and Vegetation

Ecosystem interactions between animals and plants are quite easy to observe even in areas settled by humans. This is particularly true of the so-called food-chain relationships—which is the ecological term for the "who-eats-whom" relationships in nature. For example, leaves of trees that line residential streets in New Jersey may be eaten by cankerworms or other foliage-eating insects, which in turn may be eaten by birds such as the red-eyed vireo. And if not alert, the vireo may be devoured by a hawk. Plants are the initial food source in all food chains, for in spite of the great accomplishments of the human species, the fact remains that only plants are able to convert inorganic materials of carbon dioxide and water to organic material called food.

Animals have both favorable and unfavorable effects on vegetation. Beneficial effects stem from the multitude of organisms that live in the soil. Some, like earthworms, improve the texture of the soil, and others aid in the decomposition of organic material. Animals also help plants reproduce themselves. Flying insects and birds carry pollen from flower to flower assisting in fertilization, a necessary step in plant reproduction. Seeds develop from the fertilized flowers, and these may be embedded in berries or nuts eaten by animals, or even barbed structures that easily attach themselves to animals. All three of these provide the means by which the seeds can be transported outside the range of the parent plant by a bird, squirrel, or other animal. Thus, animals help ensure successful continuation of some plant species.

Unfortunately, not all relationships between animals and plants are beneficial to plants. Leaf-chewing insects can completely defoliate small plants and even whole trees. Over a period of years, such insects may completely defoliate and kill an old, established tree in a natural forest. Other insects, such as the elm bark beetle, may carry a lethal parasite from tree to tree, causing the spread of fatal tree disease. Too much grazing or browsing either by domestic animals such as cattle or by wild animals such as deer can alter severely the plant composition of natural vegetation.

Some unfavorable animal–plant relationships have been caused or amplified by human activities. In the past, in the absence of humans, balances were often maintained by natural processes. When the population of a particular insect or animal destructive to vegetation grew too large, it often fell rapidly by starvation (because the local food supply was used up) or by predator control. As will be discussed later, when humans upset the balance of animal–plant relationships, the results may be disastrous to natural vegetation. This is evidenced in New Jersey as well as in other parts of the country and the world.

Relationships Between Human Activities and Vegetation

Worldwide, there is a growing interest in and awareness of the relationship to human beings to the components of their ecosystem—climate, geologic and soil features, animals, and vegetation. Regarding only the relationships of humans and plants, several points are obvious. Without natural vegetation, humans in their present form would not have developed at all. This is true for several reasons. First, oxygen in the form needed for human respiration did not always exist in the atmosphere, developing only after the advent of plant life, as a product of plant photosynthesis. Next, humans thus far have been unable to duplicate the photosynthetic activity of plants whereby nonliving materials are transformed into organic food. Thus we depend upon plants as the initial source for all our food as well as for much of the material used for our shelter and clothing. We may eat plants directly or indirectly—indirectly when we eat animals that in turn have depended on plants as the initial source of food in their food chain. While humans are totally dependent on plant life for their existence, their actions from the beginning of time on earth have been destructive to vegetation.

Many human activities have an impact on natural vegetation. Some of these are obvious, and some are not. It is evident, for example, that natural vegetation is destroyed when land is used for agricultural crops, for dwellings, for industrial buildings, or for networks of highways. The accommodation of a larger and larger world population together with the trend toward more industrialization and urbanization means that each year less natural vegetation is left. That which remains is fragmented into smaller and smaller pieces that do not have as much biological diversity as the original larger tracts.

Less obvious are other actions that have an impact on vegetation. For example, whereas forests that are cut over lightly may show little change in species composition, lumbering activities that involve more extensive cutting of trees may change the composition of a particular forest so that it becomes quite different from what it was before it was first cut. Extensive grazing of domestic animals also causes changes in natural vegetation, and the consequences are an impoverishment in the plant life of grazed land. This has happened in many parts of the western United States as well as in Europe.

In still other ways humans have had a dramatic impact on natural vegetation. For example, by the use of fire, humans have greatly modified natural vegetation. It is believed that our ancestors learned to create fire hundreds of thousands of years ago. Having acquired this skill, they quickly became great arsonists and caused fires throughout the land.

Primitive humans caused broad fire damage by abandoning campfires then ignited surrounding vegetation, and they also probably started fires on purpose to facilitate hunting. As a result, extensive areas of the Old and New Worlds were burned many thousands of years ago.

In New Jersey the Indians burned the land to clear it for agriculture and settlement, to drive game in hunting, or to keep the forest open for travel. Frequent fires have greatly modified the natural vegetation in the state. This is so for several reasons. By nature of their bark, some trees are more insulated from heat than others and are therefore less suscep-tible to fire damage. Seeds of some plants are destroyed by fire, whereas the seeds of others germinate more quickly when exposed to the heat of fire. Also, some trees and shrubs are able to sprout quickly after fires, while others have no resprouting capability (Figure 1-1). New Jersey of-fers excellent examples of the effect of fire on vegetation, and these are described in Part III of this book.

The twentieth century brought a new dimension to the impact of hu-man activities on the landscape—the widespread contamination of the atmosphere, water, and soil—the results of which can be seen every-where. Atmospheric pollution is causing the dieback of forests; pollu-tants have spoiled rivers and streams, killing off desirable aquatic species; and erosion or contamination have left soils without nutrients to support vegetative regrowth. Another source of serious damage to vegetation stems from the indiscriminate use of pesticides. These have been designed to control destructive insects or fungus diseases of plants, but in many cases the results have had a boomerang effect, causing greater rather than less insect or disease damage to plants because they interfere with the balance inherent in nature's food chains.

Ecosystem Characteristics

All ecosystems, those in New Jersey as well as those in other parts of the world, have two characteristics common to all living biological systems. These characteristics, depicted graphically in Figure 1-2, are as follows:

1. Each ecosystem is continually changing in time. In any one place on earth, the interactions among climatic elements, geologic and soil-forming processes, animals, plant populations, and humans are not the same today as they were yesterday. In all ecosystems each of these com-ponents is changing continually, although at differing rates from time to time. Thus, the natural environment may be said to be "dynamic," mean-ing that climate, landforms and soils, animals, plants, and all human beings changed each day in the past and will continue to do so in the future.

2. Each ecosystem is distinctive: that is, the conditions in any one place, such as one small area within a state, are not exactly the same as in any other area. This is because particular combinations of climate, geologic history, and interactions of animals, plants, and humans found

Figure 1-1. Multiple stems sprouting from the stump of a chestnut oak tree that previously had been cut back to the ground. Not all tree species have this ability to "resprout" after being cut or burned back.

at any one place will not be exactly duplicated in any other place. Thus, ecosystems and their components vary in space.

These two characteristics apply to each component in an ecosystem as well as to the total ecosystem itself. Thus it should be expected that the plants growing on any one site will change in time, thereby resulting in a continual natural change of vegetation. Ecologists may call this process of change in vegetation with time "ecosystem development"; if the change in vegetation occurs because a site has been disturbed, however, the process is often called "succession." In addition, the plants

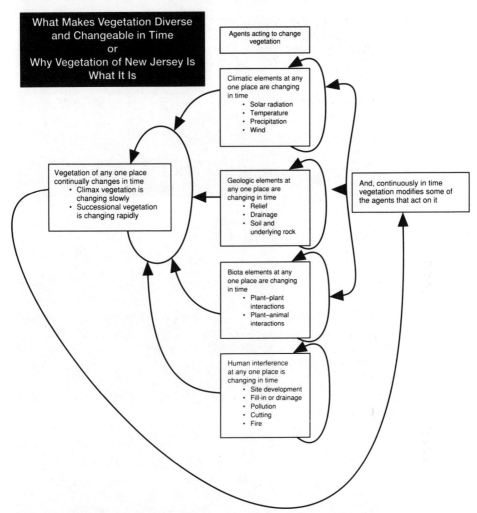

Figure 1-2. Schematic diagram showing ecosystem relationships that cause change in natural vegetation over time. Because these relationships also differ from one place to another, there is spatial variety (diversity) in natural vegetation.

growing on any one site are not exactly the same as those growing on another site, thereby making for variety in vegetation. This variety is called "diversity." These two notions—vegetation change and diversity— are among the more important concepts of ecology, and knowledge of them is necessary to an understanding of vegetation of New Jersey or of any other region.

The Natural Change of Vegetation in Time

Without human interference the vegetation of any particular site does change in time. This can easily be verified by observations of real events. For example, Dr. Gily Bard, an ecologist who studied land near New

Figure 1-3. The process of natural change of vegetation in fields left abandoned. This change is called succession.

1st year of field abandonment Field in Somerset County that was plowed and left unseeded in early summer is covered in late fall by an annual herb, wild mustard. (Photo by Dr. Mary Leck.)

3 years after abandonment Field is densely covered with perennial herbs, mostly goldenrod with some fleabane. (Photo by Dr. Mary Leck.)

6 years after abandonment Red cedar trees have invaded the field, along with a few multiflora rose, sumac, and pin cherry. Queen Anne's lace and goldenrod are the dominant herbs. (Photo by Dr. Mary Leck.)

Brunswick, New Jersey, that once had been cultivated for agriculture but then left idle, found that the following natural changes took place (Figure 1-3).

When a field that had been cultivated is left abandoned, seeds that have been dormant in the soil or that have come from plants growing in nearby areas start to germinate. The first plants to grow successfully are

12 years after abandonment Red cedar trees are abundant, and a wild grass (little bluestem) has replaced the pioneer herbs. Field is in Somerset County but is not the same as that shown in the first three photos.

About 30 years after abandonment Red cedar trees are still dominant, with bayberry, blackberry, and sumac shrubs in the foreground. Red maple, black cherry, and pin oak trees are present and eventually will shade out the lower growing red cedar trees and the shrubs. Field is in Mercer County.

About 50 years after abandonment A woodland now occupies this abandoned field in Mercer County. Red maple, black cherry, sassafras, and pin oak trees are abundant and have shaded out most of the lower-growing red cedar trees and the shrubs except along the edges of the field.

those with short lives. Of these, ragweed, the annual plant whose pollen causes the hay fever allergy, is the most abundant. Annual plants are so named because they live only one year and then die. Other common invaders in the first year are the wild radish and wintercress; the mass presence of the latter can often be seen in May and June as a blanket of yellow blooms on an abandoned field in New Jersey.

By the second year other plants develop in the field, such as the goldenrods and asters. These are perennial plants that have a lifespan of more than 2 years, and their continued spread over several years results in their gaining almost complete dominance after a period of time. Other herbs start to grow in the field, one of the most abundant being a high-growing wild grass known as little bluestem. Less common but conspicuous for their flowers are the herbs known as Queen Anne's lace, common mullein, daisy, and black-eyed susan.

For as many as 10 years, the mixture of low-growing herbaceous plants gives the appearance of a natural flower garden. Then the scene changes, for seeds of woody shrubs and trees successfully germinate in the field and develop into plants that grow taller than the herbs. In mid New Jersey the first woody plant to show up conspicuously in an abandoned field is the red cedar tree, a narrow, pyramid-shaped tree with small evergreen leaves that remain on the tree the year round. As these grow to a maximum height of about 30 feet, they are joined by seedlings of other trees such as the red maple, wild black cherry, and sassafras. In addition, lower-growing shrubs such as bayberry occupy places in the field, and scattered thickets of shrubs and young trees interwoven by vines such as poison ivy become conspicuous. In 20 to 30 years, either the little bluestem grass crowds out the showy flowering herbs that once grew so abundantly in the field or the trees shade them out. Finally, in 50 to 60 years' time, the piece of ground that had been an abandoned field will be changed into an open woodland of fairly tall trees.

Some of the reasons for natural succession as just described become obvious when one remembers that all ecosystem components change in time. For example, as taller plants occupy a site, less light falls on the surface of the soil. This makes the environment less favorable for plants that have a high requirement for light. Some plants cannot reproduce or even develop successfully in shady conditions and thus die off as trees grow up around them. On the other hand, many trees that can develop under shady conditions cannot seed themselves in an abandoned field until it has first been occupied by herbaceous plants. Changes in vegetation also are accompanied by alterations in soil conditions and in climatic conditions close to the ground (the microclimate). There is a constant struggle or competition among plants for resources of water, soil nutrients, light, or whatever may be in short supply. Slight changes in environmental conditions can favor one or more species over others.

As long as changes are occurring relatively rapidly in the plant growth of a particular site, the vegetation continues to be referred to as "successional" vegetation. On the other hand, if and when a point is reached at which change becomes extremely slow, the plant growth may be called a "climax" type of vegetation. For example, the extensive forests of spruce and fir trees that cover a great part of the undisturbed land of Canada are considered climax vegetation.

Until recently many ecologists believed that a so-called climax stage

Figure 1-4. Blowing down many older trees, a windstorm created a gap in this Atlantic white cedar swamp forest in Lebanon State Forest. The forest floor in the gap is exposed to open sunlight, creating different habitat conditions for plant growth from those that had previously existed. (Photo by the N. J. Bureau of Forest Management.)

of vegetation represents an end to succession and an almost permanent type of vegetation, assuming no drastic climatic changes. Climax types of vegetation were said to be stable, with the community populations at an equilibrium point. Furthermore, they believed that given enough time all ecosystems in a region would show succession to a single climax type controlled by the regional climate.

Today most ecologists talk less about stability and equilibrium of ecosystems and acknowledge instead the dynamic nature of natural communities that are continuously being subject to disturbances from natural as well as human sources. For example, a severe windstorm that can uproot large trees or an insect infestation that can completely defoliate large trees may create a gap in a forest canopy, allowing sunlight to penetrate the forest floor (Figure 1-4). In this patch of sunlight a group of species other than those typical of the mature forest may flourish. A forest ecosystem then may consist of different patches of vegetation. For this reason, in place of a "balance-of-nature" view, many ecologists have adopted a "flux-of-nature" view, in which an ecosystem is seen as a mosaic of variegated pieces that change character and function over time.

Diversity: The Change of Vegetation in Space

The distinctiveness or individuality of each ecosystem stems from the spatial differences that exist from place to place in climatic factors, geologic and soil features, and interrelationships of animals, plants, and humans. This is what creates variety or diversity in vegetation. Because each plant species has different requirements and different ranges of tolerance regarding various environmental factors, we should expect some variety in plant composition as changes occur in environmental conditions. Obviously, then, the degree of variation in vegetation from one geographical location to another (or even from one site to another within the same geographical area) will depend in great part on the relative differences in climate, geologic and soil features, animal–plant interrelationships, and the extent of human interference. More will be said about this in Chapter 5.

Summary

The concept of vegetation as one, and only one, component of the ecosystem explains the two basic characteristics of all natural vegetation—its change in time and its change in space (diversity). The chapters in Part II deal more fully with each of the ecosystem components individually—geologic and soil features, climate, human actions and other biological influences (plant–plant and animal–plant relationships) as each has affected the vegetation of New Jersey.

References and Source Material

Balance of Nature? What Balance Is There? October 22, 1991. *New York Times*, sec. C.

Bard, Gily E. 1952. Secondary Succession on the Piedmont of New Jersey. *Ecological Monographs* 22:195–215.

Dansereau, Pierre. 1957. *Biogeography: An Ecological Perspective*. New York, N.Y.: Ronald Press.

Kareiva, Peter, Joel G. Kingsolver, and Raymond B. Huey, eds. 1993. *Biotic Interactions and Global Change*. Sunderland, Mass.: Sinauer Associates.

New Eye on Nature: The Real Constant Is External Turmoil. July 31, 1990. *New York Times*, sec. C.

Odum, Eugene P. 1989. *Ecology and Our Endangered Life-Support Systems*. Sunderland, Mass.: Sinauer Associates.

Pyne, Stephen J. 1982. *Fire in America*. Princeton, N.J.: Princeton University Press.

Treshow, Michael. 1970. *Environment and Plant Response*. New York, N.Y.: McGraw-Hill.

Wilson, Edward O. 1992. *The Diversity of Life*. Cambridge, Mass.: Harvard University Press.

Part II

Influences on the Natural Vegetation of New Jersey

Chapter 2

❦ *Geologic and Soil Features of New Jersey*

Small as it is, New Jersey bears the imprint of numerous highly varied geologic processes operating throughout hundreds of millions of years. Some of the results are easily recognized today by the diverse relief, varied parent rock and other surface material, and complex drainage patterns found in the state. It is also primarily these three geologic features that both influence and interact with vegetation. Relief is important because higher elevations have lower temperatures, greater exposure to winds, and usually thinner, less fertile soil—and steep slopes have greater water runoff. Because soils are formed primarily from the disintegration of parent rock or surface deposit material, they can vary widely in qualities of texture, water-holding capacity, and nutrients—all important to plants. Finally, drainage patterns including water table levels, coastal tidal areas, and inland river systems all influence vegetation.

This chapter examines the ecosystem relationship of geologic and soil features to vegetation in New Jersey. It starts with a simple explanation of the geologic time scale and a definition of the present geologic divisions of New Jersey. This is followed by a brief outline of the state's geologic history and a description of each geologic region from the standpoint of characteristics that have an impact on vegetation.

The Geologic Time Scale

Geologists date past events on a scale in which time is divided into major divisions called eras, and each era, in turn, is subdivided into smaller units called periods. While the earth is now thought to be more than 4 billion years old, describing accurately geological events dating back to earliest times is still not possible. Instead, for purposes of geological and historical biological descriptions, many scientists go back only 570 million years to begin their fine breakdown of history. Anything that happened before 570 million years ago is said to have occurred in Precambrian time. Everything more recent than that is classified in three eras. The *Paleozoic era*, the era of "ancient life," is the time that stretches from approximately 570 million to 225 million years ago. The *Mesozoic era*, the era of "middle life," starts at about 225 million years ago and

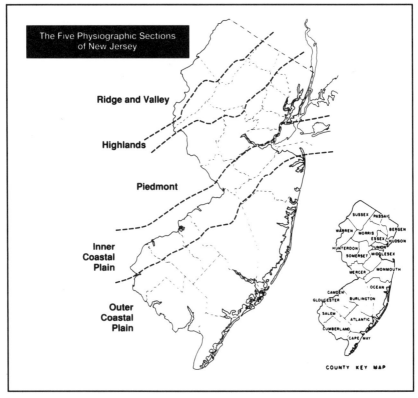

The Five Physiographic Sections of New Jersey

Ridge and Valley

Highlands

Piedmont

Inner Coastal Plain

Outer Coastal Plain

COUNTY KEY MAP

Figure 2-1. The five physiographic sections of New Jersey overlaid on county boundaries.

continues to about 65 million years ago. And the *Cenozoic era,* the era of "new life," starts about 65 million years ago and includes the time in which we live. Rather than burden the reader with full details of the division of eras into periods and still finer classifications (the subdivision of periods into epochs), only those specific periods most relevant to geologic development in New Jersey will be identified and discussed herein. The references at the end of the chapter include publications containing more complete descriptions of the geologic history of New Jersey.

Physiographic Land Regions of New Jersey

As a framework for explaining the geologic history that follows, it is necessary to delineate the present physiographic land divisions of New Jersey. The state is divided into five very different physiographic regions known as:

> Ridge and Valley section
> Highlands section

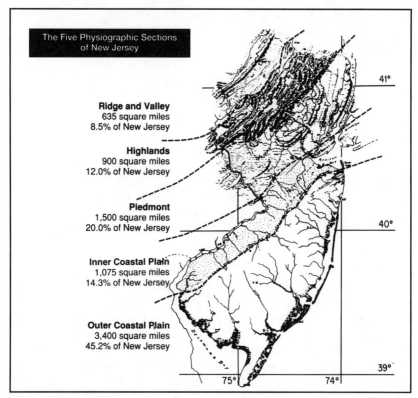

The Five Physiographic Sections
of New Jersey

Ridge and Valley
635 square miles
8.5% of New Jersey

Highlands
900 square miles
12.0% of New Jersey

Piedmont
1,500 square miles
20.0% of New Jersey

Inner Coastal Plain
1,075 square miles
14.3% of New Jersey

Outer Coastal Plain
3,400 square miles
45.2% of New Jersey

41°

40°

39°

75°   74°

Figure 2-2. The distribution of land area in New Jersey by the five physiographic sections of the state.

    Piedmont section
    Inner Coastal Plain section
    Outer Coastal Plain section

Figure 2-1 shows the boundaries of the five regions in relation to a county map of New Jersey, and Figure 2-2 imprints the boundaries on a relief map of the state.

Geologic History of New Jersey

Because we live in such a relatively tiny time span compared with the earth's history, it may be difficult for us to recognize that geologic processes, like the other components of the ecosystem, are operating continually. Mountain building, erosion, glaciation, and wave action on coastal dunes, important geologic processes in New Jersey's past, are still sculpturing landforms. Change is taking place continuously. And as illustrated in Figure 1-2, geologic and soil features, climatic elements, and living organisms, while changing continuously in time, are all interacting with each other as well. We look back briefly into the geologic history of New Jersey to identify those events that have had the greatest impact on the landscape of the state.

Earliest History: The Precambrian Era (More Than 570 Million Years Ago)

The oldest rocks known in New Jersey are of Precambrian age and date back to over 1 billion years ago. Precambrian rocks make up the backbone of the Highlands. Some were the result of lava flows or volcanic eruptions; others were igneous or sedimentary rocks, the latter formed while the land was covered by seas. After their original formation, nearly all Precambrian rocks were subject to intense heating and pressure and became what are known as metamorphic rocks.

Early History: The Paleozoic Era (About 570 to 225 Million Years Ago)

According to geologist Peter Wolfe, at the end of the Paleozoic era, North America, with New Jersey on its eastern margin, was attached to Africa and Europe as a single land mass now called Pangaea. North America then drifted away, and an ocean basin called the Proto-Atlantic formed, separating North America from Africa and Europe. Water covered New Jersey for millions of years. The present Ridge and Valley section of New Jersey shows the imprint of the Paleozoic era prominently in its sedimentary rock formations. Layer upon layer of sediments accumulated on the ocean bottom, and when these were uplifted in the course of mountain building, extensive limestone and sandstone rock formations became exposed land. The age of land areas previously covered by oceans is identified through the fossils of past marine animal and plant life found embedded in the rock formations.

In the later part of the Palezoic era, the drifting North American continent collided with Africa and Europe and again formed a supercontinent, also called Pangaea. The pressure of the continents pushing against one another resulted in the folding of the sedimentary deposits to form the Appalachian Mountains. These were subsequently refolded and eroded.

The sediments deposited when the seas cover the land are always subject to subsequent erosion. This erosion occurs because, when the land is uplifted and the seas withdraw, streams drain the land for millions of years and wear away the rocks. Because rocks have different degrees of hardness, the process of erosion produces relief in landforms, that is, ridges and valleys. Harder rocks form the ridges, while the softer rocks are eroded down to valleys or plains. Uplift of land and subsequent erosion is a continuing process (Figure 2-3). It happened in the past, it is happening today, and it will continue as long as the earth exists.

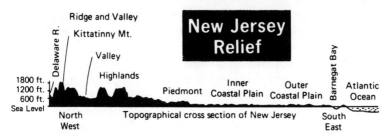

Figure 2-3. Erosion is the process that has carved out the present relief of New Jersey. Diagram shows a cross section of the state from its northwest corner to Barnegat Bay in the southeast.

Middle-Age History: The Mesozoic Era (225 to 65 Million Years Ago)

Two of the three subdivisions of the Mesozoic era, which spans about 160 million years, are particularly important in the geology of New Jersey. The first is the Triassic period, which started about 225 million years ago and lasted about 30 million years. During this period, the red sandstone and shales that presently form the surface of the Piedmont were deposited. This happened when the land again was covered by the seas. The modern Atlantic Ocean had begun to open up about 180 million years ago when the supercontinent Pangaea broke up again and North America, with New Jersey on its eastern margin, separated from Africa and Europe and drifted westward. As the Atlantic opened up, the interior of New Jersey held a succession of lakes, swamps, and sand and mud flats. Large three-toed dinosaurs roamed the mud flats, leaving their footprints in the red Triassic shales. Some of these footprints can be seen at the Rutgers Geology Museum.

After most of the sandstone and shales were deposited, volcanic (or igneous) activity with lava flows occurred in the Piedmont section of New Jersey in the Jurassic period, 195 million to 135 million years ago. The lava flows resulted in the formation of the present Watchung Mountains. Magma intrusions formed the diabase Palisades along the Hudson River, Cushetunk Mountain, the Sourland Mountains, and other smaller land masses that rise above the Piedmont plain. During the Mesozoic era, as before and after, uplift of whole areas of land continued and was followed by millions of years of erosion by inland rivers. The erosional processes etched out the present relief of the Piedmont, leaving the harder volcanic rocks to form the ridges and hills and the less resistant shales and sandstones to form the plains.

The Jurassic period was followed by the Cretaceous period, a very important period in New Jersey geologic history. In the early part of this period (135 million to 65 million years ago), the New Jersey Coastal Plain became a zone for deposition of sediments carried down rivers from uplifted land to the north. Then later in this period the seas again encroached upon the land of southern New Jersey and withdrew, only to return again and again. This alternation of encroachment and withdrawal of the sea happened many times, and each time the water covered the land, it left behind sedimentary deposits composed mainly of clays, silts, sands, and gravels, forming the Inner Coastal Plain. And, each time the sea withdrew, erosion proceeded and streams carried away some or all of the sediments, depending upon the hardness of the material.

Recent History: The Cenozoic Era (From 65 Million Years Ago to and Including the Present)

The imprint of the Cenozoic era, too, is visible in New Jersey today. This era is divided into two time intervals, the first of which is called the Tertiary. Tertiary time started 65 million years ago and continued to 1.75 million years ago. The marine processes operating in the Cretaceous continued into the Tertiary period. New Jersey was uplifted only to be submerged again. Many times during this interval the seas invaded that part of southern New Jersey known as the Outer Coastal Plain. With each invasion, clays, silts, sands, and gravels were deposited, and subsequent erosion carried some of the deposits back to the sea. While these deposition and erosion processes were occurring on the Outer Coastal Plain, the land in other parts of New Jersey was being uplifted, eroded, and sculptured into ridges and valleys. Since the last time the land was uplifted, streams have carved out the present valleys and ridges in the northern part of the state.

A very important part of New Jersey's geologic history took place in Quaternary time, the second time period of the Cenozoic, usually dated from 1.75 million years ago to the present. The Quaternary includes the period of the Pleistocene glaciation. Over a million years ago, a world wide preglacial cooling trend started, and about 700,000 years ago a sharp drop in world temperatures took place. The accumulation of snow exceeded summer melting, and huge ice masses formed in Canada (and northern Europe). These moved southward to the United States (and through Europe). Four major ice advances have occurred. They are referred to as the Nebraskan, Kansan, Illinoian, and Wisconsin ice ages, the Wisconsin advance being the most recent. In addition, there have been minor but locally important ice movements. Between the successive ice advances, extended periods of warmer weather have occurred, causing snow to melt and sea levels to rise. During these interglacial periods, patches of yellow sand and gravel from fluvial and some marine deposition were left on parts of the Inner and Outer Coastal Plains.

At least three of the four ice advances—the Kansan, Illinoian, and Wisconsin—reached northern New Jersey. As the ice sheets moved across New Jersey, they smoothed out rock formations and cut scratches and grooves in underlying bedrock, some of which remain. All existing vegetation was destroyed. Rock fragments were picked up and carried south

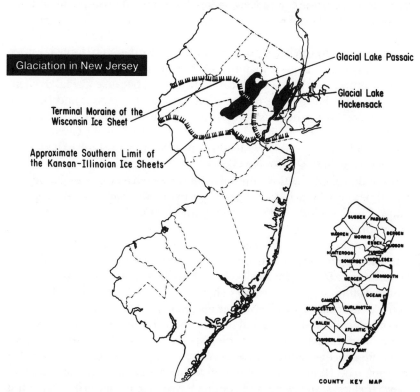

Figure 2-4. The location of glacial terminal moraines and former glacial lakes in New Jersey. (Map redrawn from Kemble Widmer, *The Geology and Geography of New Jersey*) [Van Nostrand, 1964].)

with the ice sheets. When the ice melted, the rocks carried from the north were left in the south. Glacial streams also transported smaller rock debris from the north to more southern areas having different underlying parent rock formations. The glacial deposits were thickest at the southernmost end of the ice sheets, and these are known as the "terminal moraines." The terminal moraine of the Wisconsin glacial ice sheet stretched in an irregular belt almost 1 mile wide from Perth Amboy at the east, through the Plainfield area, to Belvidere in the western part of the state (Figure 2-4). The terminal moraine as it still exists today is a heterogeneous mixture of rocks and gravel, as deep as 300 feet near Dover.

In addition to changing the landscape by its sculpturing force and deposits, glaciation left an impact on stream drainage patterns. In New Jersey, as in other areas, natural lakes were formed because glaciers scoured out depressions in rock beds, and glacial deposits blocked previous stream drainage channels. The state's largest lakes, Hopatcong, Greenwood, and Budd lakes, are glacially formed lakes, and more than two-hundred present-day New Jersey lakes and thousands of wetland acres owe their existence in large part to Ice Age changes in drainage patterns.

In addition to the lakes just mentioned, two other very large lakes existed in glacial times—Glacial Lake Passaic and Glacial Lake Hackensack (Figure 2-4). These lakes came into being because glacial deposits blocked and changed the drainage patterns of the Passaic and Hackensack rivers. While these two glacial lakes have since drained, their mark is left in distinctive marsh or swampland areas such as the Great Swamp near Chatham and the Troy Meadows near Whippany, both of which are remnants of Glacial Lake Passaic.

Remains of now-extinct animals that inhabited New Jersey during glacial times have been found in peat bogs in the north and in Salem county mud. These include the woolly mammoth and the giant, elephantlike mastodons.

By their presence or absence, glaciers affect sea levels, which are lowest when glaciation is at its maximum and highest when glacial ice is at a minimum. The lowest sea levels off New Jersey moved the shoreline to about 100 miles east of today's shoreline. At present, sea levels on the New Jersey coast are still rising as glacial ice continues to melt.

The glacial ice sheet started to melt about 18,000 years ago, retreating from New Jersey, and some geologists distinguish the Holocene epoch from Pleistocene time as representing the last 11,000 years of the earth's history. The Holocene has generally been a time of climatic warming; nevertheless, some periods of cooling have occurred as well. During this epoch some of the land that had been depressed by the weight of the ice sheet was uplifted. Since the uplift, marine erosion and deposition processes, primarily in the forces of wave and tidal action, have been at work sculpturing coastal land. Nowhere in New Jersey are the processes of geologic chance more apparent today than on its coast. The results are described in Chapter 13.

Present Landforms in New Jersey

The geologic history just described has left New Jersey with a naturally diverse and complex landscape. Within its small area, considerable variation is found in landforms, in surface and parent rock materials, and in the soils derived from them. All these, combined with complex drainage patterns, have an impact on vegetation. The highlights of these features in each of the five physiographic regions are illustrated in Figures 2-5 and 2-6 and are described in this section. Serving as supplements to the text descriptions are two maps, Figures 2-7 and 2-8. Figure 2-7 shows in simplified form the geologic bedrock of New Jersey, and Figure 2-8 a classification of New Jersey soils.

Ridge and Valley Section

The Ridge and Valley section of New Jersey (also called the Valley and Ridge section or simply the Valley section) is part of a larger Ridge and Valley geologic province that extends from Canada to the southern United States as a narrow belt of ridges and interconnecting valleys having a northeast–southwest orientation. In the far west of the state is the valley of the Delaware River, which marks the western border of the state. At its northern end in New Jersey, the Delaware Valley is about 500 feet above sea level. Kittatinny Mountain separates the Delaware Valley from another and broader valley in the east; it is a flat-topped ridge varying in width from 1 to 5 miles. Kittatinny reaches a maximum height of 1,803 feet, the highest altitude in the state, in the northwest, at High Point. To the east of the mountain is Kittatinny Valley, which is part of the eastern United States Great Valley. This valley section in New Jersey is 40 miles long and about 12 miles wide. It has a broad, undulating contour varying in elevation from about 400 to 1,000 feet above sea level.

Altogether the Ridge and Valley section contains 635 square miles or about 8.5 percent of the total land in New Jersey. It occupies a large part of Warren and Sussex counties. Ridges and valleys occur in this section because different parent rock formations underlie the ridges and the valleys. As mentioned earlier, softer rocks such as limestone and shale erode faster than the more resistant sandstone and conglomerates. The lowest valley levels occur wherever limestone underlies the surface; the areas of shale, a slightly more resistant rock, are about 200 to 400 feet higher than the limestone, and ridges occur whenever the bedrock is of the more resistant sandstone or conglomerate rock.

The differences in parent rock material account not only for the variation in relief but also make for contrasts in the kind and amount of soil coverage. In general, from the standpoint of vegetation, the soil covering the Kittatinny and other ridges in this section is poor in quality. The soil layer is thin on the ridges, with bedrock exposed in many places. Also, the ridge soil tends to be very acidic and of low fertility, and often it is very stony.

In contrast, the soils in the valleys, derived from limestone and shale that were covered by glacial till, are for the most part deeper, more fertile, and well drained. Peat or large muck deposits (thick layers of organic material) may occur where shallow glacial lakes once existed. The peat or muck was created by the remains of vegetation that had invaded these glacial lakes.

Highlands

Southeast of the Ridge and Valley section is the Highlands, a part of a larger geologic province called the New England Uplands, which includes the Green Mountains of Vermont. In New Jersey the Highlands

Figure 2-5. Landforms of northern New Jersey.

In the Ridge and Valley section, looking northward from the air along Kittatinny ridge with Kittatinny Lake on the left and Culvers Lake on the right. (Photo by the N.J. Bureau of Forest Management.)

Lake in Allamuchy State Park in the Highlands section. (Photo by Greg Johnson.)

Aerial view of the Highlands in Warren County. (Photo by the U.S. Soil Conservation Service.)

In the Piedmont section looking eastward toward the Watchung Ridges. (Photo by the U.S. Soil Conservation Service.)

Figure 2-6. Landforms of southern New Jersey.

Aerial view of the Inner Coastal Plain—Assunpink Creek near Windsor. (Photo by the U.S. Soil Conservation Service.)

On the Coastal Plain east of Mt. Holly, looking northward toward Arney's Mount, a cuesta hill formation, which marks the separation here between the Inner and Outer Coastal Plains.

Above left, a sand road stretches through an upland pine forest in the Pine Barrens of the New Jersey Outer Coastal Plain. Above right, a Pine Barrens cedar swamp wetland on the Wading River, Outer Coastal Plain. (Photo by the Pinelands Commission.)

Sand dunes on an offshore island on the New Jersey coast, Outer Coastal Plain.

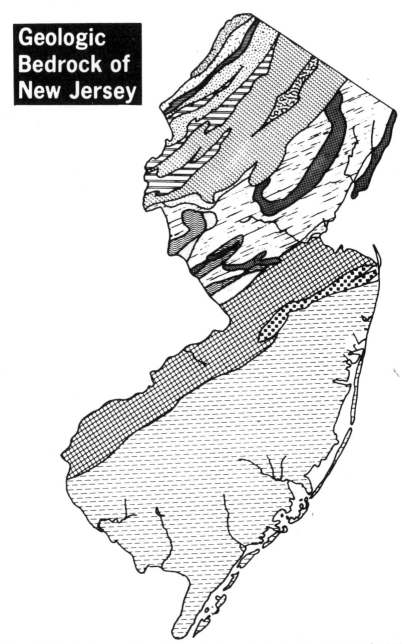

Geologic Bedrock of New Jersey

Figure 2-7. Geologic map of New Jersey showing major bedrock formations. (Copied from one prepared by J. C. F. Tedrow [1962]. The source of the map key also was from Tedrow 1962, with 1993 written comments, and additional data was extracted from the official geologic map of New Jersey prepared by J. V. Lewis and H. B. Kummel in 1910–12 and revised by Kummel and others.)

KEY TO GEOLOGIC MAP
(Age of bedrock is shown in parentheses)

Sandstone and shale sediments with some limestone, gray in color (Devonian).

Bloomsburg formation of hard red sandstone and soft red shale (Silurian).

Shawangunk Conglomerate, hard, dark gray (Silurian).

Martinsburg Shale, dark gray slaty shale (Ordovician).

Kittatinny Limestone, gray (Cambro-Ordovician).

Gneiss, granite and related rocks (Precambrian).

Green Pond and Skunnemunk Conglomerates—red; Bellvale Sandstone—gray, and Pequanac Shale—gray (Devonian and Silurian).

Basalt and diabase—igneous rocks called "traprock" (Triassic).

Stockton formation of gray, feldspathic sandstone, conglomerate, and some red shale (Triassic).

Lockatong formation of hard, reddish to blue-gray argillite and argillitic shale (Triassic).

Hammer Creek (Passaic) formation of red shale and carbonate-bearing conglomerate (Triassic).

Brunswick (Passaic) formation of soft red shale and sandstone (Triassic and Early Jurassic).

Sediments of unconsolidated sand, silt, and clay, many high in glauconite (Cretaceous and Lower Tertiary).

Sediments of reddish sand, colored and consolidated in places by iron oxide (Cretaceous).

Sediments of unconsolidated, yellow to gray, quartzose sands with a few clay lenses (Tertiary and Quaternary).

---

have an area of about 900 square miles, or 12 percent of the total land area in the state. As shown in Figure 2-1, this section is broader at the north, where it is about 20 miles wide; at its southern end bordering the Delaware River valley it is only 10 miles wide. The Highlands also has parallel ridges and valleys, but these differ from the Ridge and Valley section in the type of parent rock underlying the surface. Also, the ridges of the Highlands are more massive and generally much broader, while the valleys are narrower and have steeper slopes. Rock outcroppings occur frequently. Glacially formed lakes, such as Lake Hopatcong and Green Pond, contrast with adjacent ridges to make the Highlands a very scenic area of New Jersey.

The elevation in the Highlands averages about 1,000 feet above sea level, with a ridge maximum in the northwest of about 1,500 feet. The southern part of the Highlands shows a gentler contour, with the valleys reaching a low of 350 feet. While the oldest rocks in the state are in the Highlands, the ridges in this section have resisted erosion because they are made primarily of gneiss, a very hard rock material. The Highland valleys are of softer limestone or shale. The soil derived from the gneissic parent rock differs within the Highlands according to whether the underlying bedrock was covered by glacial drift. More important to vegetation, however, are the variations in relief, soil drainage, and stoniness that occur within the area.

Figure 2-8. Soil association map of New Jersey. (Copied from STATSGO [State Soil Geographic Data Base], USDA, Soil Conservation Service, 1993. The text for the legend was provided by the Soil Conservation Service, New Jersey, 1993.)

KEY TO SOIL MAP

- Hazen–Chenango–Riverhead
- Swartswood–Oquaga–Rock Outcrop
- Arnot–Oquaga–Lordstown
- Carlisle–Palms–Wallkill
- Stockbridge–Georgia–Farmington
- Nassau–Bath–Rock Outcrop
- Wethersfield–Urban Land–Watchung
- Holyoke–Wethersfield–Rock Outcrop
- Carlisle–Sloan–Palmyra
- Rockaway–Rock Outcrop–Hibernia
- Washington–Wassaic–Bartley
- Urban Land–Dunellen–Riverhead
- Urban Land–Boonton–Wethersfield
- Boonton–Urban Land–Wethersfield
- Parker–Gladstone–Califon
- Urban Land–Parsippany–Haledon
- Washington–Annandale–Bartley
- Pattenburg–Berks–Rowland
- Penn–Reaville–Klinesville
- Quakertown–Chalfont–Lehigh
- Penn–Bucks–Rowland
- Rowland–Pope–Birdsboro
- Neshaminy–Mount Lucas–Lawrenceville
- Urban Land–Nixon–Klinesville
- Mattapex–Matapeake–Chillum
- Hammonton–Woodstown–Mullica
- Downer–Evesboro–Klej
- Mullica–Sulfaquents–Manahawkin
- Freehold–Collington–Adelphia
- Lakehurst–Lakewood–Atsion
- Atsion–Manahawkin–Berryland
- Keyport–Elkton–Freehold
- Marlton–Kresson–Pemberton
- Westphalia–Freehold–Pasquotank
- Downer–Sassafras–Hammonton
- Sulfaquents–Udorthents–Psamments
- Hooksan–Psamments–Urban Land
- Woodmansie–Atsion–Downer
- Aura–Downer–Sassafras

SOIL DESCRIPTIONS

Hazen–Chenango–Riverhead Deep and very deep, well drained, nearly level to strongly sloping gravelly loams and gravelly, sandy, loamy soils overlying stratified outwash on outwash plains and terraces.

Swartswood–Oquaga–Rock Outcrop Moderately deep and deep, well drained and moderately well drained, gently sloping to very steep, very stony loams formed in sandstone, shale, quartzite, and conglomerate glacial till on uplands.

Arnot–Oquaga–Lordstown Shallow and moderately deep, excessively drained to moderately well drained, gently sloping to very steep, channery loams formed in shale and sandstone glacial till and residuum on uplands.

Carlisle–Palms–Wallkill Very deep, very poorly drained, nearly level mucks and loams formed in organic deposits and alluvium over organic deposits occurring on depressions and floodplains.

Stockbridge–Georgia–Farmington Gently sloping to moderately steep, well drained, deep to shallow, loamy soils derived from limestone, shale, slate, and siltstone glacial till over limestone bedrock on uplands.

Nassau–Bath–Rock Outcrop Shallow, deep and very deep, somewhat excessively drained and well drained, gently sloping to very steep gravelly loams formed in shale, slate, and sandstone glacial till on uplands.

Wethersfield–Urban Land–Watchung Very deep, well drained and moderately well drained, gently sloping to steep stony loamy soils formed in basalt, red sandstone, conglomerate, and shale glacial till over basalt and red sandstone bedrock on uplands.

Holyoke–Wethersfield–Rock Outcrop Shallow and very deep, somewhat excessively drained and well drained, rolling to very steep stony, loamy soils formed in basalt, red sandstone conglomerate, and shale glacial till over basalt and red sandstone bedrock on uplands.

Carlisle–Sloan–Palmyra Nearly level to gently sloping, very poorly drained and well drained, very deep mucks and loams formed in organic deposits in depressions, silty alluvium on flood plains, and sandy, calcareous outwash on outwash plains and terraces.

Rockaway–Rock Outcrop–Hibernia Gently sloping to very steep, well drained to somewhat poorly drained, very deep stony loams formed in gneissic glacial till and alluvium over granitic gneiss bedrock on uplands.

Washington–Wassaic–Bartley Nearly level to moderately steep, well drained and moderately well drained, very deep and moderately deep, loamy soils formed in lime-influenced glacial till over limestone bedrock on uplands.

Urban Land–Dunellen–Riverhead Nearly level to strongly sloping, well drained, deep and very deep gravelly, sandy loams formed in sandy, stratified glacial outwash on outwash plains and terraces.

Urban Land–Boonton–Wethersfield Gently sloping to moderately steep, well drained and moderately well drained, very deep and deep gravelly loams formed in acid, reddish sandstone, shale, basalt, and conglomerate glacial till over shale and basalt bedrock on uplands.

Boonton–Urban Land–Wethersfield Gently sloping to very steep, well drained and moderately well drained, very deep and deep gravelly loams formed in acid, reddish sandstone, shale, basalt and conglomerate glacial till over shale and basalt bedrock on uplands.

Parker–Gladstone–Califon Gently sloping to very steep, excessively drained to somewhat poorly drained, deep and very deep, stony sandy loams and loams formed in granitic gneiss residuum, glacial till, and colluvium over granitic gneiss bedrock on uplands.

Urban Land–Parsippany–Haledon Nearly level to strongly sloping, poorly drained and somewhat poorly drained, very deep silt loams formed in lacustrine sediments in depressions and in sandstone, shale, and basalt glacial till over shale and basalt bedrock on uplands.

Washington–Annandale–Bartley Nearly level to strongly sloping, very deep, well drained and moderately well drained loamy soils formed in limestone, shale, and granitic gneiss glacial till and alluvium over limestone and granitic gneiss bedrock on uplands.

Pattenburg–Berks–Rowland Nearly level to very steep, well drained to somewhat poorly drained, very deep to moderately deep, gravelly loams formed from conglomerate, shale siltstone and sandstone residuum on uplands, and silt loams formed from silty alluvium on floodplains.

Penn–Reaville–Klinesville Gently sloping to moderately steep, somewhat excessively drained to somewhat poorly drained, moderately deep to shallow channery silt loams formed from red shale, siltstone, and fine-grained sandstone residuum on uplands.

Quakertown–Chalfont–Lehigh Nearly level to strongly sloping, well drained to somewhat poorly drained, deep and very deep silt loams formed from sandstone and shale residuum and metamorphosed sandstone and shale residuum on uplands.

Penn–Bucks–Rowland Nearly level to strongly sloping, well drained to somewhat poorly drained, moderately deep to very deep, channery silt loams and silt loams formed in red shale, siltstone and fine-grained sandstone residuum and in loess mantles over shale and sandstone on uplands, and in silty alluvium on floodplains.

Rowland–Pope–Birdsboro Nearly level to gently sloping, well drained to somewhat poorly drained, very deep silt loams and sandy loams formed in silty and sandy alluvium on floodplains and river terraces.

Neshaminy–Mount Lucas–Lawrenceville Nearly level to very steep, well drained and somewhat poorly drained, deep and very deep stony silt loams and silt loams formed in diabase and basalt residuum and in silty loess mantles overlying shale on uplands.

Urban Land–Nixon–Klinesville Nearly level to strongly sloping, well drained and somewhat excessively drained, very deep and shallow loams formed in acid, coarse-textured alluvial sediments over shale bedrock and shaly loams formed in red shale, siltstone and fine-grained sandstone residuum on uplands.

Mattapex–Matapeake–Chillum Nearly level to moderately steep, well drained and moderately well drained, very deep silty soils on Coastal Plain uplands.

Hammonton–Woodstown–Mullica Nearly level to gently sloping, moderately well drained to very poorly drained, very deep loamy and sandy soils on Coastal Plain uplands and lowlands.

Downer–Evesboro–Klej Nearly level to gently sloping, excessively drained to somewhat poorly drained, very deep sandy and fine sandy loam soils on Coastal Plain uplands.

Mullica–Sulfaquents–Manahawkin Nearly level, very poorly drained, very deep organic soils over loamy subsoils on Coastal Plain lowlands.

Freehold–Collington–Adelphia Nearly level to steep, well drained to somewhat poorly drained, very deep loamy soils formed from glauconite on Coastal Plain uplands.

Lakehurst–Lakewood–Atsion Nearly level to moderately sloping, excessively drained to poorly drained, very deep sandy soils on Coastal Plain uplands.

Atsion–Manahawkin–Berryland Nearly level, poorly drained and very poorly drained, very deep organic and sandy soils on Coastal Plain lowlands.

Keyport–Elkton–Freehold Level to moderately steep, poorly drained to well drained, very deep loamy and silty soils overlying slowly permeable clays on Coastal Plain uplands.

Marlton–Kresson–Pemberton Nearly level to moderately sloping, well drained to somewhat poorly drained, very deep clayey or sandy over loamy soils formed from glauconite on Coastal Plain uplands and intermediate positions.

Westphalia–Freehold–Pasquotank Nearly level to steep, well drained and poorly drained, very deep loamy soils on Coastal Plain uplands and lowlands.

Downer–Sassafras–Hammonton Nearly level to steep, well drained and moderately well drained very deep soils that have a loamy subsoil on Coastal Plain uplands.

Sulfaquents–Udorthents–Psamments Nearly level to steep, well drained to very poorly drained, very deep mineral and organic soils on tidal flats.

Hooksan–Psamments–Urban Land Nearly level to gently sloping, excessively drained, very deep sandy soils on the barrier islands.

Woodmansie–Atsion–Downer Nearly level to sloping, well drained and poorly drained, very deep sandy and loamy soils on Coastal Plain uplands and in depressional areas.

Aura–Downer–Sassafras Nearly level to moderately sloping, well drained, very deep loamy, sandy, and gravelly soils on Coastal Plain uplands.

Piedmont

East and south of the Highlands is the section called the Piedmont, or the Triassic lowlands. The New Jersey Piedmont belongs to a larger belt of rock formation that extends almost 1,000 miles from the Hudson River southward through New Jersey and Pennsylvania, where it is separated from a similar, more southerly formation that extends through Maryland into Virginia. Detached areas of the same formation also occur northward in Connecticut and Massachusetts.

The Piedmont of New Jersey occupies 1,500 square miles, or about 20 percent of the land area and is composed mostly of shale, sandstone, and argillite formations that typically are brownish-red in color. These formations are less resistant to erosion than the adjacent Highland gneissic rock is, so in comparison to the Highlands the Piedmont is, in fact, a lowland. The Piedmont section in New Jersey slopes gently southeastward from about 400 feet above sea level at its northwestern margin, to an elevation of less than 100 feet at its southern margin bordering the Delaware, and to sea level at Newark Bay. Though flat in some areas, the Piedmont contour is slightly rolling, with mostly gentle slopes, but in some areas rivers have cut rather steep-sided valleys.

Interestingly, on the Piedmont several ridge formations tower over the adjacent lowlands—the three Watchung Mountains (850, 650, and 350 feet high), Cushetunk Mountain, the Sourlands, and the Palisades. These ridges are made of intrusive or extrusive lava material known as diabase and basaltic rocks, both of which are much harder than the shale and sandstone of the Piedmont. While the diabase and basalt have resisted erosion, the less resistant shale and sandstone have been worn down, resulting in the lower elevations.

Differences in the rock formations combined with the fact that glacial deposits of varying age covered only part of the Piedmont have resulted in a variety of soil types within the area. However, these variations appear to be less important to vegetation than the differences in soil water drainage.

Inner and Outer Coastal Plains Sections

The Coastal Plains area is the most easterly and southern part of New Jersey and constitutes about 60 percent of the total land area of the state. It belongs to a larger geologic province of the eastern United States that extends northward through Long Island to Cape Cod and southwesterward along the coast into Mexico.

Although both the Inner and Outer sections of the Coastal Plain in New Jersey have their origin in the deposition of clays, silts, sands, and gravels, the two areas are distinctive particularly with respect to soils. The land identified as the Inner Coastal Plain represents Cretaceous period sedimentary deposits that were covered for the most part with later deposits made in interglacial Pleistocene time. It consists of 1,075 square miles, or 14.3 percent of the state's land. The Outer Coastal Plain, on the other hand, consists of sedimentary deposits dating from Tertiary time but with overlying patches of sand and gravel deposits that also date back to interglacial time. It is the largest of New Jersey's physiographic regions, occupying 3,400 square miles, or 45.2 percent of the state.

The Inner Coastal Plain is separated from the Outer Coastal Plain by a belt of hills that extends in a southwesterly direction from the Atlantic Highlands (the Highlands of the Navesink) overlooking Raritan Bay to the Delaware River lowlands in the southwest. The hills are remnants of a particular landform called a "cuesta." On the lower elevations of the Coastal Plain the clays, silts, sands, and gravels, for the most part, are unconsolidated; that is, the particles are not cemented together as in a sandstone rock. On the cuestas, however, some of the sands and gravels are cemented together to form a rocklike cap on the hills. The larger cuestas include the Beacon Hill formation, which reaches a height of 373 feet; Arney's Mount, 230 feet; Mount Holly, 183 feet; and Mount Laurel, 173 feet. These larger cuestas contrast with most of the rest of the Coastal Plain area, which is less than 100 feet in elevation.

The Inner Coastal Plain lies to the west of the cuestas, and on it, water drains westward to the Delaware River or northward to the Raritan Bay. On the Outer Coastal Plain, which lies to the east of the cuestas, water drains mostly eastward on a gentler slope to the ocean or southward and southeastward to the Delaware Bay. (The Rancocas Creek is one exception; it flows westward from its source in the Pine Barrens to drain into the Delaware River.) Thus the whole surface of the Coastal Plain may be pictured as rising gradually from seal level on the east, west, and south to elevations as high as nearly 400 feet where the Inner and Outer Coastal Plains join at the cuestas.

Just as the continual process of differential erosion determined the relief in the other three physiographic sections of New Jersey, so has it determined the present landforms of the Inner and Outer Coastal Plains. In addition, changes in sea level between glacial and interglacial periods, combined with continuing wave erosion and deposition, have sculptured the coastal area of New Jersey.

As a result of many natural processes, the present soils of the Coastal Plain show much variation in their mixtures of clays, silts, sands, and gravels. The difference among the four rests in the size of the particles— clay being the smallest and gravel the largest of the four. The Inner Coastal Plain has a larger proportion of clay in its soil than does the Outer Coastal Plain, which is much sandier. Also, the Inner Coastal Plain contains deposits of marl, commonly called greensand. It consists of a sand-sized aggregate of the green-colored mineral glauconite.

Some of the Coastal Plain soils provide better growing conditions for plants than others do. For the most part, the soils of the Inner Coastal Plain are more fertile than those of the Outer Coastal Plain, which contain a much higher amount of quartz sand. Although the Outer Coastal

Plain does have some fertile soils, the largest part of it, nearly 2,000 square miles, is made up of very sandy soil of low fertility that retains little of the moisture needed for plant growth. This area is known as the Pine Barrens (Figure 10-1).

On both the Inner and Outer Coastal Plains, wide variation in drainage conditions can be observed. High water tables cause extensive areas of wetlands, and at the other extreme there are very dry, sandy soil conditions, as in the Pine Barrens. Finally, on the coast from Bay Head south to Cape May, one finds a shifting chain of barrier islands that are sometimes separated from the mainland by bays, tidal ponds, and marshland.

Summary

From Precambrian time to the present, varied and complex geologic processes have produced a landscape of startling diversity in New Jersey, considering the small size of the state (Figures 2-5 and 2-6). Within its borders, New Jersey exhibits many variations in relief, in soil parent rock and surface deposit materials, in soil types, and in land drainage; all these have an impact on vegetation.

References and Source Material

Kummel, H. B. 1940. *The Geology of New Jersey*. New Jersey Department of Conservation and Development. Geological Series Bulletin 50.

Mitchell, Alison E. 1992. *The New Jersey Highlands: Treasures at Risk*. Morristown, N.J.: New Jersey Conservation Foundation.

Pielou, E. C. 1991. *After the Ice Age: The Return of Life to Glaciated North America*. Chicago, Ill.: University of Chicago Press.

Quakenbush, G. A. 1955. *Our New Jersey Land*. New Jersey Agricultural Experiment Station Bulletin 775, New Brunswick, N.J.

Schuberth, C. J. 1968. *The Geology of New York City and Environs*. Garden City, N.Y.: Natural History Press.

Stanley, Steven M. 1986. *Earth and Life Through Time*. New York, N.Y.: W. H. Freeman.

Tedrow, J. C. F. 1963. *New Jersey Soils*. Rutgers College of Agriculture Circular 601, New Brunswick, N.J.

———. 1986. *Soils of New Jersey*. Malabar, Fla.: Robert E. Krieger.

Widmer, Kemble. 1964. *The Geology and Geography of New Jersey*. Princeton, N.J.: Van Nostrand.

Wolfe, Peter E. 1977. *The Geology and Landscape of New Jersey*. New York, N.Y.: Crane Russak.

Chapter 3

❧ *Climate of New Jersey*

Located at a latitude between the 39th and 41st parallels, New Jersey is in the same north–south position as areas of northern California, southern Italy, and Turkey, but climatic conditions in the four places are quite different. This is evidence that latitudinal position is only one of a number of factors that determine the climate of a region. In addition to the angle of the sun's rays and the length of daylight—factors determined by latitude—an area's altitude and proximity to oceans and mountain ranges have an influence on its climate. Also important are the source and direction of air masses that flow over the region. This chapter describes the climatic conditions that affect vegetation in New Jersey, beginning with the reasons for the particular climate conditions.

Why the Climate of New Jersey Is What It Is

One might reasonably expect that New Jersey, with a coastline of about 125 miles, would have the type of climate known as maritime, in which there is little change between summer and winter temperatures and little variation in daily temperatures. Areas in California, for example, at the same latitude as New Jersey and adjacent to the Pacific Ocean, have a relatively uniform climate throughout the year and only small variation in daily temperature. In contrast, New Jersey has a continental type of climate, one more typical of midwestern states.

A continental climate is characterized by significant variation between summer and winter temperatures and by relatively large daily and day-to-day temperature fluctuations. In all parts of New Jersey there is a difference of more than 40°F in temperature from the warmest to the coldest month of the year, reflecting the continental nature of the climate. The reason for this is the direction of the prevailing winds. In winter the winds are from the northwest, and cold air masses from subpolar areas of Canada move over New Jersey (Figure 3-1). In the months from May through September, again because of the prevailing winds, the state is blanketed with moist tropical air masses that originate over the Gulf of Mexico, flow inland, and then travel over very warm land before reaching New Jersey. California weather, on the other hand, is more uniform because the air-mass exchange is from ocean to land daily and from land to ocean nightly. The same air-mass exchange also occurs on a seasonal cycle and causes a moderating effect on the air temperature of the land, making it cooler in the summer (and in the daytime) and warmer in winter (and at night) than otherwise would be expected.

Temperatures in New Jersey

The annual temperature in New Jersey averages about 53°F for a normal year, but from the standpoint of vegetation, two considerations are important—variation by locale within the state and deviation from the average annual temperature from month to month.

For reporting of its weather data the U.S. government groups the official weather-reporting stations in New Jersey in three classes—northern, southern, and coastal stations. All weather stations slightly north of the line that separates the Piedmont from the Inner Coastal Plain are classed as northern, and with four exceptions, all those south of the line are grouped as the southern stations; the exceptions include the weather stations at Cape May, Atlantic City, Sandy Hook, and Long Branch, which make up the third category, the coastal group. The monthly average temperatures for each of the three groups are plotted in Figure 3-2. Two characteristics of New Jersey temperatures are apparent from these figures. First, the statistics reflect the continental nature of the climate by the wide variation between January, normally the coldest month, and July, the warmest month. Second, it is evident that the temperature differences between northern and southern locales in the state are greater in winter than in summer.

Over a period of the last 30 years, the January temperature of the northern New Jersey stations averaged 27.9°F; of the southern, 31.5°F; and of the coastal, 33.2°F. In July, the temperature averaged 73.2°F in the north, 75.1°F in the south, and 74.6°F on the coast. The coastal averages in both cases reflect the moderating influence of the ocean. At extreme ends of the state, the differences in winter temperatures are even more pronounced, with January averaging as low as 23°F at the Sussex weather station, in the far northwest, and over 33°F at Cape May, in the southeastern part of the state.

The winter variations between the northern and southern sections of New Jersey are particularly important from the standpoint of vegetation, when one considers differences in the average length of the vegetative growing season, that is, the number of consecutive days on which the average temperature is about 43°F, the point above which it is believed that most plant growth starts. In a discussion of the climate of New Jersey, Erwin Biel describes the differences that occur in the growing season in New Jersey in terms of the starting date, the ending date, and the

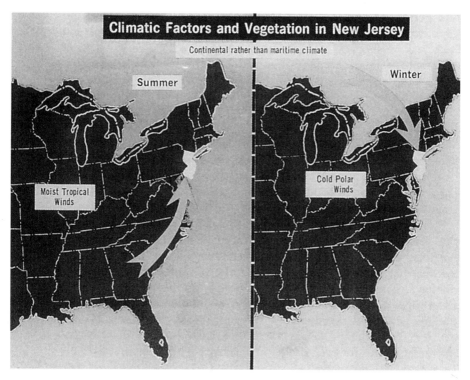

Figure 3-1. The direction of air-mass movement over New Jersey accounts for the continental nature of its climate. (Redrawn from Erwin Biel, "The Climate of New Jersey," in *The Economy of New Jersey* [New Brunswick, N.J.: Rutgers University Press, 1958].)

length of the period in which the daily temperature averages 43°F or more. Figure 3-3 plots the information in graphic form on a New Jersey county map. As the data indicate, the temperatures in the southern part of New Jersey permit plant growth to start earlier in the spring and to continue later in the fall, making the duration of the growing season as much as 5 weeks longer in the south.

Another way of looking at the temperature differences between northern and southern New Jersey is in terms of the length of the frostfree period, the interval in which the daily temperature remains above 32°F. The 1992 data published by the National Climatic Data Center show that the average date of the last killing frost in Sussex County is May 12, whereas at Cape May it is April 19. As the first killing frost in the fall comes much sooner in Sussex County than in the south, the duration of the intervening period without killing frost is significantly shorter in northern New Jersey.

Both sets of statistics point up the "biological" differences between the climate of North and South Jersey. For comparison, Cape May, in southern New Jersey, has a normal January temperature about equal to that

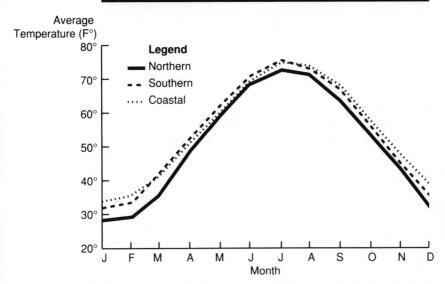

Figure 3-2. Thirty-year (1961–90) monthly temperature norms for the northern, southern, and coastal sections of New Jersey. (SOURCE: "Climatological Data, New Jersey," *1992 Annual Summary* 95, no. 13, 1993. U.S. Department of Commerce, National Oceanic and Atmospheric Administration—National Climatic Data Center.)

of southern Virginia; in contrast, the normal January temperatures in the most northern extremity of New Jersey are about equal to those in northern Ohio. The impact on vegetation of these differences in the cold weather temperatures is discussed in Chapter 5.

Several other variations in temperature occur within the state. Ecologists have observed significant climatic differences on slopes of different exposures. For example, differences in temperature between the north-facing and south-facing slopes of Cushetunk Mountain, 600 feet high in central New Jersey, are enough to cause differences in the natural vegetation growing on the two slopes.

Variations in climate also occur between cities and surrounding countrysides, as reflected in differences in temperature, humidity, precipitation, fog, and wind speed as well as in atmospheric pollution. That the temperatures in cities tend to be higher than in surrounding areas is explained by the combined result of city activities and substitution of building structures and pavement for vegetation. Urban concentration of people means a concentration of heat-creating sources whether required for the operation of heating or air-conditioning systems or of industrial plants and vehicles. This heat, as well as solar radiation, is reflected and stored by pavement and building structures. Weather Bu-

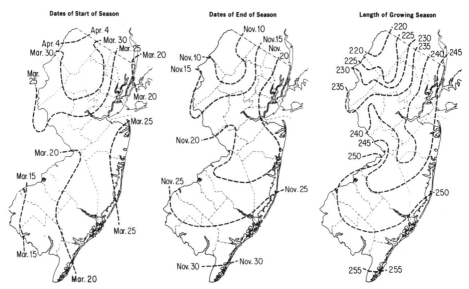

Growing Season Period in New Jersey

(period in which temperatures average 43F°, or more)

Dates of Start of Season

Dates of End of Season

Length of Growing Season

Figure 3-3. Dates of the start and the end of the growing season in New Jersey and length in days of the season. The growing season is the period in which the temperature averages 43°F or more. (Redrawn from Erwin Biel, "The Climate of New Jersey," in *The Economy of New Jersey* [New Brunswick, N.J.: Rutgers University Press, 1958].)

reau data indicate that the highest average annual temperatures recorded by the weather stations in the northern New Jersey area occur in Newark. Here the elevated average temperatures are particularly noticeable in the months of July and August; in these months the average temperatures in Newark are almost as high as in areas much farther south in New Jersey. Scientists report that the temperature differentials between Newark and less developed areas around it have increased continuously for the last 50 years.

In addition to temperature differences, other climatic variations between cities and their less settled surroundings exist. The former director of climatology of the U.S. Weather Bureau, Helmut Landsberg, estimates that as compared with the surrounding countryside cities have 10 percent more precipitation, 10 percent more cloudiness, 30 percent more fog in summer, and 100 percent more fog in winter.

Precipitation in New Jersey

As compared with most other regions in the United States and in the world, New Jersey has a relatively high rainfall. Annual precipitation

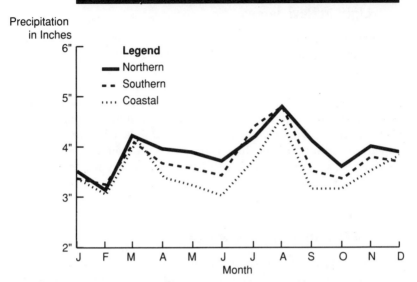

Monthly Average Precipitation for the Northern, Southern, and Coastal Sections of New Jersey

Precipitation
in Inches

Legend
▬ Northern
▬ ▬ Southern
.... Coastal

Month

Figure 3-4. Thirty-year (1961–90) monthly precipitation norms for the northern, southern, and coastal sections of New Jersey. (Source: "Climatological Data, New Jersey," *1992 Annual Summary* 95, no. 13, 1993. U.S. Department of Commerce, National Oceanic and Atmospheric Administration—National Climatic Data Center.)

ranges from an average low of about 40 inches at the southeastern corner of the state to over 48 inches in an area in the north that seems to receive the heaviest brunt of storms coming up the coast from tropical areas. Throughout the state, rainfall normally is distributed fairly uniformly over the twelve months, with slightly more falling in the months of July and August and less in February. Also important for vegetation is the fact that over a long period of time there have been only relatively slight fluctuations in the total amount of rain recorded from year to year.

The official precipitation figures for the northern, southern, and coastal sections of the state for the last 30 years are plotted in Figure 3-4. Northern New Jersey normally averages 46.94 inches of precipitation in a year, southern New Jersey, 44.58 inches, and the coastal area, 42.65 inches. Most of the difference occurs in the growing season, April through July. However, differences that do exist in the amount of rainfall between sections of New Jersey appear to be less important to vegetation than the water-holding capacity of different soil types and the varying water table levels. The effect of these on vegetation is discussed in Chapter 5.

In winter, nearly 50 inches of snow normally fall in northern New Jersey, while in the south the average is only about 14 inches. New Jersey is located in a belt with a relatively high frequency of sleet and glaze storms; these have a damaging influence on vegetation, particularly in forests, where limbs or whole trees can be destroyed by the weight of ice.

Light in New Jersey

The length of daylight in New Jersey as measured at New Brunswick varies from about 9½ hours in January to nearly 12 hours in March and in September, and the longest day of the year, 15 hours, occurs in June. Of the total daylight hours, it is estimated that in the nonpolluted areas of the state, the percentage of clear, sunny days to total days averages 65 percent in the summer, 60 percent in the autumn and spring, and 55 percent in the winter. Before concentrated industrial areas were developed, the amount of sunshine throughout the state did not vary significantly. Now skies over industrial areas frequently become clouded with pollution wastes at the same time less highly developed locales in the state are enjoying sunshine.

Air Pollution and Vegetation

When compared with the other forty-nine states, New Jersey has poor air quality. This results from a set of unique circumstances: the state is heavily industrialized and home to some of the country's major petrochemical firms; it has the densest population of all fifty states; and it has more miles of highway per square mile and more cars per mile of highway than any other state.

Certain types and levels of air pollution cause serious medical problems to human beings, but even levels of pollution seemingly not harmful to humans can cause serious damage to some plants. Plants filter out dust, soot, and fly ash from the air. Too much pollutant material absorbed from the atmosphere or from the soil through root hairs can be toxic to a plant, however. Plant species differ in their tolerance to pollutants: some trees, shrubs, and even agricultural crops show no sensitivity to certain types or doses of pollutants that cause serious injury or even death to other types of plants.

Pollutants known to damage plants include ground-level ozone, acid depositions (wet and dry), sulfur dioxide, fluorides, nitrogen oxides, PAN (peroxyacetyl nitrate), and particulates such as lead and soot. Scientists are particularly concerned with the effects of the first two types of atmospheric pollution on vegetation.

Ozone is formed naturally in the stratosphere as incoming solar radiation interacts with oxygen. As is discussed in Chapter 14, the ozone layer in the upper atmosphere shields plants and other living organisms from deadly ultraviolet radiation. On the other hand, excessive ozone in the lower atmosphere, ground-level ozone, has become a major pollutant.

More than half of our ground-level ozone, a major component of what is called smog, is formed as a result of oxidation reactions that stem from automobile and industrial emissions. In 1993 every New Jersey county failed to meet national standards for ground-level ozone, and eighteen of the state's twenty-one counties exceeded the ozone standard by more than 50 percent. This, of course, can cause a human-health problem, but it also is of concern to forest managers and agriculturists. Scientists have found that excessive ground-level ozone in the atmosphere may damage foliage and root tissues, interfere with growth processes, and generally weaken trees and crops.

Acid depositions are caused primarily by emissions of sulfur and nitrogen oxides into the lower atmosphere. Coal-fired power plants and smelters as well as automobiles are major sources of these emissions, which interact with water to form toxic acids. Acid pollution may mix with water in the atmosphere and fall as acidic precipitation, but it may be deposited on earth in its dry form, too. Both forms of acid depositions are referred to as acid rain. Eastern North America and much of Europe in particular have suffered from acid depositions, which may cause damage to leaf surfaces, leaching of essential nutrients, and accumulation of aluminum to toxic levels in the soil, adversely affecting tree roots and growth. Foresters in Canada, for example, report a decline in sugar maples because of acid rain damage. There has, however, been some disagreement among scientists regarding the relative impact of acid rain on forests, for example, whether it is acid rain that is responsible for the decline of red spruce trees throughout the eastern United States. This uncertainty appears to be because the presence of multiple contaminants in the atmosphere makes distinguishing the cause and effect of a single pollutant difficult.

At this time, New Jersey's Bureau of Forest Management reports no evidence that, as yet, excessive ground-level ozone levels or acid depositions are damaging state forests. Nevertheless, they agree on the need for a monitoring system to give early warning of such damage should it occur.

A Changing Climate: Global Warming

As we well know, climate can be variable. The long-range temperature and precipitation norms for New Jersey already discussed hide variations that frequently occur in both, one particular month or year being hotter or colder, wetter or drier than another. As an example, December 1990 was one of the warmest Decembers on record, yet December 1989 had been the coldest ever recorded. Scientists disagree about the meaning in terms of future trends in climate of these variations from norm.

Studies of temperature trends in New Jersey show warming during the first half of the twentieth century followed by cooling during the 1950s and 1960s. A less pronounced continuation of the cooling followed in the next two decades. But overall the scientific evidence now points to a gradual warming of the atmosphere by the so-called greenhouse effect, caused primarily by the burning of wood and fossil fuels (coal, oil, and gas) and by tropical deforestation, activities that release carbon dioxide (CO_2) into the atmosphere. Excessive carbon dioxide in addition to other atmospheric emissions such as methane, nitrous oxide, and chlorofluorocarbons (taken together, commonly known as the "greenhouse gases") allow the sun's rays to pass into the atmosphere but then trap the radiant heat reflected from the earth, resulting in increased global temperatures. Incidentally, in 1989 the then commissioner of environmental protection reported that New Jersey accounted for .5 percent of the world's total global carbon dioxide emissions.

If it occurs, warming of the atmosphere will have profound effects on the landscape and natural vegetation of New Jersey. More about these effects and also those resulting from the depletion of ozone in the upper atmosphere will be considered later in the book.

Summary

Within the state of New Jersey variation in climatic conditions of temperature, precipitation, and light occur. Of these, the most important from the standpoint of vegetation is variation in temperature, as it influences the length of the growing season and the duration of the frostfree period. Atmospheric pollution is a growing threat to the vegetation of the state.

References and Source Material

Biancomano, Vincent J., and Mark D. Shulman. 1991. A Temporal Investigation of an Urban Heat Island. *Bulletin of the New Jersey Academy of Sciences* 36(2): 13–18.

Biel, Erwin R. 1958. The Climate of New Jersey. In *The Economy of New Jersey*, 53–98. New Brunswick, N.J.: Rutgers University Press.

Cantlon, J. E. 1953. Vegetation and Microclimates on North and South Slopes of Cushetunk Mountain, New Jersey. *Ecological Monographs* 23: 241–270.

Lowry, William. 1967. The Climate of Cities. *Scientific American* 217(2): 15–23.

Owenby, James R.. and D. S. Ezell. 1991. *Monthly Station Normals of Temperature, Precipitation, and Heating and Cooling Days 1961–1990.* Asheville, N.C.: U.S. Department of Commerce, National Oceanic and Atmospheric Administration, National Climatic Center.

U.S. Department of Commerce. 1993. *Climatological Data, New Jersey 1990's Annual Summary,* vol. 95, no. 13. Asheville, N.C.: National Oceanic and Atmospheric Administration, National Climatic Center.

Zimmermann, George L., et al. 1986. *Forested Ecosystems: A System for Monitoring the Effects of Acid Rain Deposition.* A final report for the N.J. Department of Environmental Protection, Division of Parks and Forestry.

Chapter 4

❦ *Human and Other Biological Influences on the New Jersey Landscape*

In addition to geologic processes and climatic elements, biological inter-relationships have played an important role in the shaping of the present New Jersey landscape. This chapter pinpoints some of the ways in which human activities have used, and misused, the land. Then, the impacts of other biological interrelationships—animal–plant and those among plants themselves—are examined for their effect on the vegetation of New Jersey. As a starting point, we look backward at the development of vegetation in New Jersey.

Early History of Vegetation in New Jersey

The earliest real evidence of plants in New Jersey consists of fossils, the remains of plants that lived a long time ago and have been preserved in rock or swamp material. The time at which a fossilized plant lived is identified by scientific dating of the rock or other material in which the plant is embedded.

The earliest known forms of life existed in Precambrian time, more than 570 million years ago, yet few fossils have been found dating back to this period. But Kemble Widmer, in a book on the geology of New Jersey, suggests that

> unproved as it is in New Jersey, it would seem reasonable to as-sume from evidence elsewhere in the world that the graphite in the Franklin formation (rocks in the Highlands) is all that is left of very ancient Precambrian marine life which once existed in New Jersey.

Fossils of primitive plants and animals dating back to the Paleozoic era, more than 225 million years ago, have been found in New Jersey, though they are not as plentiful here as in neighboring states. More fossils are available from Triassic times, the first period of the Mesozoic era, in which the climate for the most part was warm and moist. The type of flowering plants that we know today did not exist at that time. Instead, more primitive plants, some of them huge trees with a fernlike appearance, grew in the swamps through which dinosaurs roamed and left a record in the form of footprints embedded in the Triassic shale. It was in the later Cretaceous period, 65 million to 135 million years ago, that plants somewhat similar but still ancestral to those of today grew in New Jersey. Fossils dating back to Tertiary times (1.75 to 65 million years ago) give evidence that during this time, plants growing in New Jersey were quite similar to those now found in the latitude of Virginia.

When the glacial ice started to move over the northern part of our state about 1 million years ago, it must have destroyed existing vegetation in a manner similar to that strikingly illustrated in a photograph taken in Alaska (Figure 4-1). Advancing ice completely overruns a forest, destroying all trees that lie in its path. During the period of extensive glaciation in North America, some plant species were able to continue their existence by migrating southward. Those species unable to migrate were exterminated.

While the boundaries of land covered by glacial ice in New Jersey have been clearly identified, disagreement about the climate and the vegetation that continued to exist south of the ice sheet remains. Some believe that it was so cold in southern New Jersey that only a treeless vegetation similar to that found in the Arctic today could have existed. Others think that while either the arctic tundra type of vegetation or spruce–fir forests now typical of Canada may have grown in a belt 10 to 50 miles wide adjacent to the glacial edge, a more temperate type of vegetation survived farther south in the state. In any event, there is enough evidence to conclude that because of the colder climate, vegetation different from that today must have existed in the part of New Jersey that was south of the ice sheets.

In the last 1 million years the glacial ice has alternately advanced and retreated, depending upon temperatures. In extended cold periods, the glacial ice advances, and in warmer periods, such as we are now enjoying, glacial ice melts, causing higher sea levels. As a result of glacial ice melt, land areas previously covered with vegetation now are inundated by sea water. Evidence of the changing sea level has been found in the Hackensack Meadows, where remains of a former cedar tree forest are now overlain with tidal marsh grass.

The last ice sheet, which at its maximum was as much as 2,500 to 3,500 feet in thickness, started to melt and retreat from New Jersey about 18,000 years ago. After this date, vegetation reestablished itself on those parts of the Ridge and Valley, Highlands, and Piedmont sections that had been covered by ice. In addition, the type of vegetation growing south of the ice sheet changed composition; most of the species now more typical of colder regions migrated northward and were replaced by those presently found in New Jersey. A record of changes in vegetation types of New Jersey is preserved in peat bogs and lakes. As long as a bog or lake has existed, pollen grains from the plants growing around the area have

Figure 4-1. Glacial ice sheet advancing over a forest. In 1966 the north margin of Meares Glacier in south central Alaska overran trees in a 300-year-old forest in the same manner that the ice sheets must have advanced on forests in New Jersey in Pleistocene time. (Photo by W. O. Field, American Geographical Society, taken September 2, 1966.)

been deposited in the bog or lake. Thus, pollen from plants currently growing in the area accumulates in a layer above that of plants growing in previous times. By analyzing sample cores from bogs and lakes, scientists can reconstruct from the preserved pollen grains a history of the groups of plants that grew in the past. From the pollen-recorded sequence of changing vegetation types, the history of climatic changes that must have occurred in the past can be postulated. Some of the species now remaining as relics of the Ice Age and plant immigrants from areas farther south are identified in later chapters.

Long-term climatic changes such as those just described are one reason for changes in the natural vegetation of an area. This happens because lower (or higher) temperatures are more favorable to some species than others. Thus, long-term cooling or warming trends have always been accompanied by gradual changes in the plant species composition of an area. The vegetation of New Jersey 15,000 years ago may have resembled that now present in the Arctic or in Canada, but some 15,000 years in the future, if the warming trend continues, the present vegetation may be replaced by plant immigrants more typical of warmer climates, such as those now in the southeastern United States.

Vegetation of New Jersey at the Time of European Discovery

The date of the first arrival of humans or their ancestors in New Jersey has not yet been firmly established. Humans as we know them today are thought to have arrived in the eastern United States only as early as 10,000 or 11,000 years ago—a few thousand years after the last glacial ice had disappeared from New Jersey. The climate then is thought to have been a good deal cooler than at present, and although dinosaurs no longer roamed the state, the now-extinct mastodons, close relatives to the elephants, were plentiful.

The first real evidence of the presence of the human species in the state is derived from Indian artifacts found along the upper Delaware River valley. These have been scientifically dated, indicating their use about 7,000 years ago. There is no accurate record of the number of Indians who lived in New Jersey before the Europeans came into the state; some authorities believe that the permanent Indian population was only 2,000 or 3,000, but others think that it was as high as 8,000 to 12,000. The Indians who occupied New Jersey at the time of the European settlement belonged to the tribe known as the Lenape (or Delawares). Their numbers were distributed unevenly throughout the state, concentrating in sites accessible by water, such as the valleys of the Delaware, Passaic, Hackensack, and Raritan rivers, the same areas that later were to be crowded by the European settlers.

In the course of living in New Jersey, the Indians disturbed the natural vegetation. Sites had to be cleared for villages and for the cultivation of agricultural crops, particularly maize. According to Gordon Day, who studied the impact of Indian activities on the forests of northeastern United States, the Indians cut the forests extensively to provide the wood and bark used for utensils, weapons, canoes, shelters, and especially for fuel.

In addition to destroying the forest in some locales, the Indians modified its composition in larger areas, mostly by setting fires. They recognized that many types of game such as deer prefer open woods to dense forests. Also, hunting can be made easier by the use of fire to drive game. Travel to and from hunting and fishing areas throughout the state was made easier when dense thickets of forests were cleared by burning. Once fires were started, they were allowed to burn until extinguished by physical barriers or by other natural means.

The Lenape Indians deliberately burned the woods in spring and fall, and many early explorers of the New World including Henry Hudson observed smoking forests when approaching the coast. The report of a Dutch navigator nearing the coast of New Jersey in 1632 stated that those on shipboard

> smelt the land, which gave off a sweet perfume, as the wind was from the Northwest, which blew off the land, and caused these sweet odors. This comes from the Indians setting fire, at this time of year, to the woods and thickets, in order to hunt; and the land is full of sweet smelling herbs, as sassafras, which has a sweet smell. When the wind blows out of the northwest, and the smoke is driven out to sea, it happens that the land is smelt before it is seen. The land can be seen when in from thirteen to fourteen fathoms.

This is one of several similar observations collected in a book of narratives of early Pennsylvania, western New Jersey, and Delaware by Albert Myers.

The results of the Indian-set fires in New Jersey are believed to be similar to those in New England, described by Thomas Morton in 1637:

> The Salvages are accustomed, to set fire of the Country in all places where they come; and to burne it, twize a year, vixe at the Springe, and the fall of the leafe. The reason that mooves them to doe so, is because it would other wise be so overgrowne with underweedes, that it would be all a copice wood, and the people would not be able in any wise to passe through the Country out of a beaten path . . . for this custome hath bin continued from the beginning. . . . For when the fire is once kindled, it dilates and spreads it selfe as well against, as with the winde; burning continually night and day, until a shower of raine falls to quench it. And this custome of firing the Country is the meanes to make it passable, and by the meanes the trees growe here, and there as in our parks.

Opinion differs about the extent to which the activities of the Indians actually impacted the landscape of New Jersey. It is likely, however, that they cleared accessible river valleys for settlements and crops and also that they set fires. The effect of Indian-set fires, like those of their successors and like those caused by lightning, was to modify the composition of New Jersey forests. This is because some species of trees are more resistant to fire damage than others.

European Colonization and Its Impact on Vegetation

Although the Indians undoubtedly left some imprints on the landscape of New Jersey, it was the European settlers and their descendants who truly disturbed the vegetation of the state.

The Delaware River valley was the first area settled by the Europeans, for they, like the Indians, favored sites accessible to water. Located as it is between two large rivers, the Hudson on the east and the Delaware on the west, New Jersey offered relatively easy access and invited early settlement. As early as 1620 the Dutch started settling along the shores of the Hudson River and the Swedes along the Delaware, but the land of the state was officially claimed by England in 1664. Thereafter settlement of the state rapidly increased.

Colonization proceeded at different rates. Pioneers spread out from the initial sites of settlement, the Delaware, Hudson, Hackensack, Passaic, and Raritan River valleys, and occupied the rest of the lowlands in the Piedmont and Inner Coastal Plain sections. Although it was both accessible by water and fertile, the Kittatinny Valley was not settled initially because it was occupied by hostile Iroquois Indians.

Soon, most of the upland on the Piedmont and Inner Coastal Plain was cleared for agricultural use. The forests on higher slopes or ridges or in areas too wet for cultivation were kept as the source of wood needed for shelter, fencing, household utensils, and heating. From the time of initial settlement, however, domestic animals such as cattle, horses, and hogs were allowed to graze freely in the woodlands.

In 1726, the date of the earliest census, the population of New Jersey was 32,442; by 1784 this had jumped to 149,435. To facilitate clearing of land for settlement or for cultivation, the Indian practice of setting fire to the forests was continued by some European settlers. By the time New Jersey became a state in 1778, no extensive areas of land well suited to farming remained wooded in the central part of the state.

Nineteenth Century: Human Activities and Vegetation in New Jersey

As the population of New Jersey continued to grow, so did the need for wood. Until the middle of the nineteenth century, wood was the only source of fuel. In addition to accommodating the household needs of the growing population, wood was needed in enormous quantities as fuel for the operation of steamboats and locomotives and for the early New Jersey industries of lumbering, iron making, charcoal production, and the manufacture of glass. In 1783 a visitor from Europe observed that a single iron furnace in Union, New Jersey, had exhausted a forest of nearly 20,000 acres in about 12 or 15 years, and the works had to be abandoned for lack of wood.

Settlers spread out into less fertile areas of the Highlands and the Ridge and Valley sections, but because of the poor soil conditions, agricultural subsistence on the ridges was never really successful. For the same reason the major part of the Outer Coastal Plain, the area of the Pine Barrens, was not attractive to the early settlers. However, to meet the enormous demand for wood, the forests in these areas were cut frequently and repeatedly for cordwood. The indiscriminate cutting of woodlands at 20- to 25-year intervals was accompanied by continuing damage by wildfires. In 1874 an estimated 100,000 acres of forests were burned, and in 1885 another 128,000 acres were lost.

Fortunately, with the introduction of coal in 1850 and other fuel material later, the demand for wood from the forests of New Jersey decreased. However, repeated cutting of wooded areas combined with fire damage had already so altered the composition of the forests that the effects can be seen in New Jersey today. As an example, cedar swamps are now relatively rare in South Jersey even though early settlers reported that they were commonly found there. Unfortunately, the Atlantic white cedar, the dominant tree in these swamps, does not have the ability to resprout after being damaged by fire or cut for timber. Also, this species is only able to reestablish itself by seeding under special conditions. For this reason, after cutting, cedar swamps are often replaced by hardwood swamps with different species of trees. Like the cedar, sugar maple and hemlock also cannot resprout after cutting. Those species that can resprout after fire damage or cutting, such as the oaks and pitch pine, typically develop multiple stems (Figure 1-1). These are commonly seen in New Jersey forests today.

Starting in 1850, the population of New Jersey increased rapidly and grew from a total of 489,000 in 1850 to slightly under 2 million by 1900 (Figure 4-2). During this time, however, because of the substitution of anthracite coal for wood and charcoal, humans did less damage to the natural vegetation of New Jersey than in the preceding 50 years. That the forests of the state were able to recover, in part, from some of the past misuses is reflected in the 1899 report of the New Jersey State Geologist:

> Reviewing all the evidence which we have collected, therefore, we state with confidence that there was progressive cutting and clearing-up of the original forest all over the State, from its settlement until 1860, but that at the latter date very little original forest remained. This cutting was most severe about 1850, and from 1850 to 1860 was the period of maximum deforestation. The forest was then younger and smaller, with a larger proportion of stump and brush land than has prevailed at any time since. The

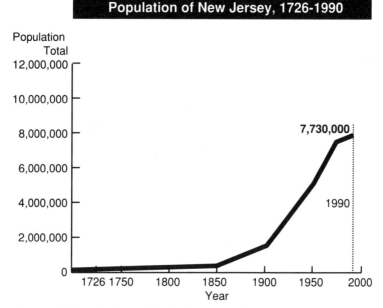

Figure 4-2. Growth of population in New Jersey from 1726 to 1990. (Source: Figures for 1726 to 1950 from John Brush, *The Population of New Jersey* [New Brunswick, N.J.: Rutgers University Press, 1956]. Figures for later years from the N.J. Department of Labor, State Data Center.)

cutting of very young growth has decreased to a marked extent in recent years, and the average size and age of the forest has increased. At present not two per cent of the forest is cut annually, so that at the present rate of cutting all of the forest may attain an age of fifty years.

In the same report the State Geologist stated that in 1899, 46 percent of New Jersey land was covered by forest—as much as had existed in 1860. An almost equal amount of land was used for farming.

As might be expected, even in 1899 the wooded areas were not distributed evenly throughout the state. At this time, only 15 percent of the Inner Coastal Plain and 23 percent of the Piedmont area consisted of wooded land. In contrast, 68 percent of the Outer Coastal Plain, 56 percent of the Highlands, and 45 percent of the Ridge and Valley section were forested.

Twentieth Century: Population Growth and Dispersal

From 1900 to 1990 the population of New Jersey more than tripled (Figure 4-2), and New Jersey has become known as the most urban state of the union. The statistics that support this reputation are staggering: New

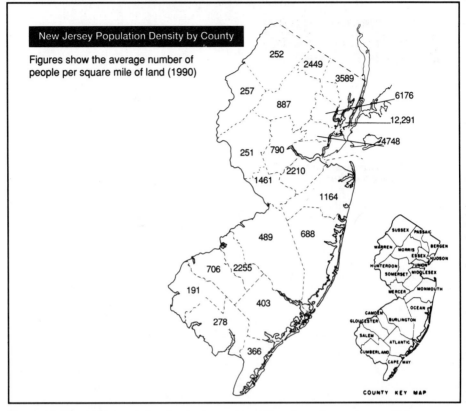

Figure 4-3. The 1990 population density (average number of people per square mile) in each county of New Jersey. (SOURCE: Census of Population and Housing, March 1991. New Jersey Department of Labor, State Data Center.)

Jersey has a population density averaging 1,042 people per square mile, the highest of the fifty states; 8.9 percent of the total population of the United States lives within a 50-mile radius of New Brunswick, located in central New Jersey; and the state has more miles of highway per square mile and more cars per mile of highway than any other state. Fortunately, until recently, increases in population have tended to follow the distribution pattern established originally by the Indians and followed by European colonists. Certain areas of the state have been heavily settled while others remain more sparsely populated. Two sets of statistics highlight this fact: the population density by county, shown in Figure 4-3, and the county percentages of total population as compared with the percentages of total land area, shown in Figure 4-4. Both sets of figures indicate that as of 1990, the population of New Jersey is concentrated in three areas.

1. By far the highest concentration of people is in the seven counties that border the New York metropolitan region: Bergen, Passaic, Hudson,

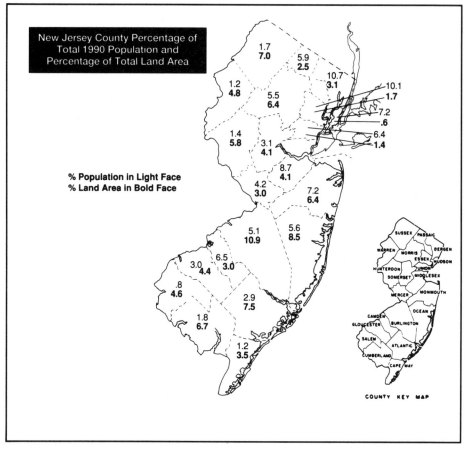

Figure 4-4. A comparison for each county of its percentages of the total 1990 population of the state with the total land area of the state. (SOURCE: Census of Population and Housing, March 1991. New Jersey Department of Labor, State Data Center.)

Essex, Union, Monmouth, and Middlesex. In 1990, the population of the seven counties totaled 4,328,468, or 56.2 percent of the total population of the state, although these counties account for only 19.8 percent of the total land in the state.

2. A much less concentrated center is in Camden County, the county that adjoins the Philadelphia area. Camden County has 6.5 percent of the population but only 3 percent of the land area of the state.

3. Population is also concentrated, though to a still lesser extent, in the Trenton, Mercer County, area, which has 4.2 percent of the population but only 3 percent of the land.

Altogether, the nine counties enumerated above have densities of over 1,000 people per square mile and in 1990 accounted for about 67 percent of the total population of New Jersey but only about 26 percent of the land area. In contrast, of the remaining twelve counties in New Jersey, all average population densities well under the state norm, and all but four have fewer than 500 people per square mile.

It is because the population is not equally distributed that significant natural areas remain in New Jersey in spite of its high degree of urbanization. How long this will remain true is questionable; since 1960 areas of the state that were sparsely populated have begun to experience population growth, some at a very accelerated rate. For example, in just 30 years the population of Ocean County grew from 38,000 to over 433,000; it won what might be considered an unfortunate distinction, that of being the fastest-growing county in the whole United States in the last two decades. Other counties that historically have also been sparsely populated—Burlington, Cape May, Sussex, and Morris—are now growing at an accelerated rate, while the more urbanized counties of Bergen, Essex, Hudson, Union, and Mercer actually lost population in the last decade as people and businesses moved away from cities and older suburbs to more rural places in the state.

Population Growth and the New Jersey Landscape

The explosive population growth of the twentieth century accompanied by the recent dramatic shift of people from cities and older suburbs to more rural areas has left significant imprints on the New Jersey landscape. Hundreds of thousands of acres of valuable farmland, forestland, and other open space have been swallowed up by development.

Housing, shopping malls, and other commercial and industrial buildings with their acres of paved parking lots now stand where once there were woodlands, wetlands, sand dunes, or farms. As late as 1930 New Jersey had about 27,000 farms, but by 1991 this had fallen to about 7,500; fertile farmland soils particularly on the Piedmont and Inner Coastal Plain have been eroded away. In just two decades, between 1970 and 1990, New Jersey lost more than 180,000 acres of farmland and other open space.

Even the wetlands have not escaped development pressures. The state has lost by drainage or fill-in much of its saltwater marshlands and freshwater wetlands. Now less than 325 square miles, or about 4.3 percent of the state, consist of tidal land, or salt marshland on which a nonforest type of natural vegetation prevails. The degree to which human activities have invaded and destroyed much of our original marshland can be observed when riding on the turnpike or train through the Newark and Jersey City area. Much of the natural marshland in this region has been lost to drainage systems or destroyed by landfill operations, and that which remains is threatened by pollution. The Atlantic white cedar swamps that early settlers thought characterized the Coastal Plain of New Jersey had been reduced to about 50,000 acres as the twentieth century began, and now less than half of that remains.

Destruction of the natural ecosystems by development has meant the loss of habitats for plant species as well as for wildlife. Without the appropriate environmental conditions (or habitat) a species may no longer be able to survive. The state Department of Natural Lands Management reported in 1993 that 130 plants that once grew naturally in New Jersey no longer survive here; also, 308 additional species have populations so small that their survival is in jeopardy. Such species are listed on New Jersey's endangered species list. Scientists are concerned too about the increasing fragmentation of the natural ecosystems into smaller-sized, often isolated, units to accommodate development. This has occurred, for example, in the Pine Barrens, where large residential communities have been sited in the middle of forested areas. Fragmentation of a forest usually results in a reduction in the number of native species and in the genetic diversity of the entire system, thus diminishing its capability to adapt to changing environmental conditions and ultimately to survive.

Population growth and increased industrial activities have brought a legacy of air, water, and soil contamination problems to the state. The impact of atmospheric pollution on the natural vegetation was discussed in Chapter 3; pollution of surface and groundwater also threatens native plant species. Toxic wastes deposited in stream waters have reduced the variety of plants growing in streams and along their banks. The impact on streams of sewer wastes and polluted runoff from upland sites can be seen all over the state. The green scum on polluted waters actually is an aggregate of small living plants called algae. The algae population grows abnormally large in situations where excessive nutrients exist in the water; the algae then choke out other forms of plant life and fish. Later chapters take up in more detail the destructive impacts of human activities and the actions that must be taken to protect the landscape and natural vegetation of New Jersey.

Other Biological Influences on Vegetation

Biological interactions other than those involving humans may also exercise a major influence on the vegetation of an area. Both interrelationships among plants themselves and between plants and animals have had an impact on the natural vegetation of New Jersey. While such interactions existed before the presence of human beings, we will see that human actions have disturbed some of these biological interrelationships to the detriment of natural vegetation.

Plant–Plant Interrelationships

Chapter 1 described an example of what ecologists call successional change in vegetation—a piece of land was stripped of its natural vegetation, farmed, and then abandoned. The vegetation on the site gradually and naturally reverted back to forestland. In some part it is competitive action among plants that causes this type of natural change in vegetation. The plants growing in any area usually are competing among themselves—individuals within a single species and whole populations of different species—for the available resources of water, soil nutrients, and light. Whenever one or more of these resources is in short supply, some plants, and even all individuals of a whole species, may not be as successful as other plants or other species in getting their share of the needed resource. Also, slight short-term changes in environmental conditions may shift the advantage of exploitation from one species to another. Competition for a particular resource may lead to the death of certain individuals or to the extinction of whole populations of certain species at the benefit of others. These failures and successes over a period of time result in the process of succession and cause gradual changes in the plant composition of a given area.

Successional stages of vegetation may originate from forces other than those of human origin; glaciation in New Jersey, for example, was responsible for the initiation of varied successional stages of vegetation because the ice sheets completely obliterated large areas of natural plant growth that probably represented the climax stage as defined in Chapter 1. Much of the land left bare of plant growth by glaciers thousands of years ago is now in various stages of successional growth. As another example, strong winds may blow down a group of trees in the middle of a forest, opening the area to light. This permits plants that need light to flourish and to compete with the shade-tolerant species already there, changing the plant composition in a small patch of the forest. Changes in species composition as they specifically occur in succession in New Jersey are described in the third part of this book.

Invasion of Exotic Plant Species   Exotic plants (also called aliens or introduced species) are those that have been introduced to an area intentionally or unintentionally by people; thus, they are not part of the original natural vegetation. Historically, such plants were brought in accidentally (in the ballast of a ship, for example) or as sources of food. More recently they have been introduced for landscaping purposes.

Some exotic plants cannot compete against native species, but many others adapt very well to their new environment and proliferate. They consume habitat space and compete with native species for germination sites, nutrients, and light, resulting in the local elimination of native species. The new environment may harbor no insects to eat the invading plant and thereby control its population. In New Jersey, exotic shrubs such as Japanese honeysuckle, Japanese barberry, and multiflora rose have crowded out many native shrubs. In the early 1800s, imported purple loosestrife was a favorite garden plant. Now it forms dense, impenetrable stands along stream banks such as along the Delaware, where it has crowded out a number of native species found nowhere else in the state. That the problem of alien plants is significant is reflected in estimates by botanists that as many as 25 percent of the plant species now present in New Jersey are exotic plants.

Figure 4-5. Example of a destructive plant–plant relationship in New Jersey. Light shines on the leaves of a chestnut tree sprout in High Point State Park. Tree sprouts will grow only about 15 feet tall and then be killed back by the fungus blight.

Other Destructive Plant Interrelationships Some organisms classified as plants can cause disease and even death of other plants. One such plant organism is a particular type of fungus known as the chestnut blight. At the beginning of the twentieth century, the American chestnut tree was a common and beautiful tree in the forests of central and northern New Jersey as well as other eastern states. In 1904 the chestnut blight fungus was accidentally brought into the United States from eastern Asia. This fungus, a parasitic organism, causes a disease in the tree bark and can kill a chestnut tree. Within fifty years of its introduction into the country, the disease spread over the entire range of chestnut trees, killing all mature trees growing in the northeastern United States. Today no fully grown chestnut tree remains in New Jersey forests. While sprouts may develop from diseased tree trunks, they rarely grow more than 15 to 20 feet high before being killed by the fungus. The die-off of the chestnut trees left gaping holes in the forests of the state, holes that are now being filled by other types of trees (Figure 4-5).

Today, in New Jersey as well as in New England, we can see the disastrous results of another tree disease, Dutch elm disease, caused by another type of fungus. The fungus is carried from tree to tree by the elm bark beetle. Not only have most of the huge elm trees that lined our streets died off in large numbers, but those growing naturally in the woods have gradually disappeared.

A more recent victim of a destructive fungus is the lovely native dogwood tree, which grows as an understory tree in the forests of central and northern New Jersey. During the 1980s the flowering dogwoods began to die off. Foresters now believe that environmental stress, including acid rain and other atmospheric pollution, extensive drought in the early 1980s, and some severe winter weather, is the primary force behind the dogwood decline. Trees weakened by these stresses are more susceptible to a particular type of fungus that then causes the death of the tree.

Animal–Plant Relationships

In New Jersey abundant evidence of both beneficial and destructive interrelationships between plants and animals exists. An example of beneficial interrelationships is the dependence of forest trees upon animals for successful survival. Earthworms, along with many other soil-inhabiting organisms, improve soil conditions for plants; still other organisms, mostly microscopic, decompose fallen logs and leaf litter in the forest, thereby returning to the soil nutrients needed for plant growth. Also, we can observe the role of flying insects, such as bees, butterflies, and moths, who aid in the perpetuation of native plants by carrying from plant to plant the pollen needed for reproduction. The results of successful reproduction are plant seeds, which may be contained in berries or berrylike fruit such as that of the native dogwood trees, or in nuts such as the acorns of the oak trees. The fruit-eating birds—robins, blue jays, and cardinals, for example—aid the spread of dogwood and other trees throughout the woods of central and northern New Jersey. In the same way, common gray squirrels, who fail to eat all the acorns that they cache away, provide opportunities for acorns to develop into trees in locations far beyond the range of the parent tree.

On the other hand, plant seeds or nuts may be destroyed as well as disseminated by animals. Scientists studying oak trees have found that each year a large proportion of the acorn crop is destroyed or badly damaged by insects. Many species of insect can be found in acorns, but most of the damage is caused by several species of weevils, moths, wasps, and flies.

Other actions of animals have even more serious impact on natural vegetation. Currently, the greatest damage to the natural vegetation of New Jersey stems from the explosive growth in populations of particular insects who feed on the foliage of our native trees. While some loss of plant parts including leaf foliage to insects is always expected, complete defoliation of all trees of a species is abnormal and raises the tree mortality rate for the species far higher than that normally expected. In recent years there have been large increases in the population of three types of leaf-eating insects—the gypsy moth, the pine looper, and the hemlock woolly adelgid (Figure 4-6).

The gypsy moth was imported into Massachusetts from Europe in 1869 by a French scientist attempting to develop a strong race of silk-producing insects by crossing gypsy moths with silkworm moths. Unfor-

Figure 4-6. Examples of destructive animal–plant relationships in New Jersey. (Photos by the N.J. Bureau of Forest Management.)

Above left, an eastern pine looper nibbling on a needle of a pitch pine tree, 1993. Above right, defoliation of pitch pine trees at Double Trouble State Park by eastern pine loopers, 1993.

The defoliation of Mixed-Oak forest on Sunrise Mountain, Sussex County, New Jersey, by the gypsy moth caterpillar, 1969.

Tops of trees in hemlock forest at Sparta Glen have been defoliated by the hemlock woolly adelgid in 1993.

Above left, trees cut down by beaver building a dam to create a pond in High Point State Park, 1993. Above right, destructive deer browse on needles on lower branches of Atlantic white cedar trees in Lebanon State Park, 1993.

tunately, in a windstorm gypsy moth eggs were accidentally blown out of the laboratory into the surrounding area and hatched into caterpillars, which had no natural enemies to control their numbers. Since this catastrophe, the gypsy moth has spread into other eastern states, including New Jersey.

The gypsy moth has four life stages—egg, larva (or caterpillar), pupa (resting stage), and adult (moth). It is the caterpillar life stage that causes severe damage to vegetation. Gypsy moth caterpillars feed heavily at night on tree foliage, in New Jersey particularly on oaks and pines, and in a short time can completely defoliate a whole tree. Although a white oak tree can survive one complete defoliation, it becomes weakened and its natural growth becomes impaired. If defoliated in two or three successive years, the tree may die. The other common oaks in New Jersey—red, black, and scarlet—are slightly more resistant but will also die from successive defoliation. On the other hand, a single severe defoliation of a pine or hemlock tree may cause its death. Other species of trees in New Jersey killed by gypsy moth defoliation include the beech, birch, willow, poplar, and red maple.

Although gypsy moth egg masses were discovered in New Jersey as early as 1919, only 5 acres of woodland were defoliated in 1966. By 1971 this figure had grown to 180,000 acres and reached its highest level in 1981, when 800,000 acres were eaten by gypsy moths. On average, for the past 30 years, the insect has infested an average of 187,000 acres annually. The outbreak of these infestations is cyclic: 1992 had a lower incidence of damage than usual, but foresters expect a resurgence in coming years. By 1993, however, the Bureau of Forest Management reported that as yet no catastrophic damage had been done to New Jersey forests by the gypsy moth, but small patches of trees killed by successive defoliations can be seen in forests throughout the state, particularly in northern forests such as those at High Point, Stokes, and Farny. And many of the old oaks in Jockey Hollow Park near Morristown are said to have been killed by insect defoliation.

Another insect, the eastern pine looper, is causing damage by nibbling on the needles of pitch pine trees, the dominant tree species of the Pine Barrens. The needles then brown out and drop off, and unless the tree can develop new needles, it will die. Outbreaks of this insect seem to occur in 10- to 20-year cycles: in 1975 an infestation occurred; in 1991, 300,000 acres were damaged, and an additional 250,000 acres were damaged in 1992. State foresters cannot predict what tree loss will occur if defoliation continues in the same areas.

In the northern part of the state the dominant tree in ravine forests, the hemlock, is being destroyed by the hemlock woolly adelgid, referred to as HWA. This insect, a native of Asia, was introduced into the Pacific Northwest forests and then invaded the Northeast in the 1980s. The tiny adelgids suck juices from the base of the tree needles, causing the tree to lose vigor and then die in 3 to 5 years. The Bureau of Forest Management estimates that in 1993, of the approximately 26,000 acres of hemlock forests in New Jersey, about 1,000 acres have already died off and another 12,000 acres are seriously infested. As yet, there is no known satisfactory treatment for the hemlock trees.

The growing evidence in New Jersey as in other states is that recently the more damaging of the insect population explosions have resulted from human interference with the natural processes by which insect populations normally would be controlled. Usually after a few years of explosive growth, an animal population will naturally "crash" (or reduce in numbers) because of lack of food, attack by predators and parasites, climatic conditions, and disease. Ecologists believe that with the indiscriminate use of chemical pesticides humans interfere with these natural forces. For one thing, pesticides kill off predators (such as birds) and parasites that would feed on destructive insects. For this reason attempts are now being made to control by means other than chemical sprays the excessive outbreaks of gypsy moths and other damaging insects.

Instead, biological pesticides, such as *Bacillus thuringensis* are being used to control insect infestations, including the gypsy moth. The toxic bacillus attacks the egg, larval, and pupal stages of the moth. Scientists have discovered recently, however, that pest populations can become resistant to biological as well as chemical pesticides. To avoid this, a new approach to control insect infestations, called integrated pest management (IPM), is being used. Through a variety of technologies an IPM program can be designed to reduce rather than totally eradicate a pest population so that a population of natural enemies is also preserved to keep the pest under control.

Insects are not the only animals destructive to plants. By building dams, beavers can change the drainage conditions along a stream; areas not previously flooded may become submerged by a beaver-created pond (Figure 4-6). This has an impact on the vegetation as described in Chapter 5. The only larger animal now causing extensive damage to our natural vegetation is deer. Without natural predators such as wolves to control their population, overpopulation of deer occurs even in New Jersey. In these years extensive damage can be done to forest vegetation in both northern and southern New Jersey by deer that nibble on wildflowers, ferns, shrubs, and small trees. One of their preferred species is the Atlantic white cedar, which has suffered severely from deer browse. In recent years, large deer herds have been invading residential areas in search of food.

Summary

Since their initial occupation of New Jersey, humans have proceeded to destroy totally or to modify the natural vegetation of the state. The forest primeval has long been gone. More than half of the state previously covered by forest or marshes is now paved, or settled with houses or industrial buildings. In the past, the population has been highly concentrated in the most accessible and, fortunately, least diverse land of the state. This explains why New Jersey, the most densely populated state, continues to have diverse natural vegetation.

Other biological interrelationships have shaped the vegetation of New Jersey. Continued competition among plants has resulted in changes that reflect the successes and failures of particular species. Animals have had both beneficial and destructive impacts on the vegetation; in recent decades insect infestations have been particularly damaging to New Jersey's forests.

References and Source Material

Brush, John E. 1956. *The Population of New Jersey.* New Brunswick, N.J.: Rutgers University Press.

Buell, Murray F. 1970. Time of Origin of New Jersey Pine Barrens Bogs. *Bulletin of the Torrey Botanical Club* 97:105–108.

Daines, R. H., I. A. Leone, and E. Brennan. 1960. Air Pollution as It Affects Agriculture in New Jersey. New Jersey Agricultural Experiment Station Bulletin 794, New Brunswick, N.J.

Day, Gordon M. 1953. The Indian as an Ecological Factor in the Northeastern Forest. *Ecology* 34:329–346.

Deer on Your Doorstep. *New York Times Magazine,* April 28, 1991, p. 29.

Gibson, Lester P. 1972. Insects That Damage White Oak Acorns. U.S.D.A. Forest Service Research Paper NE-220. Northeastern Forest Experiment Station, Upper Darby, Pa.

Kegg, John D. 1970 and 1971. Results of 1971 Gypsy Moth Aerial Survey, N.J. *New Jersey Forest Pest Reporter,* vol. 4, nos. 2 and 5. Department of Agriculture. Division of Plant Industry, Trenton, N.J.

McCormick, Jack. 1966. *The Life of the Forest.* New York: McGraw-Hill.

Moore, E. B. 1939. *Forest Management in New Jersey.* Trenton, N.J.: New Jersey Department of Conservation and Development.

Morton, T. 1637. New English Canann. Boston, Mass.: John Wilson and Son. 1883.

Muntz, Alfred P. 1959. The Changing Geography of the New Jersey Woodlands. Ph.D. diss., University of Wisconsin, Madison.

Myers, Albert. 1912. *Narratives of Early Pennsylvania, West New Jersey, and Delaware.* New York: Scribner's.

New Jersey Department of Labor. 1991. *1990 Census of Population and Housing.* N.J. State Data Center.

Pyne, Stephen J. 1982. *Fire in America.* Princeton, N.J.: Princeton University Press.

Rogers, Georgia M. May 1969. The Menace of the Gypsy Moth. *New Jersey Municipalities.*

———. October 1970. The Gypsy Moth. *New Jersey Municipalities.*

Shafer, Elwood L., Jr. 1964. *Deer Browsing of Hardwoods in the Northeast:*

A Review and Analysis of the Situation and the Research Needed. Northeast Forest Experiment Station, Upper Darby, Pa.

Vermeule, C. C., A. Hollick, J. B. Smith, and G. Pinchot. 1900. Report on Forests, in *Annual Report of the State Geologist for 1899.* Trenton,, N.J.

Widmer, Kemble. 1964. *The Geology and Geography of New Jersey.* Princeton, N.J.: Van Nostrand.

Chapter 5

𝕵 *Diversity of Plant Habitats and Communities in New Jersey*

In Chapter 1 the ecosystem factors that influence vegetation of any region—climate, geologic and soil features, human actions and other biological interrelationships—were identified, and reasons given to explain why landscape variety or diversity occurs and why vegetation continually changes. Chapters 2 to 4 dealt individually with each ecosystem component as it relates specifically to the vegetation of New Jersey. This chapter analyzes the total impact of all ecosystem components on vegetation to identify the particular factors that cause differentiation of plant habitats in New Jersey. This leads to a delineation of the types of natural terrestrial habitats in New Jersey, which, in turn, provides a framework for the following chapters' descriptions of plant community types. To provide a basis for understanding what follows, the chapter opens with definitions of a few basic ecological terms.

Plant Habitat and Plant Community Type

The word "habitat" is used in a variety of ways; plant ecologists generally understand it to mean the place in which one plant or a group of plants live. As physical space, then, a plant habitat is defined in terms of its particular environmental characteristics such as soil type, soil moisture or drainage, temperature, and other conditions that may be critical for plant existence and growth. The degree of variety of plant habitats in a locality or in a whole state such as New Jersey depends therefore upon the amount of diversity in the environmental conditions within the locale or region. An area having uniform relief and climate and similar soil types and water drainage conditions throughout has little opportunity for variation in plant habitat conditions. On the other hand, in some places within a relatively small area there can be wide variation in relief, soil types, and drainage conditions, creating different types of plant habitats. This is the case with New Jersey.

Even though as noted in the first chapter every plant species has its own distinctive tolerance range and requirements for light, water, heat, nutrients, and other resources, almost always in nature some overlapping of these tolerance ranges occurs. As a result, within any one habitat plants of different species usually grow together. Generally, ecologists refer to the group of plants that live together as a "plant community." A plant community and the animals occupying the same habitat compose what is called the "biotic community"; thus, the biotic community represents the living part of an ecosystem. The well-known scientist Edward O. Wilson more precisely defines community as "all organisms—plants, animals, and microorganisms—that live in a particular habitat and affect one another as part of the food web or through their various influences on the physical environment."

Some ecologists have observed that under similar habitat conditions within a region as large as a state, or even several or many states, the same plant species, more or less, may occur together as a plant community in more than one place. For example, many of the same plant species growing together on sand dunes of the New Jersey coast also grow together on the coast of Long Island. This has led some ecologists to classify vegetation into groups called "vegetation types." Simply stated, a vegetation type (or plant community type) is a distinctive group of plant species that may be expected to grow naturally together in more or less the same population proportions under particular habitat conditions.

The natural vegetation of New Jersey, like that of other regions, may be described in terms of its plant community types. Before describing these, however, it is necessary to delineate the specific types of distinctive plant habitats that are typically found in the state, based on various combinations of environmental factors.

Moisture Differentiation of Plant Habitats

The factor most important for differentiation among plant habitats within the state of New Jersey appears to be the amount of water in the soil substrate, the medium in which the plant is rooted. As already noted, plants differ in their requirements for water and in their ability to tolerate extremes, whether excessive water or drought. Some plants can live only in standing water; others, such as desert or sand dune species, can exist only under extremely dry conditions. Still others are best adapted to gradations of soil saturation between these two extremes. As examples, in New Jersey the Atlantic white cedar tree grows mostly in sites that are covered with standing water for at least part of the year, while the chestnut oak tree is usually found on rather dry soils.

The amount of water in a plant substrate is controlled by the relief of the land surface, the soil type, the height of the water table, and the site's exposure to wind and sun. For example, rainwater rapidly runs off steep slopes, and thus little water penetrates below the surface of the soil. On the other hand, standing water may remain in depressions most of the year. Also, soils vary in their capacity to hold the water needed for plant growth. Rainwater drains quickly through very sandy soils, leaving little moisture in the soil for plant growth. In contrast, soils that contain a

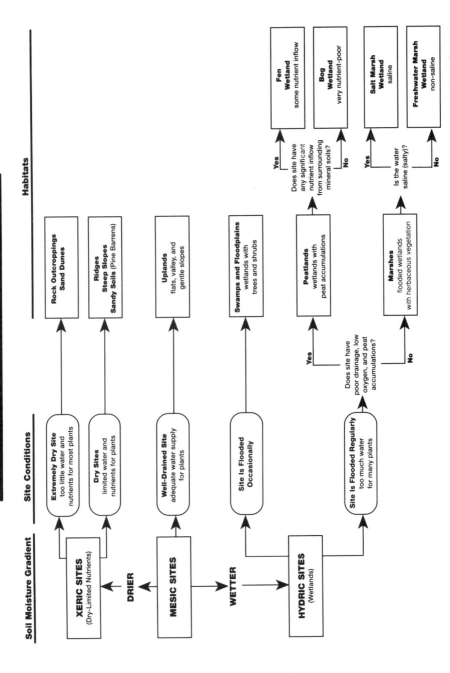

Figure 5-1. Amount of soil moisture as the primary influence causing differentiation of terrestrial plant habitats in New Jersey.

large amount of clay usually hold a great deal of water. The amount of moisture in the soil is also affected by the level of the water table. A high water table, as found frequently in parts of the Coastal Plain, may provide standing water at the level of deep-rooted plants. Finally, the amount of sun and wind a particular site receives influences the soil moisture content. A slope that faces south or is exposed to strong winds will be drier than one of similar soil that faces north or has less wind exposure.

The amount of moisture in soil can be considered in terms of a relative gradient ranging from extremely dry to a more or less permanent standing-water condition. Five categories in this gradient are suggested for an initial differentiation of plant habitats in New Jersey. These categories and their assigned place on the moisture gradient scale are depicted in Figure 5-1, and each category is assigned a habitat name. Grading from the driest soil condition (which ecologists call "xeric") to the wettest (or "hydric") condition, the five habitats are as follows:

Rock outcroppings and sand dune habitats represent the xeric extreme of habitats. In New Jersey rock outcroppings occur mostly at the higher elevations in the northern part of the state. These are very dry habitats because they lack a soil cover. Just about at the same point on the moisture gradient are the sand dunes of the New Jersey coast, on which limited moisture is available for plant growth.

Ridgetops and slopes of higher elevation and excessively drained flat habitats are dry sites, but not as dry as those of the previous category. Ridgetops and slopes of higher elevations are drier for two reasons: rainwater is quickly lost because of rapid runoff, and soil water evaporates because of exposure to sun and wind. In New Jersey these conditions are found mostly at higher elevations in the Highlands and the Ridge and Valley sections. The flat sites included in this category are those that are excessively drained primarily because of soil characteristics. For example, rainwater quickly drains through sandy soils because they have a limited water-holding capacity, and such soils therefore provide little soil moisture for plant growth. Excessively drained soils occur on the Outer Coastal Plain in the Pine Barrens.

Upland habitats are well-drained substrates representing an idealized midpoint on the moisture gradient and are referred to as mesic. In contrast to drier sites, mesic upland habitats retain a good supply of rainwater for use by plants, but unlike wetland sites, they usually have no standing water. In relief, mesic sites include land of flat or undulating contour including gentle slopes and hilltops that are not excessively drained and valleys and ravines that are not as wet as swampy lowlands or floodplains.

Wetlands occasionally flooded habitats are sites on which there is standing water on the soil surface for only certain parts of the year, most often in spring and early summer. For example, in the spring, standing water may accumulate in depressions of land or above the soil surface where the water table level is unusually high. By late summer the water on such sites normally drops to below the soil surface. On lowlands adjoining a river, called a floodplain, the land will be covered with water only occasionally, at times of unusually heavy rains when the river overflows its banks. This category includes swamps, which unlike marshes are flooded only occasionally and which are dominated by trees and shrubs.

Wetlands regularly flooded habitats are sites on which there is standing water on the soil surface most of the year or that are subject to flooding regularly year round if only for a few days each month or for some part of each day. Included in this category are tidal areas and the edges of estuaries, rivers, and ponds. In New Jersey marshes occur in inland areas as well as along the coast. By definition, a marsh is a frequently or continuously flooded wetland characterized by emergent herbaceous vegetation.

Further Differentiation of Wetland Habitat Types

Wetlands are an important component of the New Jersey landscape, estimates being that 19 percent of the state, about 900,000 acres, consists of wetlands, and they provide many different types of plant habitats. Plants that are adapted to wetland conditions are called hydrophytes, and different species of hydrophytes are found in different types of wetlands.

Thus far in this book, two types of wetland sites have been identified based solely on the amount of soil moisture in the substrate: sites flooded regularly and sites flooded occasionally. From the standpoint of vegetation, further differentiation must be made with respect to type of water, saline or fresh, and whether peat formations are present. Water salinity on a site distinguishes saltwater from freshwater wetlands, and the presence of peat in the substrate distinguishes the peatlands from other wetland types.

Saltwater and Freshwater Wetlands

While some plants (called halophytes) can successfully grow and reproduce in soil covered or saturated by salt water, others that flourish under standing freshwater conditions will die if salt water invades their habitat. Thus, for the purpose of categorizing wetlands vegetation, a distinction must be made between saltwater and freshwater habitats. For this purpose, then, in New Jersey the saltwater marshland is placed in a category separate from that of freshwater marshland. The same distinction is not needed for the other wetland habitats, such as swamps and floodplains, because they are saturated only with freshwater. Although some marshland can be said to have brackish water (an arbitrary midpoint between the extremes of fresh water and saline water), for purposes of this book such sites are included in the salt marsh category.

Peatlands: Bogs and Fens

In some wetlands, because of poor drainage (creating a condition of little or no movement of water and little oxygen) dead plant and other organic remains do not fully decompose to become part of the soil material but rather accumulate to form layers of material called "peat." Accumulations of peat are accompanied by very acidic conditions and low fertility, to which some plants are intolerant. Because plants have a varying tolerance to peat conditions, wetland habitats must be further differentiated to include this characteristic.

Wetlands with peat accumulations are called peatlands; and two types of peatlands, both found in New Jersey, are bogs and fens. The word "bog" dates back to medieval times and has been used through the years to distinguish a wide variety of soggy, spongy, and wet sites around the world. Ecologists now have restricted the use of the word "bog" to a particular type of wetland, a peat-accumulating wetland that has no inflow or outflow of water and is nutrient-poor. In contrast to a bog, a fen is a peat-accumulating wetland that receives some drainage inflow from surrounding mineral soils or from streams or springs and thus is not as nutrient-poor as a bog.

As in the case of other classifications, the differentiation between bogs and fens and between both of these and swamps cannot always be made with scientific exactness, and even ecologists might argue about whether a particular wetland is a bog or swamp. Also, on a higher level, there is no single, universally accepted definition for the identification of wetland sites.

Defining a Wetland

Up until 1989, different government agencies had individual ways of defining wetland sites. The U.S. Fish and Wildlife Service used three criteria—type of vegetation (the presence of hydrophytes), type of soils, and the water saturation condition. In contrast, the U.S. Army Corps of Engineers, under the permit system required by Section 404 of the 1977 Clean Water amendments, used only one criterion—vegetation.

As a general definition, wetlands are lands transitional between uplands and aquatic systems where the water table is at or near the surface or the land may be covered by shallow water and include marshes, swamps, bogs, fens, and similar areas. A more precise working definition of a wetland is contained in a manual issued in 1989 by four federal agencies, the Environmental Protection Agency, Department of Agriculture, Army Corps of Engineers, and the Interior Department. In that manual, wetlands are defined as areas that have mucky or peat-based soils, are havens to specific plants that thrive in moist soils (hydrophytes), or have water within 18 inches of the surface for at least 7 days during the growing season.

The definition of wetlands is very important because both federal and New Jersey state legislation protecting wetlands depends upon a legally accepted definition of wetland sites. Recent actions to weaken the definition, and therefore the protection efforts, are discussed in Chapter 14.

Influence of Climate on Plant Habitats

Variations in several other environmental conditions, while exerting less influence than soil moisture, still have an impact on vegetation in New Jersey. Among these are the variations in temperature as described in Chapter 3. The differences in the length of the growing season and the frostfree period in particular appear to be important for plants. The combination of lower temperatures and shorter growing seasons characteristic of northern New Jersey is more favorable to some plant species than the longer frostfree interval and growing seasons of southern New Jersey, conditions under which other types of plants appear to flourish.

It is not possible to delineate with any degree of scientific exactness a north–south geographic division of New Jersey wherein the temperature conditions on one side favor the group of plants more closely allied with northern regions over those with a more southern alliance. This is because soil and local relief conditions act together with climatic factors to produce conditions more or less favorable to northern or southern plants. However, for the purpose of describing the environmental differences that do occur in the state, a distinction is made between plant habitats of "North" and "South" Jersey based on a dividing line that coincides with the boundary that separates the Piedmont from the Inner Coastal Plain (Figure 5-2). This boundary is just south of the north–south dividing line used for the classification of weather data as described in Chapter 3; the latter division follows county rather than physiographic boundaries.

Other environmental differences, while important to some types of plants, appear to be of minor importance in development of a broad classification of plant habitats in New Jersey. For example, it has been reported for other states and appears to be true also of New Jersey that the same type of plant community can develop on a variety of soil material. There are some exceptions to plant indifference to the soil types of the state other than variations in water-holding capabilities. For one, soils derived from limestone material appear to be favorable to more different kinds of plants than any other soil type in the state.

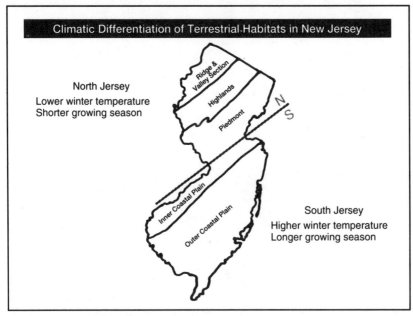

Figure 5-2. Climatic differences as a secondary influence causing differentiation of terrestrial plant habitats in New Jersey.

Terrestrial Plant Habitats in New Jersey

Based on combinations of the environmental factors of soil moisture, temperature, water salinity, and peat substrates, the natural landscape of New Jersey can be fitted into a framework of eight major types of terrestrial plant habitats, within which there are various subcategories (Figure 5-3):

   Type 1: North Jersey ridges and steep slopes of higher elevations, and rock outcroppings The ridges and slopes of higher elevations occur mainly in the Highlands and Ridge and Valley sections, though the formations of diabase and basalt on the Piedmont also have examples of this type habitat. Some parts of the ridgetops in North Jersey are still exposed rock outcroppings, a reminder of the time when the glacial ice stripped off the soil mantle and left the rock surfaces exposed.

   Type 2: North Jersey uplands This category includes the well-drained (mesic) lands of North Jersey, which are represented by the slopes, hilltops, valleys, and ravines of the Ridge and Valley and the Highlands sections as well as the flats of the Piedmont.

   Type 3: North Jersey freshwater wetlands Freshwater wetland habitats of North Jersey include marshes, swamps and floodplains, and

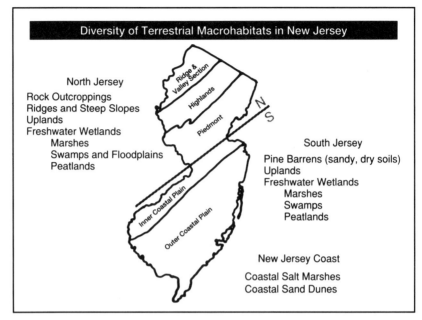

Diversity of Terrestrial Macrohabitats in New Jersey

North Jersey

Rock Outcroppings
Ridges and Steep Slopes
Uplands
Freshwater Wetlands
  Marshes
  Swamps and Floodplains
  Peatlands

Ridge & Valley Section
Highlands
Piedmont
Inner Coastal Plain
Outer Coastal Plain

South Jersey

Pine Barrens (sandy, dry soils)
Uplands
Freshwater Wetlands
  Marshes
  Swamps
  Peatlands

New Jersey Coast

Coastal Salt Marshes
Coastal Sand Dunes

Figure 5-3. Major types of terrestrial plant habitats in New Jersey.

peatlands—bogs and fens. Marshes are found next to the open water of lakes, ponds, rivers, and streams. Swamps occur mostly in glaciated areas of North Jersey, particularly in sites of former glacial lakes. An example is the Great Swamp, which is on the site of former Glacial Lake Passaic. Floodplains occur in the broad valleys of the larger rivers such as the Raritan. Bog and fen peatlands are found primarily in the area that was once covered by glacial ice. Ice sheets scoured out basins without inlets or outlets, and water from ice melt then filled them. Other bogs were created by glacial deposits that partially or wholly blocked drainage of streams or lakes, thus creating poorly drained areas.

Type 4: South Jersey freshwater wetlands The freshwater wetlands of South Jersey include marshes, swamps, floodplains, and peatlands. For the most part, all are associated with edges of meandering streams that flow through relatively flat terrain and with the estuaries on the ocean and Delaware Bay. Floodplains occur in broad valleys of the larger streams such as the Upper Millstone, and wetlands are frequently found where depressions of land are kept flooded on a regular basis by high water tables. The wetlands of South Jersey contain many species of plants not found in North Jersey.

Type 5: South Jersey Pine Barrens The excessively drained flats of South Jersey make up most of the region known as the Pine Barrens, in the sandy Outer Coastal Plain area. The land is excessively drained because of the poor water-holding capacity of the soils in this area and is thus classified as a drier habitat.

Type 6: South Jersey uplands The uplands of South Jersey, like those of North Jersey, are the well-drained lands that are not excessively dry or wet. These occur mostly on the Inner Coastal Plain but also include the parts of the Outer Coastal Plain that encircle the Pine Barrens.

Type 7: Coastal salt marshes of North and South Jersey Salt marshes occur in both North and South Jersey and range southward from the area of the Passaic and Hackensack river valleys. Marshes are present along the coastal mainland as well as on the bay side of offshore islands; the southern coast, which borders the Delaware Bay; and the tidal area of the Delaware River.

Type 8: Sand dunes of North and South Jersey Sand dunes, like rock outcroppings, represent the driest type of habitat in New Jersey. They occur along the coast primarily from Sandy Hook to Cape May.

Relationships Between Plant Habitats and Vegetation Types

The vegetation of any region such as the state of New Jersey consists of the aggregate of plant communities occupying the different types of plant habitats in the area. Since each type of habitat typically has distinctive vegetation, landscape diversity increases with habitat diversity. The plant communities typical of freshwater marshes will not have the same plant composition as those occupying upland areas. And in appearance, these different plant communities will look distinctive because of the growth form of a community's most abundant (or dominant species). For example, the characteristic appearance of the North Jersey upland type of vegetation is that of a forest, because the most abundant, or dominant, species are trees. In addition, the larger trees in these forests are mostly tall-growing, deciduous broadleaf trees: they lose their leaves in the winter and have a wide leaf compared with the narrow needles found, for example, on a pine tree. The forests of the drier South Jersey Pine Barrens form a sharp contrast in appearance. The forest canopy (the tops of the tallest trees) is not as high, and the trees themselves differ in appearance; many are evergreen-needled trees that stay green all winter.

Forests may also differ in the growth that occurs under the tallest trees. They may or may not have a lower level of smaller-growing (or understory) trees, and in addition, they may or may not have a well-developed shrub layer. (By common definition, a shrub is a plant with several woody stems but usually does not grow as tall as the understory trees.) Finally, plants without woody stems—the herbs—may form an abundant cover on a forest floor or be conspicuously absent.

Each kind of wetland—marsh, swamp, peatland—has a distinctive appearance also. Since no trees grow in marshes, they have the appearance of grassy fields. Swamps and peatlands such as bogs, on the other hand, do have tree growth but differ in their typical tree species and associated plants. The trees of New Jersey bogs are typically the narrow-needled trees (conifers) as contrasted with the broadleaf trees typical of swamps.

The typical types of plant communities that occupy the habitats of New Jersey are described in the next chapters. As will be discussed, human activities as well as natural forces have altered the development of the natural vegetation in some areas, and various stages of successional vegetation are present. In this sense, then, landscape diversity is dependent on the results of human and natural interference as well as on natural habitat diversity. This is well illustrated in New Jersey, a region long disturbed by humans and before that by glacial ice.

In the study of habitat diversity and plant community types it must be remembered that seldom in the real world are there sharp boundaries between habitats and between plant communities. Rather, more often than not a transitional zone between two habitats or two plant communities is present, combining some elements from both groups. While the composition in each habitat or community is quite different, some elements of each are found in the transition zone. Thus, it is often difficult or even impossible to determine where one type of wetland or one type of forest community ends and the next starts. Subjective interpretation then is the only basis for delineating specific boundaries of habitats or plant communities.

Distribution of Forestland in New Jersey

Forest cover is the predominant type of natural vegetation in New Jersey, and in view of the population growth described in Chapter 4, it is striking that in 1987 about 42 percent of the land in New Jersey was still forested. That so large a percentage is wooded is surprising since the population is now about nine times that of 1860, when 46 percent of the state was in forest.

There are several reasons for the continued high percentage of forestland despite explosive population growth. First, already mentioned, until recently the population increase has been concentrated in the northeastern counties adjacent to metropolitan New York. Even in 1899, when the state was still 46 percent forested, a large percentage of the land area of these counties was no longer in forest cover. Second, there has been a sizable decrease in the amount of land used for farming. In 1899, 46 percent of the land was devoted to farming activities, but according to most recent statistics, only 18 percent of New Jersey remains as farmland. While much of the lost farmland has been developed, some part of it, left abandoned, has reverted to woodland. This process has helped offset the appropriation of other forestland for development. Third, the amount of forestland conserved as part of state-owned parks and recreation areas has increased in the last 50 years.

On the whole, the locations of forest areas of New Jersey are concentrated much as they were as early as 1800. Obviously, then as now, the concentration of woodlands is in areas of the state not highly settled. At present there are about 2,007,000 acres of forestland in New Jersey; the distribution of this total by county is shown in Table 5-1. As indicated by the figures, the largest concentration of forestland in the state, 45 percent of the total, is in the five southeastern counties of Burlington, Ocean, Atlantic, Cape May, and Cumberland. This is the area of the Pine Barrens which in this century, prior to the enactment of protective legislation, lost a considerable amount of forestland (Table 5-1).

The second concentrated area of forestland, smaller than the Pine Barrens, is in the northern part of the state—the region of higher elevations in New Jersey including the ridges of the northern Highlands and the Ridge and Valley sections. In the Piedmont section, generally the only areas that are still wooded are diabase and basaltic ridges, wetland areas, and state parks. On the Inner Coastal Plain, because of urbanization and use of the fertile soils for agriculture, only the more poorly drained areas remain wooded. The distribution of forestland just described is illustrated dramatically by a map prepared by the Rutgers University Remote Sensing Center (Figure 5-4).

New Jersey Forests as Part of the Eastern Deciduous Forest Formation

The natural vegetation of the world has been classified in broad categories called formations, or biomes. When mapped, the boundaries of formations appear to coincide more or less with those of distinct climatic regions. In North America one of the major formations of natural vegetation is called the Eastern Deciduous forest, the classification to which the forests of New Jersey belong.

Simplified in the sense of number of formations and in delineation of their boundaries, the major formations of vegetation in the continental United States and Canada are mapped in Figure 5-5. Eight types of vegetation are so distinguished; these are as follows:

1. *The Tundra formation* is a very low-growing type of plant growth; many of the plants are lichens—particularly abundant is one called reindeer moss. With the lichens grow grasses, sedges, and perennial herbs, some of which produce large, colorful flowers in July and August. Only a few woody plants are found on the tundra, and these are dwarfed or grow in prostrate form, as in the case of birch or willow trees.

2. *The Northern Conifer forest formation* is a forest type of vegetation

Table 5-1. County Percentages of Total Forest Land in New Jersey, 1899 and 1987

County	Acres of forestland		Percentage of county in forest	
	1899	1987	1899	1987
Burlington	305,100	296,500	59	57
Cumberland	197,600	139,100	62	41
Hunterdon	38,200	99,600	14	36
Monmouth	90,300	90,300	30	30
Morris	138,500	141,200	46	47
Ocean	357,000	204,000	87	50
Salem	58,400	50,000	27	23
Sussex	134,500	210,000	40	62
Warren	59,700	108,900	26	47
Bergen	59,300	na	40	na
Essex	26,000	na	32	na
Hudson	1,400	na	5	na
Passaic	74,100	na	60	na
Union	15,400	na	23	na
	176,200	111,200	39	25
Camden	68,800	na	48	na
Gloucester	77,300	na	37	na
	146,100	143,700	42	41
Mercer	15,300	na	11	na
Middlesex	60,200	na	31	na
Somerset	29,900	na	15	na
	105,400	147,200	19	27
Atlantic	315,500	na	88	na
Cape May	122,100	na	73	na
	437,600	274,400	82	52

SOURCE: Figures for 1899 from C. C. Vermeule, "Report on Forests," in *Annual Report of the State Geologists for 1899,* Trenton, N.J. Figures for 1987 from Dawn M. DiGiovonni and Charles T. Scott, 1990, *Forest Statistics for New Jersey: 1987.*
NOTE: na = data not available.

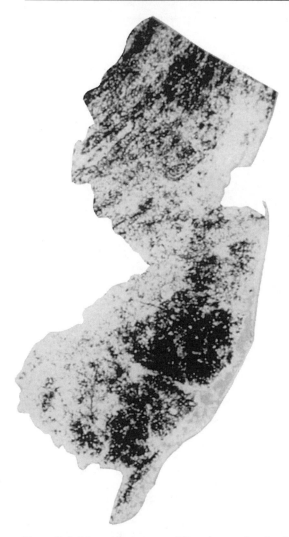

Figure 5-4. A forest cover map of New Jersey showing forest areas in black. (Derived from the classification of Landsat Thematic Mapper Imagery acquired March 17, 1991. Courtesy Cook College—Rutgers University, Remote Sensing Center.)

in which most of the trees are evergreen conifers—trees that bear seeds in cones and that have needlelike leaves that remain on the tree year round. Especially abundant are various species of spruce and fir trees, which are joined in some areas by large numbers of white (or paper) birch, trembling aspen, balsam poplar, and various species of pine trees.

3. *The Eastern Deciduous forest formation,* with which New Jersey is associated, derives its name from the fact that in the climax forests of the region the conifer trees are outnumbered by the so-called deciduous

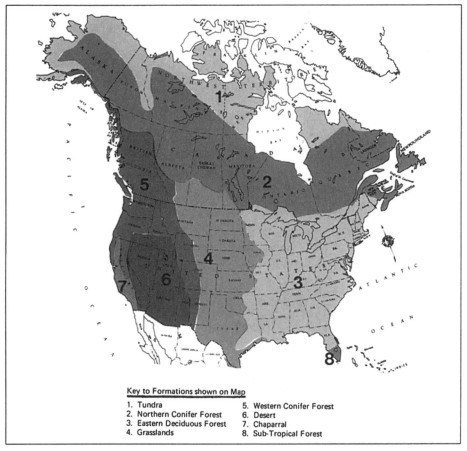

Figure 5-5. Eight major formations of natural vegetation in the United States and Canada. (Adapted with changes from Henry Gleason and Arthur Cronquist, *The Natural Geography of Plants* [New York: Columbia University Press, 1964].)

trees, which have broader leaves that fall off the tree at the start of the cold season.

   4. *The Grasslands formation* is a low-growing type of vegetation typical of the drier midwestern areas of the United States. The plants most abundant in this formation are various species of grasses, the taller of which grow in the areas of the most rainfall, or the prairies. Distinctively different in appearance are the plains—the drier grassland areas— which are covered by lower-growing grasses. Sites with moisture conditions between the prairies and the plains are covered by representative species from both groups as well as grasses of intermediate stature.

   5. *The Western Conifer forest formation* includes a number of different forest types, but all are dominated by conifer trees. These forests grow in the mountain areas of the western United States and Canada. Variations in the composition of the forest occur with altitudinal changes, but throughout various species of spruce, fir, and pine are the most abundant trees. Forests on the West Coast also include in predominant numbers the giant redwoods and western species of hemlock and red cedar.

6. *The Desert formation* includes vegetation that grows under the driest of conditions. Located between western mountain ranges, the deserts receive little rainfall; only specialized plants can survive where soil water is in such low supply. Many desert plants exhibit structural adaptations that permit their survival under dry conditions, such as the ability of the cactus plant to store water in its succulent tissues.

7. *The Chaparral formation* is a type of vegetation peculiar to lower California. The distinguishing plants in this formation are evergreen shrubs growing 3 to 10 feet tall and with rather small leaves that remain on the stems all year.

8. *The Subtropical forest formation* occurs in the continental United States only at the southernmost tip of the Florida peninsula and in the Florida Keys, where in swamps and on higher hummocks there is natural growth of some species representative of more tropical climates.

Classification of New Jersey's Upland Forests

The area circumscribed for the Eastern Deciduous forest formation includes the most densely populated and highly developed part of the country. Virgin forest once covered all the upland sites, but most of it has been destroyed. In New Jersey, and on the East Coast in general humans not only have displaced much of the natural vegetation but also through their past actions modified the composition of much that remains. Nevertheless, it is still possible to recognize distinctive subdivisions of the Eastern Deciduous forest formation, each a region of potentially distinctive climax forest types. The adjective "climax" as used here is defined in Chapter 1 and means forest types that have been relatively long-lasting in time as contrasted with "successional" forest types, which have a relatively short duration on a particular site.

Many attempts have been made to delineate acceptable subdivisions of the Eastern Deciduous forest formation. One of the classifications most widely accepted, though with some qualifications, is that developed by E. Lucy Braun. In her book *Deciduous Forests of Eastern North America*, Dr. Braun delineates nine regions of potentially different climax forest types and then further subdivides each region into varying numbers of sections. The names of the nine regions, whose boundaries are mapped in Figure 5-6, are derived for the most part from the identity of the most abundant climax trees in the region. Braun's classification scheme has some obvious shortcomings with respect to its treatment of New Jersey. For one, because of the die-off of the chestnut trees, the category entitled "Oak–Chestnut forest region" has long since been a misnomer when used for the forests of northern New Jersey as well as those in the remaining part of the region.

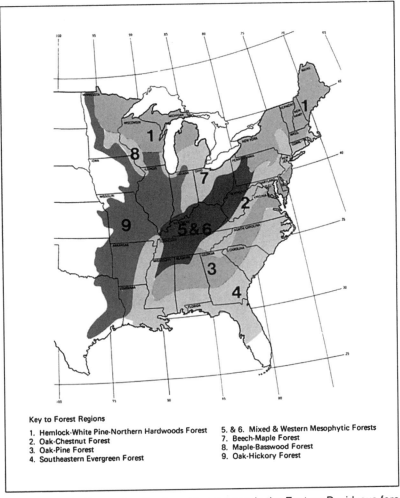

Key to Forest Regions

1. Hemlock-White Pine-Northern Hardwoods Forest
2. Oak-Chestnut Forest
3. Oak-Pine Forest
4. Southeastern Evergreen Forest

5. & 6. Mixed & Western Mesophytic Forests
7. Beech-Maple Forest
8. Maple-Basswood Forest
9. Oak-Hickory Forest

Figure 5-6. The Braun classification of forest types in the Eastern Deciduous forest formation. (Redrawn from E. Lucy Braun, *Deciduous Forests of Eastern North America* [New York: Hafner, 1960].)

Classification schemes for New Jersey forests have also been proposed by the U.S. Forest Service. These are more detailed in numbers of forest types and emphasize species of value as timberland.

We suggest that the representative climax upland forests of New Jersey as they presently exist be classified within the Eastern Deciduous Forest formation in three broad categories (Figure 5-7):

1. *The Mixed Oak forest, Northern Phase*   This type forest, described in Chapter 7, is representative of the typical upland sites in the Ridge and Valley, Highlands, and Piedmont regions.

2. *The Mixed Oak forest, Coastal Plain Phase*   Although somewhat similar to its counterpart to the north, the Coastal Plain phase of the

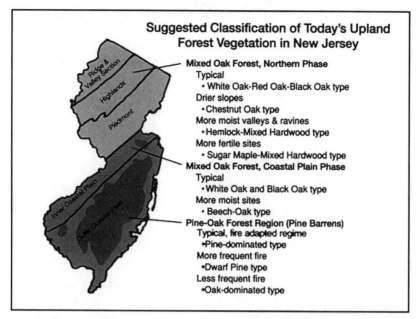

Suggested Classification of Today's Upland Forest Vegetation in New Jersey

- Mixed Oak Forest, Northern Phase
  Typical
  - White Oak-Red Oak-Black Oak type
  Drier slopes
  - Chestnut Oak type
  More moist valleys & ravines
  - Hemlock-Mixed Hardwood type
  More fertile sites
  - Sugar Maple-Mixed Hardwood type
- Mixed Oak Forest, Coastal Plain Phase
  Typical
  - White Oak and Black Oak type
  More moist sites
  - Beech-Oak type
- Pine-Oak Forest Region (Pine Barrens)
  Typical, fire adapted regime
  - Pine-dominated type
  More frequent fire
  - Dwarf Pine type
  Less frequent fire
  - Oak-dominated type

Figure 5-7. The authors suggest the classification mapped above for the upland forest vegetation of New Jersey.

Mixed Oak forest has many different components (see Chapter 11). This type forest is representative of the more mesic uplands on that part of the Coastal Plain that encircles the drier Pine Barrens.

3. *The Pine–Oak forest region*   This is the broad regional heading for the typical fire-adapted forest type found in the New Jersey Pine Barrens. Its composition is described in Chapter 10, along with that of other forest types found on the dry and sandy substrate of the Outer Coastal Plain.

The broad categories used here to classify the forests of New Jersey as part of the Eastern Deciduous Forest do not reflect the rich diversity of the vegetation of the state. This is because they ignore, intentionally so, the finer differentiations of habitat—wetlands, for example—which enrich tremendously our store of natural plant communities. The full array of New Jersey's plant communities will be described in the chapters that follow.

Summary

Despite its small size, New Jersey has diverse vegetation. This is so because of the variety that occurs within the state in landforms, temperature, parent rock and soil material, water drainage patterns, and in water salinity and peat conditions. Combinations of environmental conditions suggest eight major types of land habitats in New Jersey. Using these as the framework, the present vegetation of New Jersey is described in the chapters that follow.

The dominant form of natural vegetation in New Jersey is forest, and in spite of the state's heavy urbanization, a surprising amount of it (42 percent) remains wooded. These forests are but a small part of the Eastern Deciduous forest formation, one of the major categories of natural vegetation in North America. A broad regional classification of the climax upland forest types in New Jersey is suggested here as well.

References and Source Material

Braun, E. Lucy. 1950. *Deciduous Forests of Eastern North America.* New York: Hafner.

DiGiovanni, Dawn M., and Charles T. Scott. 1990. *Forest Statistics of New Jersey—1987.* U.S. Department of Agriculture, Northeastern Forest Experiment Station, Resource Bulletin NE 112, Radnor, Pa.

Johnson, C. E. 1985. *Bogs of the Northeast.* Hanover, N.H.: University Press of New England.

Lull, Howard W. 1968. *A Forest Atlas of the Northeast.* U.S. Department of Agriculture, Northeastern Forest Experiment Station, Upper Darby, Pa.

McCormick, Jack. 1966. *The Life of the Forest.* New York: McGraw-Hill.

Mitsch, William J., and James Gosselink. 1986. *Wetlands.* New York: Van Nostrand Reinhold.

Odum, Eugene P. 1989. Ecology and Our Endangered Life-Support Systems. Sunderland, Mass.: Sinauer Associates.

Tiner, R. W. 1985. *Wetlands of New Jersey.* Newton Center, Mass.: U.S. Fish and Wildlife Service, National Wetlands Inventory.

Wilson, Edward O. 1992. *The Diversity of Life.* Cambridge, Mass.: Belknap Press of Harvard University Press.

Part III

Plant Community Types in New Jersey Habitats

Chapter 6

⅜ *Ridgetops, Steep Slopes, and Rock Outcroppings of North Jersey*

The driest plant habitats in North Jersey are those associated with ridgetops, steep slopes, and rock outcroppings. These are dry for several reasons. Rainwater is quickly lost from ridgetops and steep slopes because of rapid runoff, which allows little time for rain to soak into the ground. In addition, the soil cover on many of these sites is thin and of poor water-holding capacity, and the water that does penetrate the soil may evaporate quickly because of exposure to sun and wind. Some rock outcroppings may lack any soil cover other than that in occasional cracks and crevices; such outcroppings are a very dry plant habitat to which only a few species are adapted.

As one might expect, ridges, slopes, and rock outcroppings are found mostly on the gneiss, shale, and sandstone in the Highlands and Ridge and Valley regions of New Jersey. However, ridges and outcrops of diabase or basalt in the Piedmont, such as in the Watchung Mountains and along the Palisades, have about the same vegetation types, with about the same dominant species, as equally dry sites in the Highlands and Ridge and Valley areas. This does not mean that every species will be the same; on the higher slopes in the Ridge and Valley section, for instance, a few northern plants not found in the Piedmont occur; and conversely, in those parts of the Highlands and Piedmont that were not glaciated, a few plants occur that are not found farther north.

Three plant communities are characteristic of ridgetops, slopes, and rock outcroppings in northern New Jersey, and the three intergrade to some extent. Two of the communities are forest types: the first, the Chestnut Oak forest, prevails on most of the slopes and ridgetops of higher elevations in North Jersey; the second, the Pitch Pine–Scrub Oak forest, is found only on the highest ridgetops in the state—Kittatinny Mountain, Bearfort Mountain, the highest spots in the Wyanokie plateau, and a few other sites. A third, found on rock outcroppings, is a long-lasting successional type that begins with a lichen–moss stage and eventually progresses to either a Pitch Pine–Scrub Oak forest or a Chestnut Oak forest.

Figure 6-1. Chestnut Oak forest growing on thin, rocky soil on an exposed ridge in High Point State Park. The sparse growth is characteristic; the understory is mostly bracken fern and black huckleberry.

Chestnut Oak Forest

The chestnut oak tree is a component of many forest types throughout New Jersey, but usually only on dry slopes at high elevations does it become the most important tree in the plant community. It appears to be able to reproduce and develop better than other oaks under the drier and poorer soil conditions characteristic of the higher slopes; the chestnut oak also regenerates readily by sprouting after fire or mechanical injury. The appearance of the Chestnut Oak forest is often rather distinctive. The trees have very thick, deeply ridged bark, and a significant percentage of them are likely to be multistemmed, indicating their origin as stump sprouts. Although the chestnut oak can grow to a large size, on the dry, rocky, infertile slopes the trees are usually somewhat stunted and misshapen. Frequently, the tops of the trees have been broken by ice storms, and in recent years some may be dead from the combined effects of drought and gypsy moth infestation (Figure 6-1). Whatever the cause, the crowns of the mature trees do not form a completely closed canopy.

The second most abundant tree in the Chestnut Oak forest may be any one of five species: red oak, white oak, scarlet oak, black birch, or pitch pine. The last three trees are more typical of sites with the thinnest soil cover. In addition to these species, black oak, red maple, pignut and shagbark hickories, sassafras, black cherry, and white pine are often associated, in smaller numbers, with the chestnut oak. That American chestnut was also once part of this community is evidenced by the sprouts that continue to come from the old, diseased stumps and roots. Some flowering dogwood is found as a lower-growing tree in the community, but it does not form a continuous understory as it sometimes does in more fertile New Jersey forests. Because of the sparse growth of the dominant chestnut oaks, considerable sunlight penetrates to lower levels in the forest, promoting the growth of a dense but often rather low-growing shrub layer.

The common shrubs of the Chestnut Oak forest are usually members of the heath family, plants typical of acid soils. Like chestnut oak, these heaths, including the early lowbush blueberry, late lowbush blueberry, deerberry, black huckleberry, pinxter flower, and mountain laurel, can resprout readily after fire. Additional shrubs found in the Chestnut Oak forest are the maple-leaved viburnum and the sweet fern. There are relatively few herbs on the forest floor on most sites, but some fairly typical species are wild sarsaparilla, bracken fern, wintergreen, and Pennsylvania sedge, a low, grasslike plant that spreads by underground stems to form a thin lawn in open places.

Many forms of Chestnut Oak forest can be seen on the higher slopes of the Ridge and Valley and the Highlands (Figure 6-2). One such slope is in High Point State Park, where the Appalachian trail crosses Deckertown Pike, the road that runs from Libertyville to Montague in Sussex County. The forest is located on the south side of Deckertown Pike about 1.3 miles east of the Sawmill Road, which goes north to the High Point monument. Here, the chestnut oak makes up about 55 percent of the tree cover. The larger trees measure 9 to 14 inches in diameter, average about 50 feet in height, and are approximately 95 years old. On this particular site, red oak is the second most abundant tree, with black oak, white oak, and black birch also common. The understory tree layer is composed of red maple, downy juneberry, sprouts of American chestnut, pignut and shagbark hickories, and many young chestnut oaks. Shrubs are rather uniformly and continuously distributed in this forest, with different plants important in different areas. In some places black huckleberry and lowbush blueberries may be more important, and in others pinxter flower or mountain laurel may be more abundant. The herb layer is very sparse, with wild sarsaparilla, wintergreen, and bracken fern the most common species. Other excellent locations in the same general area for seeing this forest type are around the parking area at the Sunrise Mountain overlook in Stokes State Forest and on the slopes above the cedar swamp in the Dryden Kuser Natural Area in High Point State Park.

To the southeast, the highest slopes of the Piedmont, such as those of Cushetunk Mountain in Hunterdon County, do not approach the eleva-

Figure 6-2. Chestnut Oak forest on a sheltered, relatively fertile upland area in High Point State Park. Red oak, black oak, white oak, black birch, and several species of hickory have joined the chestnut oak as major components of the forest.

tions of those in the Highlands or the Ridge and Valley sections, but still a form of the Chestnut Oak forest can be found on the ridgetop and higher slopes. The Cushetunk, an east–west running ridge about 600 feet higher than the surrounding Piedmont, shows differences in climate and vegetation between its north-facing and south-facing slopes. The air temperature, particularly close to the ground, is consistently higher on the south side, which receives a greater amount of solar radiation.

The climatic differences between the two slopes are reflected in the vegetation in several ways. For example, trees are larger on the more-moist north slope than on the dryer south slope. And although chestnut oak and red oak are the principal trees on both slopes, black birch, tulip tree, white ash, basswood, and sugar maple are more abundant on the north side than on the south. Among the lower-growing trees, flowering dogwood is much more important on the south slope than on the north, but twice as many shrubs grow on the north side, which also has a greater variety of species in this layer. The two slopes also differ greatly in the composition of the herb layer. On the north slope grow plants more typical of northern forests, including wild ginger, wild sarsaparilla, black snakeroot, columbine, and various ferns and mosses; on the warmer, drier south slope, various species of grasses, sedges, and annuals are more abundant.

Some typical plant species of the Chestnut Oak forest are listed in Table 6-1.

Table 6-1. Some Typical Plant Species of the Chestnut Oak Forest of North Jersey

Common name	Genus and species name
Dominant trees	
Chestnut oak	*Quercus prinus*
Red oak	*Quercus rubra*
Other trees	
Black oak	*Quercus velutina*
White oak	*Quercus alba*
Red maple	*Acer rubrum*
Black birch	*Betula lenta*
Scarlet oak	*Quercus coccinea*
Pignut hickory	*Carya glabra*
Shagbark hickory	*Carya ovata*
Bitternut hickory	*Carya cordiformis*
Sassafras	*Sassafras albidum*
Black cherry	*Prunus serotina*
Downy juneberry	*Amelanchier arborea*
American chestnut	*Castanea dentata*
Few others	
Shrubs and vines	
Black huckleberry	*Gaylussacia baccata*
Early lowbush blueberry	*Vaccinium pallidum*
Late lowbush blueberry	*Vaccinium angustifolium*
Deerberry	*Vaccinium stamineum*
Pinxter flower	*Rhododendron periclymenoides*
Mountain laurel	*Kalmia latifolia*
Scrub oak	*Quercus ilicifolia*
Winged sumac	*Rhus copallina*
Maple-leaved viburnum	*Viburnum acerifolium*
Sweet fern	*Comptonia peregrina*
Virginia creeper	*Parthenocissus quinquefolia*
Few others	
Herbs	
Wild sarsaparilla	*Aralia nudicaulis*
Bracken fern	*Pteridium aquilinum*
Whorled loosestrife	*Lysimachia quadrifolia*
Hairgrass	*Deschampsia flexuosa*
Wintergreen	*Gaultheria procumbens*

continued

Table 6-1 continued

Common name	Genus and species name
Herbs continued	
White wood aster	*Aster divaricatus*
Rattlesnake weed	*Hieracium venosum*
Pennsylvania sedge	*Carex pensylvanica*
False Solomon's-seal	*Smilacina racemosa*
Spotted wintergreen	*Chimaphila maculata*
Cow-wheat	*Melampyrum lineare*
Few others	

Pitch Pine–Scrub Oak Forest

On the highest ridgetops in North Jersey, such as Kittatinny Mountain, Bearfort Mountain, and Green Pond Mountain, grows a forest community in which pitch pine is the most abundant tree. It grows here on a very thin, dry, infertile soil high in silica, which is similar in composition to the soil of the Pine Barrens of southern New Jersey, where pitch pine is again a dominant tree species. On the ridgetops the soil cover is not only poor and thin but climatic conditions are rigorous. The sites are exposed to frequent sleet and ice storms and strong winds, and in addition they have in the past often been swept by fires.

Several forms of the Pitch Pine–Scrub Oak forest can be found in High Point State Park. Under the most rugged conditions the pitch pine is the only abundant tree, and it accounts for as much as three-quarters of the total number of trees (Figure 6-3). The other trees, which occur in small numbers, include red maple, black birch, gray birch, downy juneberry, and smooth juneberry. The pitch pine trees average only about 20 feet in height even though they are 70 years old, and they are sparsely distributed. The result is a forest with a very open canopy. Because of ice, sleet, and wind storms many of the treetops are broken off, and many branches are twisted. Trees that take root in rock crevices grow at various angles to the slope. The forest understory consists of thickets of scrub oak that reach no more than 10 feet high. Lower-growing shrubs, mostly late lowbush blueberry and black huckleberry, with some early lowbush blueberry, sweet fern, mountain laurel, sheep laurel, winged sumac, black chokeberry, and bush honeysuckle, and sprouts of American chestnut, are also present. Herbs cover about 20 percent of the ground in this forest, with wild sarsaparilla, bracken fern, and Canada mayflower most common.

On more protected parts of Kittatinny Mountain, the Pitch Pine–Scrub Oak forest is better developed and contains more tree species (Figure 6-4). In these the pine is still the tallest and most abundant tree, but chestnut oak, scarlet oak, white oak, and red maple trees in varying

Figure 6-3. Pitch pine dominates some ridgetop forests of North Jersey; these are in High Point State Park. The understory is mostly hairgrass, with some lowbush blueberry and black huckleberry.

Figure 6-4. Pitch pine grows with scrub oak, black birch, gray birch, chestnut oak, and several other species of trees and shrubs on some of the more protected ridges of North Jersey.

numbers are present. Occasionally, specimens of black oak, sour gum, and sassafras are found. Seedlings of oak trees are often more common than pine seedlings, which leads to the speculation that with control of fire the oaks may someday dominate the forest. The reason for this is that for successful germination and growth, pitch pine seeds require an open, unlittered mineral soil such as is left after a fire has burned off leaf litter. Scrub oak is less common in these protected ridgetop pine forests than it is on more exposed sites, and black huckleberry is the dominant shrub. Associated with it are the same heath shrubs that are found on the ridgetop forest. The herbs are sparse; only bracken fern is abundant.

Table 6-2 lists some typical plant species of the Pitch Pine–Scrub Oak forest.

Successional Plant Communities on Rock Outcroppings

On the soil moisture scale the rock outcroppings of North Jersey are comparable to the sand dunes of South Jersey; both represent the extreme of dry-habitat conditions in the state. The higher ridgetops in northern New Jersey were stripped of their soil mantle and vegetation by the glacial ice sheets, leaving the rock surfaces exposed. Since the disappearance of the ice sheets thousands of years ago, some parts of the exposed rocks have become covered with a soil layer and with plant growth. The process by which this has happened represents another example of plant succession. The rate at which the surface of bare rock is covered by vegetation is extremely slow, though it varies with climate and substrate conditions. For this reason, some parts of the ridgetops in North Jersey are still bare rock, even though the glacial ice melted at least 12,000 years ago. Others are in various stages of vegetation succession, and still others already have a covering of Pitch Pine–Scrub Oak forest or Chestnut Oak forest.

Exposed rock outcroppings are an inhospitable environment for plant life. Without the moderating influence of plant and soil cover, extremes of temperature occur on the bare rocks. A rock surface becomes very warm during the daytime because of exposure to sun but quickly cools at night. Little water and few nutrients are available because of the lack of a soil mantle. The first life forms to colonize the exposed rocks are crustose lichens, which appear as gray, black, or yellowish stains or encrustations on rocks. Lichens are a composite of two living organisms, a fungus and an alga. The fungus is the dominant and most visible component and appears to contribute to the partnership by providing an anchor and a protected, moisture-absorbing environment for the alga cells, which are embedded in it. The alga contains chlorophyll and can manufacture food for both partners.

Crustose lichens are intimately fused to the surfaces on which they grow so cannot be peeled from them. Other species of lichens, the so-

Table 6-2. Some Typical Plant Species of the Pitch Pine–Scrub Oak Forest of North Jersey

Common name	Genus and species name
Dominant tree	
Pitch pine	*Pinus rigida*
Other trees	
Red maple	*Acer rubrum*
Chestnut oak	*Quercus prinus*
Black oak	*Quercus velutina*
White oak	*Quercus alba*
Scarlet oak	*Quercus coccinea*
Black birch	*Betula lenta*
Gray birch	*Betula populifolia*
Sassafras	*Sassafras albidum*
Downy juneberry	*Amelanchier arborea*
Smooth juneberry	*Amelanchier laevis*
Few others	
Shrubs and vines	
Scrub oak	*Quercus ilicifolia*
Black huckleberry	*Gaylussacia baccata*
Early lowbush blueberry	*Vaccinium pallidum*
Late lowbush blueberry	*Vaccinium angustifolium*
Deerberry	*Vaccinium stamineum*
Pinxter flower	*Rhododendron periclymenoides*
Mountain laurel	*Kalmia latifolia*
Sweet fern	*Comptonia peregrina*
Bush honeysuckle	*Diervilla lonicera*
Black chokeberry	*Aronia melanocarpa*
American chestnut	*Castanea dentata*
Virginia creeper	*Parthenocissus quinquefolia*
Few others	
Herbs	
Wild sarsaparilla	*Aralia nudicaulis*
Bracken fern	*Pteridium aquilinum*
Canada mayflower	*Maianthemum canadense*
Rattlesnake weed	*Hieracium venosum*
False Solomon's-seal	*Smilacina racemosa*
Pennsylvania sedge	*Carex pensylvanica*
Cow-wheat	*Melampyrum lineare*
Wintergreen	*Gaultheria procumbens*

continued

Table 6-2 continued

Common name	Genus and species name
Herbs continued	
Stemless lady's-slipper	*Cypripedium acaule*
Few others	
Mosses	
White moss	*Leucobryum glaucum*
Haircap mosses	*Polytrichum* spp.
Few others	

called foliose lichens (Figure 6-5), have distinct and usually differently colored upper and lower surfaces. At the edges, they are free from their substrate but they are otherwise anchored by rootlike structures on their lower surfaces. Umbilicate lichens, many of them known as rock tripes, are flat and attached to their substrate at just a single central point. Finally, there are fruticose lichens, which have upright stems, often simple but in some species branching to develop a shrublike or matted form.

Lichens actually penetrate rock surfaces, weakening them and hastening their decomposition into mineral soil. Also, the dead remains of lichens provide organic material for the next plants to come. But although lichens are the earliest invaders of rock surfaces, it is the mosses that contribute most to initial succession on the rocks. Mosses start to grow on the rocks mostly as small tufts in crevices where some soil has accumulated. Haircap mosses, white moss, thread mosses, and rock mosses are typical. Gradually, the mosses extend outward to form mats over the rock surfaces. Through the years, dust and debris collect in these mats, as do the leaves and old stems of mosses. The presence of more plants hastens the disintegration process of the surface rock and of the trapped particles of debris. These, combined with the plant remains, form the beginning of a soil mantle.

When enough soil has accumulated in any one place to provide both an anchorage for plant roots and some water-holding capacity, herbaceous plants start to develop successfully from seeds that blow onto the rocks (Figure 6-6). One of the first herbs to become abundant on rock outcroppings in northern New Jersey is hairgrass, an appropriately named species. Other herbs that grow in the thin soil cover or in the moss–lichen mat include poverty oatgrass, starved panic-grass, Pennsylvania sedge, wild sarsaparilla, bristly sarsaparilla, little bluestem, common polypody, hoary mountain-mint, and pale corydalis.

As herbaceous plants start to occupy the moss–lichen mats on rock outcroppings, a few low-growing shrubs, and even trees, will start to grow on the mat or in pockets of soil in crevices. These have their origin from seeds or from the spread of roots from plants growing in better soil

Figure 6-5. Foliose lichens, such as this *Xanthoparmelia* on a boulder in High Point State Park, are among the initiators of succession on bare rock.

Figure 6-6. An early stage of plant succession on bare rock. Enough soil has accumulated in the crevices of this outcrop to allow vascular plants to develop successfully.

pockets adjacent to the rocks. Early lowbush blueberry, late lowbush blueberry, black huckleberry, sheep laurel, black chokeberry, and winged sumac are among the more common pioneers. Scrub oak, the typical shrub cover in the ridgetop forest, grows successfully only when the soil has become relatively thick. As more shrubs occupy the rock outcroppings, they shade the lower herbaceous plants, which cannot survive successfully without full sunlight. By virtue of their greater bulk of annually produced litter and their many perennial woody stems that help hold the new soil in place, shrubs accelerate the process of reforestation of the outcropping. Thus, the vegetation changes its composition, and as it does, more and more organic material accumulates, creating more fertile soil conditions.

Gradually, the soil moisture and fertility conditions improve to the point at which tree seedlings that fall on the moss mat or in crevices will successfully germinate and grow. Among the first trees to grow in the habitat of North Jersey outcroppings are members of the Pitch Pine–Scrub Oak or the Chestnut Oak forest, especially the pitch pine, chestnut oak, and black birch, though representatives of such species as the more northern paper birch can be found along the higher points of the Kittatinny Ridge. For the most part the pioneer trees are stunted and crooked in shape, and some of their roots may completely straddle large boulders or run almost horizontally in the mat of vegetation covering the rock surface. Tree growth causes greater accumulation of soil but more shading, so as taller plants grow on the site many of the original herbs disappear. Inevitably, the vegetation evolves to some form of the ridgetop Pitch Pine–Scrub Oak or Chestnut Oak forest. Table 6-3 lists additional plant species that are typical of rock outcroppings.

Although these four successional stages are individually described, in actuality, gradations and overlapping of the stages occur, often on the same site. Examples of all can be seen on rock outcroppings along the trail that leads northward from the parking area near the High Point Monument in High Point State Park. Here, lichens of numerous species can be found on exposed boulders. Few of them have common names, and crustose genera represented include the grayish to black *Rhizocarpon;* yellowish *Caloplaca;* and the pale green, thick-textured *Dimelaena.* A common foliose lichen on rocks here is the pale green rock lichen *Xanthoparmelia conspersa.* Rock tripes of the genera *Umbilicaria* and *Lasallia* are conspicuous as brown, leathery-looking rosettes affixed to rock surfaces. Brittle when dry, they become flexible when wet. Around the edges of the parking area is a sparse Chestnut Oak forest, with some unusual northern shrubs and trees including American mountain ash and saplings of striped maple. Mats of haircap mosses and white moss cover some open rocky areas. Farther along the trail, open areas are dominated by hairgrass, with some little bluestem and occasional clumps of big bluestem, more typically a western prairie species. Other plants of the rock crevices and outcrops are pale corydalis, columbine, hay-

Table 6-3. Some Typical Plant Species of Rock Outcroppings of North Jersey

Common name	Genus and species name
Trees	
Pitch pine	*Pinus rigida*
Chestnut oak	*Quercus prinus*
Black birch	*Betula lenta*
Fire cherry	*Prunus pensylvanica*
Trembling aspen	*Populus tremuloides*
Few others	
Shrubs	
Early lowbush blueberry	*Vaccinium pallidum*
Late lowbush blueberry	*Vaccinium angustifolium*
Black huckleberry	*Gaylussacia baccata*
Mountain laurel	*Kalmia latifolia*
Sheep laurel	*Kalmia angustifolia*
Black chokecherry	*Aronia melanocarpa*
Winged sumac	*Rhus copallina*
Scrub oak	*Quercus ilicifolia*
Few others	
Herbs	
Wild sarsaparilla	*Aralia nudicaulis*
Bristly sarsaparilla	*Aralia hispida*
Bracken fern	*Pteridium aquilinum*
Marginal woodfern	*Dryopteris marginalis*
Common polypody	*Polypodium virginianum*
Sweet goldenrod	*Solidago odora*
Pale corydalis	*Corydalis sempervirens*
Pennsylvania sedge	*Carex pensylvanica*
Bastard toadflax	*Comandra umbellata*
Hairgrass	*Deschampsia flexuosa*
Poverty oatgrass	*Danthonia spicata*
Little bluestem	*Schizachyrium scoparium*
Starved panic-grass	*Panicum depauperatum*
Hoary mountain-mint	*Pycnanthemum incanum*
Few others	
Lichens and mosses	
White moss	*Leucobryum glaucum*
Juniper haircap moss	*Polytrichum juniperinum*
Awned haircap moss	*Polytrichum piliferum*

continued

Table 6-3 continued

Common name	Genus and species name
Lichens and mosses cont'd	
Thread mosses	*Bryum* spp.
Rock mosses	*Dicranum* spp.
Smooth rock tripe	*Umbilicaria mammulata*
Rock lichen	*Xanthoparmelia conspersa*
Dimelaena	*Dimelaena oreina*
Others	

scented fern, and common polypody. Scrub oak and pitch pine, with scattered chestnut oaks and black birch, make up most of the tree layer, and the understory is mostly black huckleberry and lowbush blueberries, with wild sarsaparilla and bracken fern.

Human Influences on the Vegetation of the Ridges, Slopes, and Rock Outcroppings

Perhaps because of their low fertility and relatively low development value, some rather large tracts of steep slopes and ridgetops in North Jersey have been incorporated into New Jersey's system of public parks and forests. The forests in some of these sites may appear to be relatively unspoiled, but this is an illusion. Fire, logging, and the selective use of land for agriculture have left a major imprint on the natural vegetation. In earlier times, these lands were farmed, or at least cleared and used for pasture, almost to the ridgetops; in places, old stone fences still mark boundaries. Even where the land was not farmed, the forests were cut for lumber, for domestic fuel, or for fuel for the New Jersey iron industry, which used charcoal until the mid nineteenth century.

Although excessive cutting and devastating forest fires have been minimal since the start of the twentieth century, the imprint of these practices remains. Because some trees are more capable of resprouting after injury than others, fire and cutting both favor certain tree species. Pitch pine and oak trees of sapling size or even smaller have the capacity to put forth new trunks and vegetative growth if the existing growth is killed. In contrast, other upland tree species, such as sugar maple, have little ability to resprout after their trunks are injured, and they usually reproduce themselves only by seed. Also, seedlings of some tree species can survive the heat of fires better than others.

Other major influences on the vegetation, indirectly the result of human intervention in natural processes, have been the chestnut blight and the gypsy moth. As noted, the chestnut blight, a fungus disease accidentally introduced into the United States in 1904, has practically eliminated this once-important tree from the forests of North Jersey. The gypsy moth was accidentally introduced into the United States in 1869 and has been defoliating New Jersey forests since about 1970. One way this insect spreads is by "ballooning" of the larvae on silken threads which are carried by the wind. Thus, the ridgetops, which are exposed to the winds and are the landing place of the larvae, are often the areas most affected by gypsy moth invasions. Some of the defoliated trees die, and mortality is higher among chestnut and white oaks than among black and red oaks. The result may be a forest with a higher percentage of black and red oaks, or one with fewer trees and more shrubs, than would otherwise be the case.

Summary

This chapter describes the common plant communities of ridgetops, steep slopes, and rock outcroppings of North Jersey. The Chestnut Oak forest forms on most of the ridgetops and slopes of higher elevation. The less common Pitch Pine–Scrub Oak forest grows only at the highest elevations that have the thinnest soils. A still drier habitat is that of the rock outcroppings, which owe their origin to the scouring action of glacial ice sheets. But even this habitat, through the process of succession, becomes covered by vegetation with a resulting change in site conditions. Passing through long-lasting gradations of four successional plant communities—lichens and mosses, herbaceous plants, shrubs, and tree pioneers—the habitat conditions of rock outcroppings are so transformed that ultimately the ridgetop forest type of vegetation develops on what was once exposed rock.

References and Source Material

Buell, M. F., A. N. Langford, D. W. Davidson, and L. F. Ohmann. 1966. The Upland Forest Continuum in Northern New Jersey. *Ecology* 47:416–432.

Cantlon, J. E. 1953. Vegetation and Microclimates on North and South Slopes of Cushetunk Mountain, New Jersey. *Ecological Monographs* 23: 241–270.

McDonough, W. T., and M. F. Buell. 1956. The Vegetation of Voorhees State Park, New Jersey. *American Midland Naturalist* 56:473–490.

Mitchell, Alison E. 1992. *The New Jersey Highlands: Treasures at Risk*. Morristown, N.J.: New Jersey Conservation Foundation.

Niering, W. A. 1953. The Past and Present Vegetation of High Point State Park, New Jersey. *Ecological Monographs* 23:127–148.

Pearson, P. R. 1961. Upland Forests on the Kittatinny Limestone and Franklin Marble of New Jersey. *Bulletin of the New Jersey Academy of Science* 5:3–19.

Vermeule, C. C., A. Hollick, J. B. Smith, and G. Pinchot. 1900. Report on Forests, in *Annual Report of the State Geologist for 1899*. Trenton, N.J.

Chapter 7

❡ *Uplands of North Jersey*

Habitats classified as uplands represent an idealized midpoint on the soil moisture gradient and are referred to as "mesic." Unlike marshes, swamps, floodplains, and other wetlands, no standing water appears on such sites. But unlike drier sites, such as the ridgetops, steep slopes, and rock outcroppings, upland sites retain a good supply of moisture in their soil. Mesic habitats in North Jersey occur on slopes, hilltops, and ravines as well as valley floors and land of flat topography. They can be underlain by a variety of parent rock materials—conglomerates, sandstones, shales, limestones, gneiss, basalt, and diabase. In addition, depending on the location, the parent rock may be covered by glacial deposits of varying age. Despite these differences, in North Jersey upland forest types tend to be similar wherever the climate and soil moisture conditions are about the same.

At present, three forest types—the Mixed Oak forest, the Hemlock–Mixed Hardwood forest and the Sugar Maple–Mixed Hardwood forest—can be found on the mesic uplands of North Jersey. The word "hardwood" here includes deciduous broad-leaved trees that lose their leaves in winter, as contrasted with most of the cone-bearing, needle-leaved trees such as the hemlock, which have softer wood and remain in leaf all winter. The Mixed Oak forest is the most common of the three upland forest types and can be found throughout North Jersey; southward, it grades into the oak forests of the Inner and Outer Coastal Plains. The Sugar Maple–Mixed Hardwood forest, now perhaps the least abundant of the three upland forest types, is found on the most fertile sites throughout the area. The Hemlock–Mixed Hardwood forest is most abundant on cool, moist sites and in general is more abundant in the more northern and western parts of North Jersey.

Although typical examples of each of the three forest types can be found in the field, they also merge into each other. In addition, on drier sites the Mixed Oak forest grades into the Chestnut Oak forest, and on wetter sites the upland forests gradually become Swamp Forest. Also in North Jersey, so-called successional (or nonclimax forest) types of plant communities can be found on land that has been disturbed and then left untouched. The composition of the vegetation in these successional communities varies considerably from site to site, depending upon the past use of the site and its current management, if any. Of course, it also varies with the time that the plant community has had to develop.

Mixed Oak Forest

Before the early 1900s the Mixed Oak forest of North Jersey was known as the Oak–Chestnut forest, for the American chestnut trees were then as abundant as the oaks. Because of the die-off of the chestnuts, this name is no longer suitable. Seventeen species of oak trees grow in New Jersey, but the Mixed Oak forest gets its name from just three species that in varying mixtures are most abundant among the large trees that form the forest canopy at a height of about 60 to 100 feet (Figure 7-1). These three are the red oak, the white oak, and the black oak. Two other oaks—the chestnut oak and the scarlet oak—are also present but are less common in the North Jersey mesic upland forests than are the other three species. Though perhaps initially confusing, the five kinds of oaks can be distinguished rather easily by differences in leaf form, bark, buds, and acorns. In addition to the oaks, other large trees that may be present in the mesic upland Mixed Oak forest of North Jersey include several types of hickories, red maple, sugar maple, white ash, tulip tree, American beech, black cherry, black birch, sour gum, and American elm.

Growing below the tops of the larger trees are smaller trees which may form a distinct understory layer at a height of about 30 to 40 feet. Throughout most of the North Jersey uplands, the flowering dogwood is the most abundant of these smaller trees. Also common locally, however, are hop hornbeam, sassafras, and ironwood trees, as are chestnut sprouts (Figure 7-2), which grow from old root crowns and are not yet infected by the chestnut blight fungus.

Under the two tree layers, the Mixed Oak forest usually has a lower-growing shrub layer (Figure 7-3). In this layer the maple-leaved viburnum, which grows to about 3 to 4 feet tall, may be very abundant, but other common shrubs include two taller viburnums—the black haw and arrowwood—as well as the spicebush, witch hazel, and beaked and American hazels. In a few places with very acid soil, heath shrubs may grow, including several species of blueberries, black huckleberry, and pinxter flower. Poison ivy, Virginia creeper, Japanese honeysuckle, and wild grapes are familiar vines of this forest.

The herbaceous plants of the Mixed Oak forest vary with time of year as well as with location. In spring the mayapple (Figure 7-4), violets of several species, wood anemone, Solomon's-seal, jack-in-the-pulpit, wild sarsaparilla, Canada mayflower, garlic mustard, and other early-flowering herbs attract attention, while in late summer and fall the woodland asters, goldenrods, grasses, and ferns are more conspicuous. In very moist spots skunk cabbage, jewelweed, and other wetland plants can be found, and in forest openings where trees are down, such plants as pokeweed,

Figure 7-1. Mixed Oak forest in the Herrontown Woods Preserve, on the Piedmont uplands near Princeton. The taller trees are mostly red oaks.

Figure 7-2. In many Mixed Oak forests, sprouts of American chestnut can be found growing from old root crowns. Sometimes they become mature enough to produce flowers and a few nuts.

Figure 7-3. Many Mixed Oak forests have a well-developed shrub layer. In the Herrontown Woods Preserve the shrubs are mostly maple-leaved viburnum and spicebush.

Figure 7-4. Mayapple is a common spring-flowering herb in Mixed Oak forests throughout northern New Jersey, and in parts of southern New Jersey as well. As shown here, it typically forms large colonies.

Table 7-1. Some Typical Plant Species of the Mixed Oak Forest of North Jersey

Common name	Genus and species name
Dominant trees	
White oak	*Quercus alba*
Red oak	*Quercus rubra*
Black oak	*Quercus velutina*
Other trees	
Chestnut oak	*Quercus prinus*
Scarlet oak	*Quercus coccinea*
Shagbark hickory	*Carya ovata*
Bitternut hickory	*Carya cordiformis*
Pignut hickory	*Carya glabra*
Sugar maple	*Acer saccharum*
Red maple	*Acer rubrum*
Black birch	*Betula lenta*
American beech	*Fagus grandifolia*
White ash	*Fraxinus americana*
Black cherry	*Prunus serotina*
Flowering dogwood	*Cornus florida*
Sassafras	*Sassafras albidum*
Ironwood	*Carpinus caroliniana*
Others	
Shrubs and vines	
Maple-leaved viburnum	*Viburnum acerifolium*
Arrowwood	*Viburnum dentatum*
Pinxter flower	*Rhododendron periclymenoides*
Mountain laurel	*Kalmia latifolia*
Black huckleberry	*Gaylussacia baccata*
Virginia creeper	*Parthenocissus quinquefolia*
Others	
Herbs	
Mayapple	*Podophyllum peltatum*
Wild sarsaparilla	*Aralia nudicaulis*
Wood anemone	*Anemone quinquefolia*
False Solomon's-seal	*Smilacina racemosa*
White wood aster	*Aster divaricatus*
Sweet cicely	*Osmorhiza claytoni*
Jack-in-the-pulpit	*Arisaema triphyllum*
Garlic mustard	*Alliaria petiolata*
White baneberry	*Actaea pachypoda*

Table 7-1 continued

Common name	Genus and species name
Herbs	
Hairy Solomon's-seal	*Polygonatum pubescens*
Christmas fern	*Polystichum achrostichoides*
Marginal wood fern	*Dryopteris marginalis*
Bracken fern	*Pteridium aquilinum*
Many others	

pilewort, and blackberries often grow. Table 7-1 lists some typical plant species of the Mixed Oak forest.

Examples of different forms of the Mixed Oak forest can be seen throughout the well-drained uplands of North Jersey. In the Piedmont it occurs both on the relatively flat expanses of red sandstone and shale as well as on the slopes of the diabase and basalt ridges, including the Watchungs, the Sourlands, and the Palisades. In the Highlands and the Ridge and Valley regions, the Mixed Oak forest is found on lower slopes and valleys whether they be made of shale, sandstone, conglomerate, or gneiss. The Mixed Oak forest differs from but intergrades with the forests on drier ridges and slopes of higher elevation described in Chapter 6.

An exceptionally fine example of a Mixed Oak forest in the Piedmont region is the Hutcheson Memorial Forest near New Brunswick. This forest dates back to precolonial times and has been preserved thanks to the United Brotherhood of Carpenters and Joiners of America, who bought the 65-acre site and gave it to Rutgers University to administer. It is located west of New Brunswick and just east of East Millstone; its entrance is on the south side of Amwell Road (Route 514) and is identified by a memorial archway and a sign. Admission is by permit only, which can be obtained from the Biology Department of Rutgers University in New Brunswick.

The soil here is derived from the red shale typical of most of the Piedmont. More than half of the bigger trees in this forest are oaks. Here, white oak is more abundant than black or red oak. Sweet pignut hickory is the fourth most abundant species of the canopy. Also present but less common are sugar maple, red maple, American beech, white ash, Norway maple, pin oak, sour gum, black cherry, and sweet cherry. Flowering dogwood trees form an almost continuous underlayer at a height of 35 to 40 feet. In better-drained areas, maple-leaved viburnum is the most common shrub, with some black haw present. Spicebush and arrowwood are abundant in more moist parts of the forest. In recent years many of the larger oaks in this forest have died due to drought, natural mortality, hurricanes, and gypsy moth damage. In the openings thus created, Japanese honeysuckle, poison ivy, and Virginia Creeper form thickets. In spring the mayapple is the most abundant herb on the forest floor, but by late summer this role is filled by enchanter's nightshade. Interestingly, it appears that while oak trees predominate in the Hutcheson Forest, few young white or black oak trees are now growing there. Those that are present are outnumbered by young sugar maple, red maple, Norway maple, and white ash trees.

In the Herrontown Woods Preserve, on the Piedmont uplands near Princeton, a mature upland forest on a moist slope is dominated by white, black, and red oaks. But in parts of this forest tulip tree and sweet gum, the latter more typical of lowland forests, are also common. Flowering dogwood is the principal understory tree, but ironwood is also frequently found. Maple-leaved viburnum is the most abundant shrub except on moist land, where spicebush is favored. The flowering herbs in the spring include mayapple, jack-in-the-pulpit, Solomon's-seal, and wood and rue anemones; in the summer and fall the asters, goldenrods, white baneberry, New York fern, and Christmas fern are conspicuous.

The forests that remain on the traprock of the Watchungs and the Palisades are also of the Mixed Oak forest type. Throughout the 2,000 acres of the Watchung Reservation, the oak forest dominates, though its composition varies with site location. On one hillside, red, white, and black oak make up 90 percent of the mature trees, with red oak the most abundant species. With this mixture are occasional large chestnut oaks and sugar maples. The smaller trees include red maple, white ash, black birch, sour gum, and flowering dogwood. On another slope, a dry, southeast-facing one, white oak and black oak predominate, with the tulip tree, red oak, American beech, sugar maple, and hickories common but less important. Flowering dogwood is also the most important lower tree in this area, but with it grows some sassafras and hop hornbeam. Again, the maple-leaved viburnum is the principal shrub. The tallest trees in the Watchung Reservation are found on a northwest-facing slope, and while the white, red, and black oaks are still the most abundant trees, the tulip tree is also very common. Also scattered through this forest are large numbers of American beech, black birch, scarlet oak, and red maple. The understory trees are mostly flowering dogwood and sassafras. The shrubs are sparse and consist mostly of maple-leaved viburnum with occasional black haw, spicebush, and pinxter flower.

Greenbrook Sanctuary, also on the Piedmont but part of the Palisades, has a Mixed Oak forest in which the red oak predominates but with white, black, and chestnut oak; black birch; sugar maple; tulip tree; and white ash also common. Scarlet oak, American elm, red maple, basswood, black cherry, and pignut and mockernut hickories are present in smaller numbers. Maple-leaved viburnum forms a shrub layer 3 to 4 feet high, and in places there is prolific vine growth, mostly of poison ivy, wild grape, greenbrier, and Asiatic bittersweet. In this forest, as in many other oak forests, young sugar maple trees appear to be more common than young oak trees.

On the gneiss and shale slopes of the Highlands the story is the same. For example, in Voorhees State Park in Hunterdon County, the Mixed Oak forest is the most extensive type found. Red oak is the most common tree but is joined by white, black, chestnut, and scarlet oaks in varying mixtures. Red maple and hickories also are present, and on the moister slopes American beech, sugar maple, tulip tree, white ash, and black birch trees frequently appear. Flowering dogwoods occur here and form a lower tree layer with hop hornbeam and ironwood. In some areas, particularly on moist gneissic slopes in the vicinity of Morristown, as on the Piedmont traprock, the tulip tree grows abundantly. However, this tree appears not to be able to perpetuate itself well in older New Jersey forests, where it must develop under very shady conditions. In this same area the beech is also a very important tree. In the Highlands, as noted previously for some Piedmont sites, the most common younger trees in the upland forest frequently are not oaks but rather red maple, sugar maple, black birch, and white ash.

In the Ridge and Valley region the Mixed Oak forest type is common in valleys and on lower slopes and hilltops, particularly those that are underlain by shale. Such forests resemble those farther south in that mixtures of oak species—red, black, white, and here, also, chestnut oak—constitute a majority of the larger trees. Red oak, particularly, is very abundant in these forests. Also present in larger tree sizes are red maple, sugar maple, American beech, white ash, black birch, tulip tree, and sour gum. Scarlet oak and hickories are not as abundant but may be important locally. The lower-growing trees include flowering dogwood, hop hornbeam, sassafras, and occasionally striped maple. The shrubs typical of the Mixed Oak forest as far north as High Point State Park include beaked hazel, witch hazel, maple-leaved viburnum, downy juneberry, and gray dogwood, along with blueberry and blackberry. In this same area, wild sarsaparilla, goldenrods, and ferns make up a rather sparse herb cover. Again, a striking feature of these Mixed Oak forests is the lack of a well-developed younger generation of oak trees to replace the older trees in the future. Instead, in many stands, red maple, white ash, black birch, and sugar maple are the more abundant younger trees.

Hemlock–Mixed Hardwood Forest

Although the Mixed Oak forest now prevails on most of the uplands of North Jersey, a much different forest called the Hemlock–Mixed Hardwood type occurs on cooler and moister sites located in ravines or on the steep, lower, north-facing slopes. Sites suitable for this forest type are found in all three sections of North Jersey—on the Piedmont as part of the traprock formations, in the Highlands on slopes of gneiss, and in the

Figure 7-5. Hemlock–Mixed Hardwood forest at Tillman Ravine in Stokes State Forest. The association with a stream in a cool ravine is typical, as is the conspicuous lack of undergrowth.

Ridge and Valley section on land underlain by shale, sandstone, or conglomerates.

In all cases the character of the Hemlock–Mixed Hardwood forest is similar (Figure 7-5). Typically, more than half the larger trees of the forest are hemlocks, a tree which grows more abundantly to the north of New Jersey in New England and New York State. The small needles of the hemlock are dark green, and the tree is evergreen, retaining its needles throughout winter. Some of the other large trees associated with hemlock are also more typical of northern than of southern forests. These include black birch, yellow birch, sugar maple, and basswood. But also common are some of the same trees that are found in the Mixed Oak forest, typically beech, red oak, white ash, and red maple. The fallen needles of hemlock create a very acidic condition on the forest floor, which, combined with the lack of sunlight year round, appears to discourage the development of dense undergrowth, whether of lower trees, shrubs, or herbs.

In the Watchung Reservation in the Piedmont region, for example, a hemlock-dominated forest occurs on both a northwest-facing valley slope and in a rocky ravine. In both, hemlock accounts for more than half the trees in the forest, with scattered representatives of beech, black birch, red maple, sugar maple, white oak, red oak, and black oak. In the Hemlock–Mixed Hardwood forest, unlike the Mixed Oak forest, flowering dogwood occurs only infrequently as an understory tree. The shrubs, mostly the maple-leaved viburnum, spicebush, and highbush blueberry, are sparse and scattered. Some vines—poison ivy, Virginia creeper, and wild grape—are found, and a few herbs cover the ground, particularly the partridgeberry and Canada mayflower. Mosses are also present.

The Hemlock–Mixed Hardwood forests of the lower north-facing valley slopes and ravines of the Highlands and the Ridge and Valley regions are much the same as those described for the Piedmont. The hemlock tree not only dominates the canopy but also successfully reproduces and develops as a smaller tree in the forest. Red oak, black birch, chestnut oak, black oak, red maple, American beech, and yellow birch are the most consistent associates of the hemlock, with white oak, sugar maple, sour gum, tulip tree, and white ash appearing only as scattered individuals. In none of these forests does a well-developed understory of trees other than the young trees of hemlock, birch, and red maple exist. Striped maple and hop hornbeam appear only occasionally, and flowering dogwood seldom. The shrub layer is also poorly developed, with witch hazel and maple-leaved viburnum most common, and locally some great rhododendron and mountain laurel. The herbs are sparse and for the most part consist of partridgeberry and Canada mayflower. Table 7-2 lists some typical plant species of the Hemlock–Mixed Hardwood forest.

A very fine example of a Hemlock–Mixed Hardwood forest in the Ridge and Valley province can be found in the Tillman Ravine section of Stokes State Forest. This ravine borders a road that runs from Wallpack Center through Stokes State Forest to Route 206; there are two parking areas along this road, marked Tillman Falls Scenic Area. From both places one can walk downslope through a hemlock-dominated forest. Almost all the trees in the forest are hemlock, including the mature trees and developing seedlings and saplings. In this forest, some of the trees are over 100 feet in height and almost 4 feet in diameter, and are thought to be over 150 years old. In openings, an occasional sassafras, yellow birch, or sprout of American chestnut may be seen. Large clumps of great rhododendron occur in this forest, and occasional plants of mountain laurel, witch hazel, and highbush blueberry are found. Spicebush may be seen along the bank of Tillman Brook. As is typical of hemlock-dominated woodlands, the forest floor is covered with hemlock needles and there is little plant ground cover; partridgeberry is the only herb of importance, although in spring trailing arbutus, Canada mayflower, and a few other species can be seen. Mosses are common on parts of the forest floor.

Unfortunately, many of the Hemlock–Mixed Hardwood forests of New Jersey are now infested by an introduced Asiatic insect, the hemlock woolly adelgid. This aphidlike insect sucks juices from the needles

Table 7-2. Some Typical Plant Species of the Hemlock–Mixed Hardwood Forest of North Jersey

Common name	Genus and species name
Dominant tree	
Eastern hemlock	*Tsuga canadensis*
Other trees	
Black birch	*Betula lenta*
Yellow birch	*Betula alleghaniensis*
Sugar maple	*Acer saccharum*
Red maple	*Acer rubrum*
American beech	*Fagus grandifolia*
Red oak	*Quercus rubra*
Black oak	*Quercus velutina*
Basswood	*Tilia americana*
Few others	
Shrubs and vines	
Maple-leaved viburnum	*Viburnum acerifolium*
Pinxter flower	*Rhododendron periclymenoides*
Mountain laurel	*Kalmia latifolia*
Late lowbush blueberry	*Vaccinium angustifolium*
Early lowbush blueberry	*Vaccinium pallidum*
Spicebush	*Lindera benzoin*
Witch hazel	*Hamamelis virginiana*
Few others	
Herbs	
Spotted wintergreen	*Chimaphila maculata*
Starflower	*Trientalis borealis*
Canada mayflower	*Maianthemum canadense*
Stemless lady's-slipper	*Cypripedium acaule*
Partridgeberry	*Mitchella repens*
Trailing arbutus	*Epigaea repens*
Shining clubmoss	*Lycopodium lucidulum*
Spinulose wood fern	*Dryopteris carthusiana*
Christmas fern	*Polystichum acrostichoides*
Hay-scented fern	*Dennstaedtia punctilobula*
Few others	
Mosses	
Broom moss	*Dicranum scoparium*
Tree moss	*Climacium americanum*
Fern moss	*Thuidium delicatulum*
Hylocomium	*Hylocomium splendens*
Others	

Figure 7-6. Sugar Maple–Mixed Hardwood forest in High Point State Park. In this particular forest, more than three-quarters of the trees are sugar maples.

of the trees, causing the trees to lose vigor and then die. Although the insect can be controlled on specimen trees, there is as yet no practical way of protecting large forest tracts. Some large areas of hemlock forest, particularly in the northeastern part of New Jersey, have already been killed, and others are likely to follow.

Sugar Maple–Mixed Hardwood Forest

It is unfortunate that most of the fertile limestone valleys in North Jersey have been cleared of natural vegetation, for it is on such sites that the Sugar Maple–Mixed Hardwood forest (Figure 7-6) flourishes. When this type of forest occurs, it is more diverse than either the Mixed Oak or Hemlock–Mixed Hardwood forest, with more plant species and with its composition more equitably distributed among species. Examples of this forest are found mostly on the Kittatinny limestone underlying the Great Valley in the Ridge and Valley region. Sugar maple is the most abundant tree in this type of forest, but associated with it in large numbers are hardwood trees typical of areas to the north and also some of those more typical of the Mixed Oak forest.

White, black, and red oak are common in the Sugar Maple–Mixed Hardwood forest, as are white ash, tulip tree, black birch, yellow birch, red maple, basswood, American beech, and several species of hickories. Scattered trees of hemlock, white pine, American elm, and black walnut can be found in some of the wooded areas. Interestingly, however, hemlock and sugar maple do not occur together with great abundance of each. Where hemlock is dominant, sugar maple is sparse, and the reverse is also true. Unlike hemlock-dominated forests, the sugar maple–dominated forests normally exhibit a well-developed layer of lower-growing trees. Although some flowering dogwood is present in these forests, even in northernmost New Jersey, hop hornbeam appears to be more common. Sassafras and ironwood trees are also present in this understory layer. Shrubs are abundant and include maple-leaved viburnum, black haw, spicebush, and beaked and American hazel. Many early-spring-flowering herbs grow on the floor of the forest, and some unusual ferns and other plants can be found in crevices of the limestone outcroppings.

Sugar Maple–Mixed Hardwood forests can be seen at many locations in High Point State Park, particularly along the Deckertown Pike and Sawmill Road. The sugar maple trees are tall and straight, reaching heights of over 90 feet. Sugar maple is the most abundant tree, but some of its associates are also common, including American beech, yellow birch, black birch, red oak, white oak, and basswood. That chestnut was also once important in this forest is indicated by huge logs that rest on the forest floor. An understory tree layer consists mostly of hop hornbeam and flowering dogwood trees with young sugar maples that are reproducing abundantly. Spicebush is the most common shrub, and others in decreasing importance are witch hazel, maple-leaved viburnum, and beaked hazel. The shrub layer is not dense, but there is more coverage than in the hemlock-dominated forest. Vines of poison ivy and Virginia creeper are present. Although the forest floor is rocky, there is a rich herb layer. Jack-in-the-pulpit is conspicuous in the early spring, and skunk cabbage is common in wet areas. There are also many species of ferns.

Some typical plant species of the Sugar Maple–Mixed Hardwood forest are listed in Table 7-3.

The same plants more or less occur together in other forests in or adjacent to the Great Valley. In some, the tulip tree may be as common as some of those already mentioned. In all the Sugar Maple–Mixed-Hardwood forests just mentioned, the sugar maple tree is reproducing prolifically and, as a result, is abundant among the smaller trees. The same is true of the other northern species—the birches, basswood, and hemlock. Except for red oak, the oaks in these forests appear less successful in assuring themselves a place in the next generation of canopy trees.

Successional Plant Communities of the North Jersey Uplands

The important ecological concept of natural change, or succession, in vegetation through time was introduced in Chapter 1 and has also been

Table 7-3. Some Typical Plant Species of the Sugar Maple–Mixed Hardwood Forest of North Jersey

Common name	Genus and species name
Dominant tree	
Sugar maple	*Acer saccharum*
Other trees	
White oak	*Quercus alba*
Red oak	*Quercus rubra*
Black oak	*Quercus velutina*
Black birch	*Betula lenta*
Yellow birch	*Betula alleghaniensis*
Red maple	*Acer rubrum*
Shagbark hickory	*Carya ovata*
Bitternut hickory	*Carya cordiformis*
Black walnut	*Juglans nigra*
American beech	*Fagus grandifolia*
Basswood	*Tilia americana*
Tulip tree	*Liriodendron tulipifera*
White ash	*Fraxinus americana*
Black cherry	*Prunus serotina*
Flowering dogwood	*Cornus florida*
Many others	
Shrubs and vines	
Maple-leaved viburnum	*Viburnum acerifolia*
Arrowwood	*Viburnum dentatum*
American hazel	*Corylus americana*
Spicebush	*Lindera benzoin*
Witch hazel	*Hamamelis virginiana*
Many others	
Herbs	
Mayapple	*Podophyllum peltatum*
Bloodroot	*Sanguinaria canadensis*
Hepatica	*Hepatica americana*
Wood anemone	*Anemone quinquefolia*
Rue anemone	*Anemonella thalictroides*
Jack-in-the-pulpit	*Arisaema triphyllum*
Wild ginger	*Asarum canadense*
Virginia stickseed	*Hackelia virginiana*
Dutchman's breeches	*Dicentra cucullaria*
Blue-stemmed goldenrod	*Solidago caesia*

continued

Table 7-3 continued

Common name	Genus and species name
Herbs	
Aniseroot	*Osmorhiza longistylis*
Solomon's-seal	*Polygonatum biflorum*
Common blue violet	*Viola sororia*
Christmas fern	*Polystichum acrostichoides*
New York fern	*Thelypteris noveboracensis*
Many others	

illustrated in the previous chapter, which deals with rock outcroppings. Throughout North Jersey, various stages of successional change in vegetation can be seen on upland sites. For the most part these have developed because land formerly cultivated or bulldozed has been abandoned and left untouched. From the time at which the human activity ceases through succeeding years, a series of different plant communities occupy the sites, culminating finally in a mature forest. Some of the plant species typical of successional upland communities in North Jersey are listed in Table 7-4.

A part of the Herrontown Woods Preserve has examples of the successional vegetation that has developed naturally on farmland abandoned 80 to 90 years ago. On this land, the first trees to occupy an abandoned field were red cedars (Figure 7-7); most of these have now died for lack of sunlight. The cedars are being shaded out by taller-growing trees such as the sassafras, big-toothed aspen, tulip tree, sweet gum, gray birch, black locust, black cherry, and red maple. All but the red maple and perhaps the tulip tree will succumb in time because they are shade-intolerant and cannot flourish when the forest matures and little sunlight penetrates the top canopy.

Farther north in Voorhees State Park, in the Highlands section, some fields left idle have immediately been filled with yellow foxtail, an annual grass, and with common ragweed. Whether foxtail or ragweed is more abundant in a new field in this area of New Jersey appears to be dependent upon the month in which the field is left idle. Other herbaceous plants that appeared in early stages of succession include smooth crabgrass, wintercress, common mullein, Canada thistle, yarrow, butter-and-eggs, and orchard grass.

Mowed roadside fields in this area may be filled with such low-growing herbs as common cinquefoil, wild strawberry, dandelion, English plantain, and a number of grasses, including Kentucky bluegrass, Canada bluegrass, orchard grass, bentgrass, and smooth crabgrass, as well as taller, more conspicuous herbs such as chicory, king devil hawkweed, gray goldenrod, and common ragweed. Many of these early-

Table 7-4. Some Typical Plant Species of Successional Upland Communities of North Jersey

Common name	Genus and species name
Dominant trees	
Gray birch	*Betula populifolia*
Black cherry	*Prunus serotina*
Trembling aspen	*Populus tremuloides*
Big-toothed aspen	*Populus grandidentata*
Red cedar	*Juniperus virginiana*
Few others	
Shrubs	
Staghorn sumac	*Rhus typhina*
Smooth sumac	*Rhus glabra*
Multiflora rose	*Rosa multiflora*
Allegheny blackberry	*Rubus allegheniensis*
Black raspberry	*Rubus occidentalis*
Gray dogwood	*Cornus racemosa*
Autumn olive	*Elaeagnus umbellata*
Few others	
Annual or biennial herbs	
Common ragweed	*Ambrosia artemisiifolia*
Nodding foxtail	*Setaria faberi*
Yellow foxtail	*Setaria glauca*
Wintercress	*Barbarea vulgaris*
Large crabgrass	*Digitaria sanguinalis*
Wild carrot	*Daucus carota*
Horseweed	*Conyza canadensis*
Common mullein	*Verbascum thapsus*
White sweetclover	*Melilotus alba*
Many others	
Perennial herbs	
Rough-stemmed goldenrod	*Solidago rugosa*
Canada goldenrod	*Solidago canadensis*
Grass-leaved goldenrod	*Euthamia graminifolia*
Canada thistle	*Cirsium arvense*
Kentucky bluegrass	*Poa pratensis*
Timothy	*Phleum pratense*
Sweet vernal grass	*Anthoxanthum odoratum*
Orchard grass	*Dactylis glomerata*

continued

Table 7-4 continued

Common name	Genus and species name
Perennial herbs continued	
King devil hawkweed	*Hieracium caespitosum*
Ox-eye daisy	*Chrysanthemum leucanthemum*
Butter-and-eggs	*Linaria vulgaris*
Wild bergamot	*Monarda fistulosa*
Common St. Johnswort	*Hypericum perforatum*
Common milkweed	*Asclepias syriaca*
Many others	

succession and old-field plants are of European origin; they came to this country as weeds in crop seed or ships' ballast, and from other sources.

As on the uplands of the Piedmont, tree seedlings invade these fields shortly after they have been abandoned. On other than limestone and some particular shale substrates, the red cedar tree is not as typical in early succession stages in the Highlands and Ridge and Valley provinces as it is in the Piedmont. Instead, the pioneer trees in the northern areas are primarily the gray birch and big-toothed aspen (Figure 7-8), with black cherry, sassafras, and red maple. Along with the first trees, thickets of gray dogwood and multiflora rose develop. Vines, particularly poison ivy and Virginia creeper, are as common here as in abandoned fields to the south. Though the species may vary, the sequence of succession is the same on the uplands of the Highlands as on the Piedmont—first, a growth of annual or biennial herbaceous plants covers the ground. These are then replaced by perennial herbs. Then shrubs and young trees appear spottily throughout the field, and in time form small thickets. The thickets expand and grow taller, and what was once an open field becomes a young woodland and finally a forest.

In the most northern uplands in the Ridge and Valley section, the successional story is the same, although some of the characters differ. In and around High Point State Park, about forty species of plants occur in abandoned fields. Among these, the Canada bluegrass, wild carrot, grass-leaved goldenrod, and common St. Johnswort are the most abundant. Hawkweeds, butter-and-eggs, wild parsnip, red clover, white clover, common cinquefoil, and a variety of grasses are also present. The first trees to invade the fields are gray birch, trembling aspen, black cherry, red maple, and scarlet oak, and these gradually form thickets with shrubs of smooth sumac, staghorn sumac, scrub oak, gray dogwood, and blackberry. As time passes, these species are joined by additional shrubs including blueberries, viburnums, and witch hazel. Goldenrods and cinquefoils are common, and in some places ground pines form a ground cover. Gradually, seedlings of oaks and hickories invade the upland area, transforming it into a mature Mixed Oak forest community.

Figure 7-7. Red cedars are often the first trees to occupy abandoned farmland in the Piedmont of New Jersey.

Figure 7-8. Big-toothed aspen and gray birch are often pioneer trees in old fields in the Highlands and Ridge and Valley provinces of New Jersey.

Human Influences on Uplands Vegetation

Upland sites in North Jersey include some of the best farmland in the state, and many of these areas were cleared early and remain cleared today, particularly in the valleys, where except for small woodlots, little natural vegetation remains. The mesic forests that do occur here are found on the less-fertile slopes or in deep ravines, and even these no longer represent virgin growth. As a result, those plant species and forest types that require the most fertile soils occur less frequently than they would have without human influence on the land.

Also, as on the drier ridgetop habitats, both fire and timbering practices have influenced forest composition on mesic sites. The cutting of forests or the regular recurrence of fire can create a more open woodland, one in which sunlight penetrates to the forest floor. In contrast, in the absence of cutting or fire, upland trees grow taller and their tops form a closed canopy, shutting out the rays of the sun. The amount of sunlight that reaches the floor of a forest is important because shade conditions are more favorable to some tree species than to others, which propagate or develop well only in sunlight. In North Jersey young trees of sugar maple, hemlock, yellow birch, black birch, beech, hop hornbeam, and dogwood appear to develop well in full shade. In contrast, seedlings of oaks, hickories, and tulip tree grow rather poorly in shade.

Many people have speculated about the probable composition of the upland vegetation in North Jersey if humans had never settled here. Obviously there would be a much larger amount of natural vegetation than there is today. But the present vegetation might be less varied. One reason this is so is that all the uplands would be completely covered with forest, and the successional vegetational stages stemming from abandoned fields would be absent. Some ecologists believe that under present climatic conditions the prevailing vegetation on the uplands would be Sugar Maple–Mixed Hardwood forest rather than the Mixed Oak type so common today. This conclusion is based on evidence that when fire and excessive cutting of the woodlands are controlled, species such as sugar maple, yellow birch, black birch, and hemlock appear to be able to successfully invade forests that were previously dominated by white, red, or black oak trees. Certainly, if present abundance of young tree seedlings and saplings indicates the trees that will dominate the future composition of the forest, this conclusion would appear to be correct. In this sense, then, the present Mixed Oak forest may represent a successional stage of forest that, if left undisturbed by human activities, eventually and naturally would progress into one of the other two forest types.

Some authorities question the validity of this speculation with respect to the dominance of sugar maple on all mesic uplands in North Jersey. It may be that the large numbers of young sugar maple trees do not necessarily reflect the future composition of the forest. And although the hemlock and sugar maple and the associated northern hardwoods may be more successful than the oaks on cooler and moister sites in northern-most New Jersey, these trees may never do as well as the black, white, and red oaks under warmer and drier conditions, as on Piedmont red shale sites or on south-facing slopes in the Highlands and Ridge and Valley sections.

Such speculation is interesting but probably can never be resolved. Only if the present forestlands were maintained without disturbance for hundreds of years would it be possible to determine what New Jersey forests would be like without human influence.

Summary

The topography and the soil parent material of the North Jersey uplands varies widely. While the Mixed Oak forest is the most common, the Hemlock–Mixed Hardwood forest dominates in cool, moist sites such as ravines, and the Sugar Maple–Mixed Hardwood forest is found on more fertile soils such as those derived from limestone. Successional stages in the uplands of North Jersey result primarily from human activity.

References and Source Material

Airola, T. M., and K. Buchholz. 1982. Forest Community Relationships of the Greenbrook Sanctuary, New Jersey. *Bulletin of the Torrey Botanical Club* 109:205–218.

Baird, J. 1956. *The Ecology of the Watchung Reservation, Union County, New Jersey.* New Brunswick, N.J.: Rutgers University Press.

Buell, M. F., A. N. Langford, D. W. Davidson, and L. F. Ohmann. 1966. The Upland Forest Continuum in Northern New Jersey. *Ecology* 47:416–432.

Collins, S. 1956. *The Biotic Communities of Greenbrook Sanctuary.* Alpine, N.J.: Palisades Nature Association.

Kramer, Richard J. 1971. *Herrontown Woods.* Pennington, N.J.: Stony Brook–Millstone Watershed Association.

McDonough, W. T., and M. F. Buell. 1956. The Vegetation of Voorhees State Park, New Jersey. *American Midland Naturalist* 56:473–490.

Mitchell, Allison E. 1992. *The New Jersey Highlands: Treasures at Risk.* Morristown, N.J.: New Jersey Conservation Foundation.

Monk, C. D. 1961. The Vegetation of the William L. Hutcheson Memorial Forest, New Jersey. *Bulletin of the Torrey Botanical Club* 88:156–166.

Niering, W. A. 1953. The Past and Present Vegetation of High Point State Park, New Jersey. *Ecological Monographs* 23:127–148.

Pearson, P. R. 1961. Upland Forests on the Kittatinny Limestone and Franklin Marble of New Jersey. *Bulletin of the New Jersey Academy of Science* 5:3–19.

Serrao, J., and N. Dicker. 1988. Flowering Plants Recorded in Greenbrook Sanctuary, 1946–1986, Exclusive of Grasses, Sedges, and Rushes. *Bartonia* 54:116–123.

Vermeule, C. C., A. Hollick, J. B. Smith, and G. Pinchot. 1900. Report on Forests, in *Annual Report of the State Geologist for 1899.* Trenton, N.J.

Chapter 8

❦ *Freshwater Wetlands of North Jersey*

Wetlands are intermediate both in soil moisture and location between the well-drained uplands and the deepwater habitats such as ponds, lakes, and streams. As described in Chapter 5, there are a variety of wetlands; some are wet for only a few days each year, and others may be more or less wet year round. In northern New Jersey most of the natural wetlands, other than floodplains, owe their origin to the glaciers of the last Ice Age. These ice sheets scoured out basins that were then filled by water from glacial melt or from streams whose drainage was altered by glacial deposits. Many of these old glacial lakes have been completely filled by silt and organic material and through the natural processes of succession are now covered with forests. Others, however, remain as marshlands or as bogs and fens.

Wetlands, which are too wet for most agricultural uses and not suitable as building lots, were once considered wasteland to be reclaimed by draining or filling. They are now recognized for the many benefits they provide to society. They offer food and breeding areas for wildlife, from fish and amphibians to waterfowl and mammals. They contain populations of unusual and sometimes endangered plants. They are aesthetically pleasing to many people and are preferred recreation sites for such activities as nature study, wildlife photography, fishing, and hunting. They may have an effect on local climate. Many wetlands help maintain water quality by absorbing excess nutrients and trapping sediments. They also act as temporary reservoirs for floodwater, reducing water turbidity and lowering water levels.

Freshwater wetland habitats of North Jersey include marshes, swamps, and peatlands, including bogs and fens. But although near-ideal examples of each of these wetlands can be found in North Jersey, in practice large areas that are permanently wet may contain examples of all these habitats; in addition, the habitats often grade into each other. The result is that even professionals might argue about whether a particular wetland should best be called a bog, a fen, a swamp, or a marsh. The differences between these habitats are particularly vague in late stages of succession, when rather similar forests may develop on all of them.

Freshwater Marshes

Marshes are wetlands on which standing water exists for most of the year or that are subject to flooding regularly year round if only for a few days each month or for some part of each day. Included in this category are the shallow edges of rivers and ponds, freshwater tidal marshes, and a variety of wet depressions that are dominated by emergent herbaceous vegetation. No trees and few woody shrubs grow in marshes, giving them the appearance of grassy or herb-covered fields.

Freshwater marshlands also develop around the shallow edges of ponds and lakes. In these waters, tiny free-floating plants such as duckweed and water meal may cover large areas of the water surface. Other aquatic plants live close enough to shore so that their roots penetrate the bottom of the pond or lake. In some of these plants, such as fanwort, the leaves or flowers stay submerged; but in other species such as cattail or water lily they emerge above the surface. Marshes form on such sites as a normal stage in pond succession; shallow waters inevitably fill with undecomposed plant remains and with silt washed or blown in from higher ground, the emergent vegetation becomes more abundant, and a freshwater marsh habitat is created.

In the zone of freshwater marsh next to the open water of lakes, ponds, or rivers in North Jersey the plant community is typically dominated by either common reed, more commonly known by its scientific name, *Phragmites,* or by cattails. Phragmites (Figure 8-1) is often particularly abundant in polluted or somewhat brackish marshes where little else grows, and it can tolerate great fluctuations in water level, even growing on rather dry ground. It can grow as tall as 10 feet, and its showy seed heads are very conspicuous in late summer through winter. Phragmites is native to North America, but its range locally has increased dramatically in the past century, for reasons not entirely understood. In the Hackensack Meadows, the site of former Glacial Lake Hackensack, this plant covers extensive areas, and it is the dominant plant seen when riding from Newark to New York along the New Jersey Turnpike.

In some parts of the Hackensack Meadows and in other freshwater marshes such as the Troy Meadows in Morris County, phragmites is not as abundant as cattails (Figure 8-2). Two species grow in New Jersey—broad-leaved cattail and narrow-leaved cattail. They occur either separately or together in freshwater marshes and occasionally even in somewhat brackish water. Unlike phragmites, cattails cannot grow on dry sites, and they do not often monopolize a marsh to the degree that phragmites does. Cattail marshes produce more wildlife food than do phragmites-dominated marshes. Other plants are usually associated with cattails and phragmites: arrowhead, arrow arum, several species of tickseed-sunflowers, common rush, woolgrass, bulrushes, bur-reed, spike-rushes, blue flag (an iris), sweet flag (a relative of skunk cabbage),

Figure 8-1. Phragmites, or reedgrass, is common almost throughout New Jersey in freshwater marshes. Unlike cattail, it can also grow on upland sites.

Figure 8-2. Broad-leaved cattail often dominates high-quality freshwater marshes.

lizard's-tail, smartweeds, and several species of water-loving grasses, including bluejoint and manna-grass, are common in many marshes. Many high-quality marshes contain a variety of grasslike plants called sedges; there are many species of sedges and one—aptly called tussock sedge—typically forms small tussocks above the water level. This species can sometimes dominate a marsh. Purple loosestrife, a European plant that has naturalized itself here, can crowd out native plants; its purple flower spikes are a beautiful but often too-common sight in marshes in late summer. On slightly higher land are found plants such as the marsh fern, swamp milkweed, joe-pye weed, and jewelweed. Beyond this herbaceous zone grow the taller woody plants of the swamp forest that will gradually invade the marsh. Some typical plant species of North Jersey marshes are listed in Table 8-1.

Freshwater marshes of various sizes occur in many places in North Jersey. Small clumps of cattails and of phragmites can be seen in depressions along roadsides, where drainage from highway embankments results in a more or less continuous condition of standing water. Larger areas of marsh can be found in detention basins and along the edges of lakes and shallow streams. The largest areas of cattail marsh now present in New Jersey are in and around the Great Swamp National Wildlife Refuge in Morris and Somerset counties. One may drive through this refuge and view cattail marshes from the road. A very accessible place from which to observe these marshes more closely is the Wildlife Refuge Observation Station, located on Long Hill Road, which runs from Meyersville to New Vernon. There is a parking lot here, and a marked trail which leads through a cattail marsh and a swampy woods.

Another fine area of marsh can be seen at the Black River Wildlife Management area, in western Morris County near Chester. An abandoned railroad right of way, which heads east from Pleasant Hill Road, parallels the south side of the Black River for several miles.

The best North Jersey examples of large freshwater marshes dominated by phragmites are seen in the Hackensack Meadows. All but a small portion of the remaining marshland here is dominated by this tall grass. There is good access to this habitat at the Hackensack Meadowlands Environmental Center in DeKorte State Park.

Swamps and Floodplains

Swamps and floodplains are typically forested sites on which there is standing water on the soil surface for only certain parts of the year, most often in spring and early summer. At such times, when rainfall or snowmelt is high and evaporation is low, runoff may accumulate in poorly drained forested depressions of land; and even on better-drained sites the water table may temporarily rise above or close to the soil surface. By late summer the water on such sites will normally drop by evaporation and slow drainage to below the soil surface. The lowland adjoining

Table 8-1. Some Typical Plant Species of North Jersey Marshes

Common name	Genus and species name
Shrubs and vines	
Buttonbush	*Cephalanthus occidentalis*
Silky dogwood	*Cornus amomum*
Smooth alder	*Alnus serrulata*
Common elder	*Sambucus canadensis*
Swamp rose	*Rosa palustris*
Meadowsweet	*Spiraea tomentosa*
Few others	
Herbs	
Broad-leaved cattail	*Typha latifolia*
Narrow-leaved cattail	*Typha angustifolia*
Phragmites	*Phragmites australis*
Tussock sedge	*Carex stricta*
Broad-leaved arrowhead	*Sagittaria latifolia*
Swamp loosestrife	*Decodon verticillatus*
Tickseed-sunflower	*Bidens* spp.
Pickerelweed	*Pontederia cordata*
Woolgrass	*Scirpus cyperinus*
Great bulrush	*Scirpus validus*
Common rush	*Juncus effusus*
Purple loosestrife	*Lythrum salicaria*
Arrow arum	*Peltandra virginica*
Blue flag	*Iris versicolor*
Yellow marsh iris	*Iris pseudacorus*
Sweet flag	*Acorus calamus*
Lizard's tail	*Saururus cernuus*
Dotted smartweed	*Polygonum punctatum*
Arrow-leaved tearthumb	*Polygonum sagittatum*
Water pepper	*Polygonum hydropiper*
Bluejoint	*Calamagrostis canadensis*
Rice cutgrass	*Leersia oryzoides*
Reed canary grass	*Phalaris arundinacea*
Manna-grass	*Glyceria striata*
Cut-leaved water-horehound	*Lycopus americanus*
Swamp milkweed	*Asclepias incarnata*
Jewelweed	*Impatiens capensis*
Boneset	*Eupatorium perfoliatum*
Bur-reed	*Sparganium* spp.
Spike-rush	*Eleocharis* spp.
Marsh fern	*Thelypteris palustris*
Many others	

a stream, called a floodplain, will be covered with water only when the river overflows its banks, which may occur several times a year or only at long intervals.

Swamps occur in glaciated areas of North Jersey, particularly in sites of former glacial lakes, such as the Great Swamp. As already noted, swamps are often a late stage in pond succession; as a shallow pond fills with vegetation and silt, it gradually becomes less wet, permitting invasion by trees and shrubs (Figure 8-3). In the same way, bogs and fens may also be transformed into swamp as forest replaces the typical bog vegetation.

Swampy areas have been both created and destroyed in New Jersey as in other areas by the activities of beavers (Figure 8-4). These animals often construct dams across small streams to create a pond deep enough so that the entrance to their lodge or burrow is beneath the water surface. The impounding of water changes the surrounding land, and existing trees may die because of the flooding. When the beavers eventually move on, usually because they deplete the local food supply, the dams gradually erode away, and the former pond becomes a swamp.

Floodplains are well-defined, flat valley surfaces that are covered with water when a stream overflows its banks. Typically, in such terrain the land closest to a stream subject to flooding is slightly higher in elevation and better drained than land farther back from the water, because the overflowing stream deposits coarser, heavier materials, such as sand and gravel, close to its banks. This natural levee traps floodwaters behind it. In addition, this land collects water because it receives seepage from the higher adjacent lands and being less sandy than the land closer to the stream it is not usually well drained. Floodplains occur in North Jersey in the broad valleys of the larger rivers such as the Raritan, Passaic, and Ramapo. The Raritan River from New Brunswick to Bound Brook has a well-formed floodplain, as do its tributaries such as the Lamington and the Millstone Rivers.

Although the frequency, duration, and depth of flooding of the floodplains may vary, the resulting condition of poorly drained land creates just about the same type of plant habitat as that of swampland of different origin, with much the same types of plants. Thus, one may talk of "floodplain swamps" or "backswamps" when referring to the more poorly drained sections of a floodplain. In dry seasons, both swamps and floodplains may appear to be mesic (Figure 8-5), but they can still be distinguished as wetlands by soil characteristics and by their typical vegetation.

Even within the area designated as North Jersey, slight differences in swamp and floodplain plant species occur between the more northern lowland habitats and those in the Piedmont section. At High Point State Park, in the northwest corner of New Jersey, two distinct zones of vegetation can often be observed in the swamps. The wettest sites are densely covered by thickets of various types of shrubs. The most abundant of

Figure 8-3. Woody plants invading a freshwater marsh in the Great Swamp. The low shrubs are buttonbush. The plants in the foreground include swamp loosestrife and arrow arum.

Figure 8-4. Marsh vegetation, dominated by sedges, developing in an abandoned beaver pond in High Point State Park. The dead trees were killed by flooding.

Figure 8-5. Floodplain forest in the Great Swamp. Even though the ground here appears dry, the vegetation indicates that this area is seasonally flooded. The tree with persistent, down-arching dead branches is a pin oak, a wetland species. The flaring bases are typical of trees that grow in wet soil.

these—the alders, willows, and buttonbush—may form pure stands or grow together. Growing with these species but less abundantly are other shrubs, including winterberry, arrowwood, nannyberry, highbush blueberry, swamp azalea, spicebush, and witch hazel. The less wet swamp sites are forested. Typically, red maple and to a lesser extent yellow birch are the characteristic trees in these forests, in some cases accounting for as much as 70 percent of the total tree cover. Other less abundant trees include hemlock, white ash, basswood, sour gum, and the lower-growing ironwood trees. Shrubs, mostly the same as those that form shrub thickets, grow underneath the tree canopy. On the floor of the swamp forest grow the herbs, most typically skunk cabbage, cinnamon fern, royal fern, and tussock sedge and other sedges. Table 8-2 lists typical plant species of swamps of northwestern New Jersey.

Moving southward to the swamps of the Piedmont in central New Jersey, a slight change in the swamp forest can be seen. Red maples are still very common, but few yellow birch trees occur. Instead, American elm, pin oak, swamp white oak, and silver maple are more abundant, and these join sour gum and white ash as the most common trees in the swamps of the Piedmont. A mixture of these species can be seen in the

Table 8-2. Some Typical Plant Species of Swamps and Floodplains of Northwestern New Jersey

Common name	Genus and species name
Trees	
Red maple	*Acer rubrum*
Yellow birch	*Betula alleghaniensis*
Eastern hemlock	*Tsuga canadensis*
White ash	*Fraxinus americana*
Basswood	*Tilia americana*
Sour gum	*Nyssa sylvatica*
Sycamore	*Platanus occidentalis*
Ironwood	*Carpinus caroliniana*
Others	
Shrubs and vines	
Buttonbush	*Cephalanthus occidentalis*
Pussy willow	*Salix discolor*
Silky dogwood	*Cornus amomum*
Smooth alder	*Alnus serrulata*
Common elder	*Sambucus canadensis*
Winterberry	*Ilex verticillata*
Arrowwood	*Viburnum dentatum*
Nannyberry	*Viburnum lentago*
Highbush blueberry	*Vaccinium corymbosum*
Swamp azalea	*Rhododendron viscosum*
Spicebush	*Lindera benzoin*
Witch hazel	*Hamamelis virginiana*
Few others	
Herbs	
Skunk cabbage	*Symplocarpus foetidus*
Jack-in-the-pulpit	*Arisaema triphyllum*
Marsh marigold	*Caltha palustris*
Jewelweed	*Impatiens capensis*
Tussock sedge	*Carex stricta*
Cinnamon fern	*Osmunda cinnamomea*
Royal fern	*Osmunda regalis*
Interrupted fern	*Osmunda claytoniana*
Sensitive fern	*Onoclea sensibilis*
Crested fern	*Dryopteris cristata*
Cut-leaved water-horehound	*Lycopus americanus*
Bluejoint	*Calamagrostis canadensis*
Wood-reed	*Cinna arundinacea*
Others	

swamps occupying the site of former Glacial Lake Passaic, as in the Troy Meadows and in the Great Swamp near Morristown. The shrubs typical of swamps in northern New Jersey also occur farther south, although they are joined by others; for example in the Great Swamp mountain laurel and shadbush are abundant. Spicebush is also very abundant on moist land of the Piedmont. The herbs of the Piedmont swamp forests are much like those of the Ridge and Valley section and include skunk cabbage, ferns, and many spring-flowering species such as marsh marigold, red trillium, jack-in-the-pulpit, spring beauty, and trout lily. Some typical plant species of Piedmont swamps and floodplains are listed in Table 8-3.

A readily accessible place to view a Piedmont swamp forest is in the Great Swamp in Morris County. A good roadside view of the typical trees in this forest is from Pleasant Plains Road, which crosses marshland and swampland. This road can be reached by going north from Stirling on Central Avenue. About 0.7 miles north of the beginning of Pleasant Plains Road, the road is bordered by a swamp forest with large pin oak, swamp white oak, and red maple trees with occasional sweet gum and shagbark hickory trees. Spicebush is a common shrub, and in the summer months ferns and skunk cabbage are conspicuous. Those who want to see more of this habitat can continue along Pleasant Plains Road or take some of the trails in the Great Swamp Wildlife Refuge.

The greatest variety in the composition of lowland forests occurs on the floodplains of New Jersey. On the better-drained sections of the floodplains of the Raritan and Millstone rivers the characteristic trees include black willow, river birch, sycamore, and box elder. On the more poorly drained areas, those trees typical of the central New Jersey lowlands grow abundantly; these include pin oak, silver maple, swamp white oak, red maple, American elm, and sour gum, with occasional representatives of more upland species. The fragrant-smelling spicebush is the most common shrub. On the forest floor among the remains of fallen trees grow many herbs. In some areas, especially along forest edges or in places where forests have been disturbed by humans or trees have been downed by strong winds, vines are common and grow almost to the treetops. These include poison ivy, Virginia creeper, Japanese honeysuckle, Asiatic bittersweet, and several species of wild grape.

On the better-drained portions of the Raritan floodplain west of New Brunswick, trees typical both of swamps and uplands intermingle, and no one species is so abundant that it can be called dominant. The result is a forest of unusual diversity, with representatives of all the trees just mentioned as well as some additional tree species such as Norway maple, honey locust, sassafras, black cherry, ailanthus, white mulberry, and hawthorn. Shrubs include spicebush, common elder, several species of viburnums, staghorn and smooth sumac, Japanese barberry, and silky dogwood. In some places Virginia bluebell forms a spring carpet, along with other species of wildflowers and ferns.

Table 8-3. Some Typical Plant Species of Swamps and Floodplains of the Piedmont

Common name	Genus and species name
Trees	
Red maple	*Acer rubrum*
American elm	*Ulmus americana*
Black willow	*Salix nigra*
Pin oak	*Quercus palustris*
Swamp white oak	*Quercus bicolor*
Silver maple	*Acer saccharinum*
Box elder	*Acer negundo*
Sweet gum	*Liquidambar styraciflua*
Sour gum	*Nyssa sylvatica*
Sycamore	*Platanus occidentalis*
River birch	*Betula nigra*
Shadbush	*Amelanchier canadensis*
Others	
Shrubs and vines	
Spicebush	*Lindera benzoin*
Silky dogwood	*Cornus amomum*
Smooth alder	*Alnus serrulata*
Common elder	*Sambucus canadensis*
Winterberry	*Ilex verticillata*
Arrowwood	*Viburnum dentatum*
Highbush blueberry	*Vaccinium corymbosum*
Swamp azalea	*Rhododendron viscosum*
Buttonbush	*Cephalanthus occidentalis*
Witch hazel	*Hamamelis virginiana*
Virginia creeper	*Parthenocissus quinquefolia*
Riverbank wild grape	*Vitis riparia*
Poison ivy	*Toxicodendron radicans*
Japanese honeysuckle	*Lonicera japonica*
Others	
Herbs	
Skunk cabbage	*Symplocarpus foetidus*
Jack-in-the-pulpit	*Arisaema triphyllum*
Marsh marigold	*Caltha palustris*
Spring beauty	*Claytonia virginica*
Trout lily	*Erythronium americanum*
Tussock sedge	*Carex stricta*

Table 8-3 continued

Common name	Genus and species name
Herbs	
Cinnamon fern	*Osmunda cinnamomea*
Marsh fern	*Thelypteris palustris*
Sensitive fern	*Onoclea sensibilis*
Clearweed	*Pilea pumila*
Wood nettle	*Laportea canadensis*
Blue flag	*Iris versicolor*
Many others	

Another beautiful floodplain forest is located along the east bank of the Raritan River at the north end of Johnson Park. One can reach it by starting at River Road (Route 18) at the foot of Hoe's Lane and walking down to the river. This is a typical forested floodplain, with a higher, well-drained portion near the river and a lower, poorly drained section on alluvial soils away from the river. The latter supports swamp species, such as pin oak, American elm, swamp white oak, box elder, and willows, while the well-drained part next to the river is a forest of basswood, sugar maple, and other trees common on mesic uplands. The most common shrub is spicebush, and vines include poison ivy, Japanese honeysuckle, and wild grape.

The impact of beavers on swamp vegetation can be seen in North Jersey where these animals are active in streams that flow in the valleys of High Point State Park and adjacent Stokes State Forest. In both these areas one can walk along streams and see beaver-constructed dams and the resulting impact on vegetation. Both active dams and abandoned beaver meadows occur along the Big Flatbrook, between the Deckertown Turnpike and Sawmill Lake in High Point State Park, and can be seen from Sawmill Road, which runs parallel to and only a few hundred feet east of the stream.

Peatlands: Bogs and Fens

Peatlands are a type of wetland quite different from the marshes, swamps, and floodplains just described. Peatland sites do not have the regularity of flooding that characterizes marshes, and their substrate conditions are different from those in swamps and floodplains. In appearance too the peatlands differ from other wetlands. Peatlands typically have a cover of mosses, sedges, and low-growing shrubs; they may also have trees, but the trees are usually conifers, as contrasted with the broad-leaved trees typical of swamps and floodplains. More precisely, peatlands are wetlands that are developed on soils primarily organic in origin. Such soils are called "peat," which forms under conditions of little or no water movement and low oxygen levels. Under such conditions plant and animal remains do not fully decompose, and the partially decomposed remains become part of the soil material. Accumulations of peat create very acidic conditions and low fertility, which many plants cannot tolerate. In addition, many microorganisms that normally perform the function of decomposition or breakdown of organic material cannot live under very acidic conditions.

Bogs and fens are two types of peatlands. A bog is a peat-accumulating wetland that has no inflow or outflow of groundwater and is therefore nutrient-poor. A fen is a peat-accumulating wetland that receives some drainage from surrounding mineral soils or from streams or springs and thus is not as nutrient-poor as a bog. As is the case with other habitats, the differentiation between bogs and fens cannot always be made with scientific exactness. For this reason many ecologists prefer to use the term "peatland" for all sites, whatever the plant cover, that have a predominantly organic soil.

Bogs and fens in North Jersey occur primarily in the area that was once covered by glacial ice. In areas well north of New Jersey, where temperatures are lower and moisture levels higher than in New Jersey, bog plants, especially peat mosses of the genus *Sphagnum,* can grow out onto the surface of the ground to form raised bogs; but New Jersey's climate does not permit this. Our bogs formed when ice sheets scoured out rocky basins without inlets or outlets, which then filled with water from ice melt. Fens were formed when glacial deposits wholly or partially blocked drainage of streams or lakes, leaving areas in which peats could accumulate.

No matter what its origin, a peatland in New Jersey will gradually change in time from an open body of water or from a permanently wet lowland into a surface covered with a dense growth of vegetation. So complete is the change that one coming upon the area for the first time could hardly believe that the site was once a wetland. The gradual change from open water to forest is just another example of the natural process of succession.

As in marshes, the extension of vegetation into shallow bogs and fens is primarily accomplished by the accumulation of peat, silt, and debris that fills the wetland from the bottom up. But bogs that form in basins with relatively steep sides may fill with vegetation in a different manner. The process starts at the water's edge, where stems of certain land plants extend out over the water surface, forming a floating branched network. One such plant that grows in New Jersey bogs in swamp loosestrife; another is a heath shrub called leatherleaf, named for the texture of its small, oval, evergreen leaves. Several low-growing plants, particularly sedges and sphagnum mosses, quickly fill up the spaces on the floating branches, and a floating mat of vegetation is gradually established. Other plants join the initial pioneers, and the mat gets thicker and thicker and extends farther outward on the water. Even shrubs and small trees may start to grow on the thicker portions of the mat.

As plant life expands on top of the mat, vegetative plant parts on the underside of the mat die, drop to the bottom of the basin, and start to fill it with a deposit of peat. Without decomposition, and particularly in basins with poor drainage, the peat layer gets thicker and the bog water more acid, and the water basin, which gradually is being filled with organic material, gets smaller and smaller. With the passage of enough time the floating mat covers the entire water surface, the basin is completely filled with peat deposits, and the vegetation changes to a forest type.

Many of the bogs and fens of northern New Jersey develop with some area of floating mat vegetation. The leaves of sphagnum mosses, of which there are about forty-five species in New Jersey, can hold a great amount of water, which imparts a springy, cushionlike character to the floating mat. The edge of the mat nearest the open water may not be strong enough to support a person's weight, but it may be possible to walk on the mat almost to that edge. Wet feet result, however, for with each step the sphagnum cushion may be depressed below the surface of the water. It is the cushionlike character of the floating mat that gives rise to the term "quaking bog."

Away from the water's edge more varied plant life is found. In this zone the ground is uneven, and sphagnum hummocks rise as much as several feet above water level. Water still stands in depressions among the hummocks, but in prolonged dry periods these depressions may dry. It is on the hummocks for the most part that trees grow in bog and fen habitats. Also occupying the hummocks at the base of the trees is a strange group of plants that actually consume small insects and for this reason are called carnivorous plants; in this way they obtain nitrogen, phosphorus, and other essential minerals in an otherwise mineral-poor environment of peat and living sphagnum moss. North Jersey carnivorous plants include pitcher plant, two species of sundews, and several species of bladderworts. Many ferns also grow in this habitat, including cinnamon fern, royal fern, and bog fern. In some bogs and fens of North Jersey are found rare examples of such northern plants as bog rosemary, bog laurel, goldthread, and small cranberry; most are at or near their southeastern limit of range here.

The shrubs of the bog shrub–tree zone include sheep laurel, swamp azalea, highbush blueberry, great rhododendron (Figure 8-6), mountain laurel, and sometimes mountain holly and witch hazel. Some of these are also found on the thicker, dryer parts of the floating mat. Less abundant but still typical are winterberry, maleberry, and smooth and speckled alder. Trees include hemlock, red maple, yellow birch, sour gum, and Atlantic white cedar, as well as two northern conifers, black spruce and American larch (or tamarack), which are more characteristic of wet-

Table 8-4. Some Typical Plant Species of Bogs and Fens of Northwestern New Jersey

Common name	Genus and species name
Trees	
Eastern hemlock	*Tsuga canadensis*
Atlantic white cedar	*Chamaecyparis thyoides*
Black spruce	*Picea mariana*
American larch	*Larix laricina*
Pitch pine	*Pinus rigida*
Red maple	*Acer rubrum*
Sour gum	*Nyssa sylvatica*
Few others	
Shrubs	
Highbush blueberry	*Vaccinium corymbosum*
Smooth alder	*Alnus serrulata*
Speckled alder	*Alnus incana*
Winterberry	*Ilex verticillata*
Arrowwood	*Viburnum dentatum*
Withe rod	*Viburnum cassinoides*
Swamp azalea	*Rhododendron viscosum*
Great rhododendron	*Rhododendron maximum*
Mountain holly	*Nemopanthus mucronata*
Mountain laurel	*Kalmia latifolia*
Sheep laurel	*Kalmia angustifolia*
Leatherleaf	*Chamaedaphne calyculata*
Witch hazel	*Hamamelis virginiana*
Others	
Herbs	
Swamp loosestrife	*Decodon verticillatus*
Wild calla	*Calla palustris*
Goldthread	*Coptis trifolia*
Red trillium	*Trillium erectum*
Skunk cabbage	*Symplocarpus foetidus*
Alpine enchanter's nightshade	*Circaea alpina*
Small cranberry	*Vaccinium oxycoccus*
Pitcher plant	*Sarracenia purpurea*
Round-leaved sundew	*Drosera rotundifolia*
Bladderwort	*Utricularia* spp.
Tussock sedge	*Carex stricta*
Spike-rush	*Eleocharis* spp.

Table 8-4 continued

Common name	Genus and species name
Trees	
Bluejoint	*Calamagrostis canadensis*
Cinnamon fern	*Osmunda cinnamomea*
Royal fern	*Osmunda regalis*
Many others	
Mosses	
Peat moss	*Sphagnum* spp.
Many others	

lands in northern New England and Canada. Some typical plant species of bogs and fens in northwestern New Jersey are listed in Table 8-4.

An excellent example of a mature bog forest in northern New Jersey that can readily be visited is the "cedar swamp" in High Point State Park (Figure 8-7). The park map identifies it as the John Dryden Kuser Natural Area. One can drive to within a few hundred yards of the area, park, and then walk along a trail that encircles much of the bog forest. Without even getting one's feet wet, it is possible to see clearly the bog vegetation that has completely filled in a lake created upon the recession of the glacial ice that covered this part of New Jersey 12,000 or so years ago. Along the trail can be seen large trees of hemlock and red maple, with some sour gum, yellow birch, white pine, and pitch pine. The dominant tree of the wetter parts of the bog forest is Atlantic white cedar, the same species that dominates fens in the Pine Barrens, and there are also a few scattered black spruces. Thickets of great rhododendron border some parts of the trail, and other shrubs include swamp azalea, highbush blueberry, sheep laurel, winterberry, and mountain holly. Cinnamon fern, interrupted fern, and royal fern are abundant. Sphagnum mosses form a carpet on the wetter parts of the site, and in it grow such herbs typical of boreal bogs as wild calla (Figure 8-8), goldthread, three-leaved false Solomon's-seal, bunchberry, and bead lily. Little open water still remains in this bog (actually a mineral-poor fen, since it is drained by a small stream), but some floating sphagnum can usually be seen from a short boardwalk that crosses the site.

In a few places in North Jersey, fens have formed over a calcareous substrate such as limestone. In this situation the organic acids formed by the decomposition of sphagnum mosses are neutralized. These mineral-rich fens often contain an assemblage of unusual plants, including such species as fringed gentian, grass-of-parnassus, shrubby cinquefoil, tufted loosestrife, yellow water crowfoot, and a variety of sedges rarely seen

Figure 8-6. Great rhododendron often grows profusely along the edges of bog forests and in the shrub–tree zone of quaking bogs in northern New Jersey. It flowers in mid July.

Figure 8-7. Part of the cedar swamp in High Point State Park. The trees are sour gum and eastern hemlock. Skunk cabbage, sedges, and other herbs grow in the saturated sphagnum moss at the bases of the trees.

Figure 8-8. Wild calla, a member of the same family as skunk cabbage, grows in floating sphagnum moss in the cedar swamp at High Point State Park.

outside this habitat. Most such sites are small, few are publicly owned, and none are readily accessible.

Human Influences on the Wetlands

Although some wetlands have been created by human activities, most human activities relating to wetlands have been primarily destructive, either by obliterating them completely through filling or draining or by degrading their quality. Some of the more obvious destructive practices have included drainage for agriculture; channelization of streams for flood control; filling for residential or commercial development or highway construction; use as dumpsites; flooding to create reservoirs and recreational lakes; and logging.

More subtle forms of degradation have occurred as byproducts of other human actions. In the nineteenth century, for example, the Hackensack Meadows were a mosaic of Atlantic white cedar swamps, floodplain forests, and cattail marshes. Logging and diking changed the character of the marshes, and a final destructive action was the construction of the Oradell Reservoir in 1922. This reduced the freshwater flow into the meadows downstream of the dam, thus allowing salt water to move up the estuary. The last Atlantic white cedars died in 1939. Phragmites moved into what had become brackish water habitat and now dominates a wetland with far less species diversity than it had originally.

Even if not taking place within a wetland, lumbering and construction typically allow siltation into wetlands, which by increasing turbidity directly affects the growth of aquatic plants. Pollutants and excess nutrients from a variety of point and nonpoint sources including sewage overflow and runoff from roads, paved areas, and lawns also affect plant growth in wetlands. In addition to changing vegetation patterns, this may also affect the rate of pond succession. More is said in Chapter 14 about the effectiveness of state actions to protect wetlands.

Summary

North Jersey has examples of swamps, marshes, bogs, and fens. Each is characterized by a particular assemblage of plants, although some of the same plants can be found in almost all of them. All these habitats are affected by the natural process of succession, which eventually will convert them all to dry land. But human activities have greatly affected wetlands, usually by destroying or degrading them.

References and Source Material

Buell, M. F., and W. A. Wistendahl. 1955. Flood Plain Forests of the Raritan River. *Bulletin of the Torrey Botanical Club* 82:463–472.

Heusser, C. J. 1949. History of an Estuarine Bog at Secaucus, New Jersey. *Bulletin of the Torrey Botanical Club* 76:385–406.

Jervis, R. A. 1963. The Vascular Plants and Plant Communities of Troy Meadows. *Bulletin of the New Jersey Academy of Science* 8:1–21.

Johnson, C. W. 1985. *Bogs of the Northeast.* Hanover, N.H., and London: University Press of New England.

Niering, W. A. 1953. The Past and Present Vegetation of High Point State Park, New Jersey. *Ecological Monographs* 23:127–148.

Sipple, W. S. 1972. The Past and Present Flora and Vegetation of the Hackensack Meadows. *Bartonia* 41:4–57.

Tiner, R. W. 1985. Wetlands of New Jersey. Newton Center, Mass.: U.S. Fish and Wildlife Service, National Wetlands Inventory.

Van Vechten, G. W., III, and M. F. Buell. 1959. The Flood Plain Vegetation of the Millstone River, New Jersey. *Bulletin of the Torrey Botanical Club* 86:219–227.

Wistendahl, W. A. 1958. The Flood Plain of the Raritan River, New Jersey. *Ecological Monographs* 82:129–153.

Chapter 9

❧ *Freshwater Wetlands of South Jersey*

South Jersey, like North Jersey, has marshes, swamps, and peatlands. Some of these wetlands have much the same qualities as those farther north, but because South Jersey has meandering rivers flowing through relatively flat terrain, extensive shorelines on the ocean and Delaware Bay, and sandy soils, it also has several types of wetland habitat found only rarely in North Jersey. Among these are the mineral-poor fens (locally called savannahs) that form along streams in the Pine Barrens. Saltwater marshes, also common in South Jersey, are described in a later chapter.

Wetland habitats in South Jersey that are ecologically similar to North Jersey habitats—such as swamps and floodplains—are likely to be dominated by, or at any rate contain, many southern species of plants not found in the corresponding habitat in North Jersey. Because of climate and other factors, South Jersey is at the northern edge of the range of many such plants. Witmer Stone, writing in 1910, noted that 164 species or varieties of plants reached their northern limit in southern New Jersey, and another 77 southern plants reached their northern limit in nearby Staten Island or Long Island, New York. The majority of these are wetland species.

South Jersey does not have some of the wetland types found in North Jersey. The region has no limestone bedrock close to the surface, so it has no calcareous fens. In addition, since South Jersey has never been glaciated and typically has well-drained soil, it has no true bogs. For the same reasons, very few natural ponds or lakes are found in South Jersey. Thus, the typical pondside freshwater marsh of North Jersey is uncommon on the Inner and Outer Coastal Plains.

As in North Jersey, the wetland types of South Jersey grade into each other to some extent, so it is not always possible to make clear distinctions between them. Also, as described in the previous chapter, different types of wetlands may succeed each other on the same site. This is particularly true of forested wetlands and also of estuarine marshes, for which the line between freshwater and saltwater marsh is often somewhat arbitrary and variable.

Freshwater Marshes

In the part of New Jersey that has never been covered by glacial ice, most freshwater marshes are found along stream borders and at the mouths of rivers. This is particularly true on the Inner and Outer Coastal Plains, where high water tables keep some of the lower valley land almost continuously flooded. About 15 square miles of freshwater tidal marshes occur along the Delaware River and its tributaries south of Trenton, and along the Mullica and other rivers draining into the Atlantic Ocean. But in addition, isolated wet depressions in open fields—particularly in the Inner Coastal Plain, where soils often contain substantial amounts of clay, which retards drainage—often develop typical marsh vegetation, at least until successional processes replace herbaceous plants with shrubs and trees. And surprisingly, freshwater or brackish marshes, though small in size, sometimes form in hollows between coastal sand dunes.

Although both phragmites marshes (see Figure 8-1) and cattail marshes (see Figure 8-2) are common in southern New Jersey, wild rice is perhaps the most distinctive plant of the marshes in this part of the state. Until the 1950s, this annual grass, which grows as tall as 9 feet, was the dominant plant in many marshlands along the streams flowing into the Delaware River and Delaware Bay, from Trenton southward (Figure 9-1). Pollution, drainage, and filling have destroyed many of these marshes, and others are now dominated by phragmites. But wild rice can still be found in abundance in some places.

One of the more northern streams to have good populations of wild rice is Rancocas Creek, which flows west out of the Pine Barrens in Burlington County. A close up look at wild rice and many other South Jersey marsh plants in a freshwater tidal marsh can be obtained from one of the trails at the Rancocas Nature Center in Westampton Township. This facility is on Rancocas Road, about 1.7 miles east of exit 45-A on I-295. Wild rice here grows with such other plants as broad-leaved cattail, water hemp, halberd-leaved and arrow-leaved tearthumbs, jewelweed, pickerelweed, arrow arum, and spatterdock. Another extensive stand of wild rice, with many of the same associated plants, can be seen at Mill Creek Park in Willingboro, also on Rancocas Road but about 3.5 miles west of I-295, where Mill Creek flows into the Rancocas.

In Gloucester County, a very fine freshwater tidal marsh along Oldman's Creek can be seen from the road that runs northward from Pedricktown toward Center Square. Wild rice grows here with both phragmites and broad-leaved cattail. Other plants that are easily seen here include spatterdock, arrow arum, blue flag, rose mallow, water hemp, nodding beggar-ticks, jewelweed, sneezeweed, rice cutgrass, and halberd-leaved and arrow-leaved tearthumbs. Around the edges of the marsh are found shrubs such as buttonbush, indigo bush, and silky dogwood, with trees of black willow, box elder, and red maple.

Figure 9-1. A stand of wild rice along Rancocas Creek. This plant is abundant in some freshwater tidal marshes of southern New Jersey. It is uncommon elsewhere in the state.

Farther south, a good place to see wild rice is along the Manumuskin Creek in Cumberland County; here it can be viewed from a railroad bridge that spans the creek northeast of Port Elizabeth. To reach this site, take Route 646 (Port Elizabeth–Cumberland Road) east from Port Elizabeth for about 2.0 miles, to a railroad crossing. Walk north along the tracks to the stream. Wild rice is dominant in this freshwater tidal marsh, but there are also some broad-leaved cattail and phragmites.

Table 9-1 lists some typical plant species of South Jersey freshwater tidal marshes.

Swamps and Floodplains

The habitat conditions in the swamp and floodplain areas of South Jersey appear to favor the growth of certain tree species that are not commonly found in North Jersey. As a result, the forest composition of the South Jersey wetlands is quite different from those of North Jersey. In addition, differences in soil conditions between the Inner and Outer Coastal Plains and in temperatures between the Cape May peninsula and the more northern parts of the Coastal Plains create differences in forest composition even within South Jersey. Three forest types can be found

Table 9-1. Some Typical Plant Species of Freshwater Tidal Marshes of South Jersey

Common name	Genus and species name
Shrubs	
Buttonbush	*Cephalanthus occidentalis*
Indigo bush	*Amorpha fruticosa*
Silky dogwood	*Cornus amomum*
Swamp rose	*Rosa palustris*
Few others	
Herbs	
Wild rice	*Zizania aquatica*
Phragmites	*Phragmites australis*
Narrow-leaved cattail	*Typha angustifolia*
Broad-leaved cattail	*Typha latifolia*
Rose mallow	*Hibiscus moscheutos*
Water hemp	*Amaranthus cannabinus*
Halberd-leaved tearthumb	*Polygonum arifolium*
Arrow-leaved tearthumb	*Polygonum sagittatum*
Blue flag	*Iris versicolor*
Nodding beggar-ticks	*Bidens cernua*
Bur-marigold	*Bidens laevis*
Great ragweed	*Ambrosia trifida*
Jewelweed	*Impatiens capensis*
Sneezeweed	*Helenium autumnale*
Pickerelweed	*Pontederia cordata*
Arrow arum	*Peltandra virginica*
Rice cutgrass	*Leersia oryzoides*
Spatterdock	*Nuphar advena*
Woolgrass	*Scirpus cyperinus*
Broad-leaved arrowhead	*Sagittaria latifolia*
Dotted smartweed	*Polygonum punctatum*
Sweet flag	*Acorus calamus*
Many others	

on these wetlands—the Cedar Swamp forest, the Hardwood Swamp forest, and the Pitch Pine Lowland forest.

Cedar Swamp Forest

Historically, many of the waterways of southern New Jersey, on both the Inner and Outer Coastal Plains, were lined with swamplands dominated by Atlantic white cedar. This tree is found from Mississippi to southern Maine, always in similar wet places. It is a valuable timber tree: the wood is light, straight-grained, easy to work, and decay resistant; wherever it grows, it is eagerly sought for lumber for shingles, poles, and other uses that involve exposure to weather. As early as 1750, Peter Kalm, a Swedish naturalist working out of Philadelphia, expressed concern that the species would be depleted by overharvesting. The concern was well founded; Atlantic white cedar is much less common now than it was even a century ago. Today, most New Jersey cedar swamps are found in the Pine Barrens, often associated with and grading into pitch pine lowlands or the fens or savannahs along the waterways.

Few habitats in New Jersey are as thoroughly dominated by a single tree species as a cedar swamp (locally also called a cedar bog) (Figure 9-2). In most, however, one can find individual trees of red maple, sour gum, pitch pine, or sweet bay magnolia struggling upward toward the light. Around the edges of cedar swamps, and in openings within them, are such shrubs as highbush blueberry, dangleberry, swamp azalea, fetterbush, and leatherleaf, all of which are members of the heath family; sweet pepperbush, whose fragrant blossoms in white spikes are conspicuous along Pine Barrens waterways in August; and inkberry and winterberry, both members of the holly family.

The forest floor in a cedar swamp often has pools of standing water, and light levels are low (Figure 9-3). The ground and the bases of the trees are often covered with several species of sphagnum mosses and liverworts. Few herbaceous plants can thrive here, though one does find several species of ferns, including cinnamon fern, netted chain fern, and sometimes the rare curly-grass fern. Clumps of sedges are common— some often-seen species are long sedge and Collins' sedge. Carnivorous plants, such as the sundews and the pitcher plant, can usually be found, although they are more abundant in more open, sunny situations. Some typical plant species of the Cedar Swamp forest are listed in Table 9-2.

Typical white cedar swamps can be seen in the Wharton State Forest, Bass River State Forest, Lebanon State Forest, and other Pine Barrens areas. In Lebanon State Forest, a good example can be reached by driving east on Shinn's road from the park office for about 0.7 mile, then turning left on an all-weather sand road. In about 0.6 mile, the road trends downhill and crosses Shinn's Branch, a small, dark-colored stream. The cedar swamp parallels Shinn's Branch. In addition to Atlantic white cedar, all the expected plants can be seen here: red maple (the local population usually has only three lobes per leaf and at times has been classed as a separate variety, the trident red maple), sweet bay magnolia, sour gum, highbush blueberry, dangleberry, swamp azalea, fetterbush, leatherleaf, sweet pepperbush, and inkberry and winterberry. A few gray birches appear along the road, but they seem out of place. On the forest floor, among the sphagnum hummocks and clumps of sedges, can

Figure 9-2. Atlantic white cedar grows along the edges of waterways in the Pine Barrens. The dark foliage and upright growth habit make this tree easy to recognize from a distance.

Figure 9-3. The dark, shady interior of a cedar swamp in Lebanon State Forest. The dense tree growth and the rather sparse understory of heath shrubs is characteristic.

Table 9-2. Some Typical Plant Species of the Cedar Swamp Forest of South Jersey

Common name	Genus and species name
Dominant tree	
Atlantic white cedar	*Chamaecyparis thyoides*
Other trees	
Pitch pine	*Pinus rigida*
Red maple	*Acer rubrum*
Sour gum	*Nyssa sylvatica*
Sweet bay magnolia	*Magnolia virginiana*
Very few others	
Shrubs and vines	
Highbush blueberry	*Vaccinium corymbosum*
Fetterbush	*Eubotrys racemosa*
Dangleberry	*Gaylussacia frondosa*
Swamp azalea	*Rhododendron viscosum*
Maleberry	*Lyonia ligustrina*
Sheep laurel	*Kalmia angustifolia*
Leatherleaf	*Chamaedaphne calyculata*
Sweet pepperbush	*Clethra alnifolia*
Winterberry	*Ilex verticillata*
Inkberry	*Ilex glabra*
Common greenbrier	*Smilax rotundifolia*
Few others	
Herbs	
Pitcher plant	*Sarracenia purpurea*
Round-leaved sundew	*Drosera rotundifolia*
Spatulate-leaved sundew	*Drosera intermedia*
Bladderwort	*Utricularia* spp.
Golden club	*Orontium aquaticum*
Starflower	*Trientalis borealis*
Arethusa	*Arethusa bulbosa*
Long sedge	*Carex folliculata*
Collins' sedge	*Carex collinsii*
Cinnamon fern	*Osmunda cinnamomea*
Royal fern	*Osmunda regalis*
Bog fern	*Thelypteris simulata*
Netted chain fern	*Woodwardia areolata*
Virginia chain fern	*Woodwardia virginica*
Others	

continued

Table 9-2 continued

Common name	Genus and species name
Lichens and mosses	
Peat moss	*Sphagnum* spp.
Santee lichen	*Cladonia santensis*
Others	

be found cinnamon fern, royal fern, Virginia chain fern, and netted chain fern.

A small but not uninteresting cedar swamp can be found in Cheese-quake State Park. This is perhaps the northermost cedar swamp still remaining on the Coastal Plain of New Jersey. Again, the dominant white cedars are mixed with some red maple, sour gum, and pitch pine. Sweet bay magnolia is abundant in the understory. Other shrubs include high-bush blueberry, swamp azalea, and a few shrubs of sweet pepperbush and winterberry. The most obvious herbs are cinnamon fern and long sedge.

Hardwood Swamp Forest

On the Inner Coastal Plain, sweet gum is the most typical tree of swamp forests (Figure 9-4). In New Jersey this species is mostly confined to the Coastal Plain, although scattered individuals also grow in swamp or floodplain areas in the southern part of the Piedmont. With the sweet gum is usually found red maple, pin oak, swamp white oak, willow oak, tulip tree, and sweet bay magnolia. American holly is frequently present. The shrubs growing in the more mature lowland forests of the Inner Coastal Plain include arrowwood, spicebush, highbush blueberry, sweet pepperbush, and swamp azalea. Poison ivy and Japanese honeysuckle are often abundant and form dense thickets. Table 9-3 lists some typical plant species of the Hardwood Swamp Forest of the Inner Coastal Plain.

On the Outer Coastal Plain the natural succession on swamp and floodplain habitats is from shrub thicket to Atlantic white cedar swamp, and finally to a southern swamp hardwood-forest type. This forest is typically dominated by red maple (in its three-lobed variety), sour gum, and sweet bay magnolia. Of the three, red maple is usually the most common and sometimes accounts for as many as 80 percent of the trees making up the forest canopy (Figure 9-5). Though not as abundant, other trees are found in the swamp forest, including sweet gum, Atlantic white cedar, pitch pine, American holly, willow oak, and Spanish oak. In the lowlands of Cape May and Cumberland counties, several additional tree species characteristic of swamp forests in the southeastern United States are occasionally found, including the basket oak and water oak.

Figure 9-4. Sweet gum, with star-shaped leaves, is typical of swamp forests on the Inner Coastal Plain.

Table 9-3. Some Typical Plant Species of the Hardwood Swamp Forest of the Inner Coastal Plain

Common name	Genus and species name
Dominant trees	
Sweet gum	*Liquidambar styraciflua*
Red maple	*Acer rubrum*
Sour gum	*Nyssa sylvatica*
Other trees	
Willow oak	*Quercus phellos*
Pin oak	*Quercus palustris*
Swamp white oak	*Quercus bicolor*
Sweet bay magnolia	*Magnolia virginiana*
American holly	*Ilex opaca*
River birch	*Betula nigra*
Few others	
Shrubs and vines	
Highbush blueberry	*Vaccinium corymbosum*
Fetterbush	*Eubotrys racemosa*
Arrowwood	*Viburnum dentatum*

continued

Table 9-3 continued

Common name	Genus and species name
Shrubs and vines continued	
Swamp azalea	*Rhododendron viscosum*
Spicebush	*Lindera benzoin*
Sweet pepperbush	*Clethra alnifolia*
Winterberry	*Ilex verticillata*
Common greenbrier	*Smilax rotundifolia*
Poison sumac	*Toxicodendron vernix*
Poison ivy	*Toxicodendron radicans*
Japanese honeysuckle	*Lonicera japonica*
Others	
Herbs	
Tussock sedge	*Carex stricta*
Swamp dewberry	*Rubus hispidus*
Skunk cabbage	*Symplocarpus foetidus*
Woodreed	*Cinna arundinacea*
Eulalia grass	*Microstegium vimineum*
Slender spike-grass	*Chasmanthium laxum*
Primrose-leaved violet	*Viola primulifolia*
Partridgeberry	*Mitchella repens*
Cinnamon fern	*Osmunda cinnamomea*
Royal fern	*Osmunda regalis*
Bog fern	*Thelypteris simulata*
Netted chain fern	*Woodwardia areolata*
Others	
Mosses	
Peat moss	*Sphagnum* spp.
Others	

Table 9-4 lists some typical plant species of the Hardwood Swamp Forest of the Outer Coastal Plain.

Pigeon Swamp in Middlesex County is an excellent example of an Inner Coastal Plain Hardwood Swamp forest, with large specimens of the trees typical of this habitat. The swamp can be reached from Route 130 by taking Fresh Pond Road, which goes northeast from Route 130, just north of the turnoff marked Dayton–Jamesburg. Continue northeast on Fresh Pond Road to the first intersection, which is Rhode Hall Road. To the right, for about half a mile along Rhode Hall Road, can be seen a forest dominated by sweet gum and red maple, with some black, white,

Figure 9-5. A red maple–dominated swamp fringes Sluice Creek, on the Outer Coastal Plain in Cape May County.

scarlet, and pin oaks. There are also a few large willow oaks, close to the northern limit of their range here. The shrub understory is mostly fetter-bush and sweet pepperbush, with some highbush blueberry and arrow-wood. Some small sweet bay magnolias and sour gums form part of the understory as well. Japanese honeysuckle, common greenbrier, and poison ivy are found. Little herbaceous flora occurs—mostly cinnamon fern and eulalia grass, with some swamp dewberry and a few sedges.

On the Outer Coastal Plain, a good example of a Hardwood Swamp forest can be seen in Cape May County at Timber and Beaver Swamp, in the Beaver Dam Wildlife Management Area in Dennis Township. The area can be reached by taking Beaver Dam Road, which goes to the east off Route 47 about 0.6 miles south of South Dennis. The trees present in this forest are, in order of decreasing dominance, American holly, red maple, sweetgum, sour gum, loblolly pine, Spanish oak, sweet bay magnolia, and willow oak, with some American beech and sassafras. The gently undulating terrain makes possible this diverse composition of lowland trees. The loblolly pine is particularly interesting since it is close to its northern limit here. Understory shrubs include arrowwood, highbush blueberry, fetterbush, wax myrtle, American strawberry-bush, sweet pepperbush, swamp azalea, and common greenbrier. On the forest floor can be found New York fern, slender spike grass, glaucous greenbrier, primrose-leaved violet, and sedges of several species. In its overall appearance, this forest much resembles some forests in Virginia or southern Maryland.

Table 9-4. Some Typical Plant Species of the Hardwood Swamp Forest of the Outer Coastal Plain

Common name	Genus and species name
Dominant trees	
Red maple	*Acer rubrum*
Sweet gum	*Liquidambar styraciflua*
Sour gum	*Nyssa sylvatica*
Other trees	
Atlantic white cedar	*Chamaecyparis thyoides*
Pitch pine	*Pinus rigida*
Spanish oak	*Quercus falcata*
Pin oak	*Quercus palustris*
Sweet bay magnolia	*Magnolia virginiana*
American holly	*Ilex opaca*
Few others	
Shrubs and vines	
Highbush blueberry	*Vaccinium corymbosum*
Fetterbush	*Eubotrys racemosa*
Arrowwood	*Viburnum dentatum*
Swamp azalea	*Rhododendron viscosum*
Spicebush	*Lindera benzoin*
Sweet pepperbush	*Clethra alnifolia*
Winterberry	*Ilex verticillata*
Naked witherod	*Viburnum nudum*
Poison sumac	*Toxicodendron vernix*
Poison ivy	*Toxicodendron radicans*
Common greenbrier	*Smilax rotundifolia*
Japanese honeysuckle	*Lonicera japonica*
Few others	
Herbs	
Swamp dewberry	*Rubus hispidus*
Woodreed	*Cinna arundinacea*
Slender spike grass	*Chasmanthium laxum*
Primose-leaved violet	*Viola primulifolia*
Cinnamon fern	*Osmunda cinnamomea*
Royal fern	*Osmunda regalis*
Bog fern	*Thelypteris simulata*
Netted chain fern	*Woodwardia areolata*
Virginia chain fern	*Woodwardia virginica*
Others	
Mosses	
Peat moss	*Sphagnum* spp.
Others	

Another Outer Coastal Plain lowland can be seen from paths that branch from the red trail in Allaire State Park. This trail parallels the swamp. Almost all the large trees in this swamp are red maples and sour gums, though a few river birches and sweet gums appear as well. Sweet bay magnolia is common. There is a dense shrub layer, composed mostly of arrowwood, sweet pepperbush, highbush blueberry, and winterberry, with some fetterbush, spicebush, and naked witherod. Herbs include cinnamon fern, rice cutgrass, woodreed, skunk cabbage, swamp dewberry, woolgrass, tussock and other sedges, spinulose woodfern, and slender spike grass. Sphagnum mosses are abundant on the forest floor.

Pitch Pine Lowland Forest

In many parts of the Pine Barrens, a pitch pine forest has developed on lowland depressions. Here, the land is wet because the soil surface is at or close to the water table. Such forests are typically on somewhat drier ground than the cedar swamps and fens that often border them, but they still contain an assemblage of moisture-loving plants. Like the upland pine forests, Pitch Pine Lowland forests are vulnerable to fire, which as in the uplands has the effect of maintaining pitch pine as the most abundant tree in them. Growing with the pines may be scattered individuals of red maple, sour gum, and Atlantic white cedar. Shrubs such as highbush blueberry, sweet pepperbush, fetterbush, sheep laurel, swamp azalea, inkberry, leatherleaf, and sand myrtle are likely to be common. There is also a sparse but often interesting herbaceous layer in the forest, often including bracken fern, wintergreen, and turkeybeard. Sphagnum mosses are common and often form a deep mat of organic matter over the sandy subsoil.

This common forest type occurs in many Pine Barrens areas. In Lebanon State Forest, good examples can be seen along the headwaters of McDonald's Branch and in many other locations. In the Wharton State Forest, a small sample can be seen along a self-guiding nature trail that runs north along the east shore of Batsto Lake. In general, these lowlands can be distinguished from upland pine forests by their dense, usually rather tall shrub cover (Figure 9-6). Plants particularly indicative of the habitat are highbush blueberry, dangleberry, sweet pepperbush, and sheep laurel, with leatherleaf in the wettest sites.

Table 9-5 lists some typical plant species of Pitch Pine Lowlands.

Peatlands: Fens (Savannahs)

On the Coastal Plains of South Jersey, particularly the Outer Coastal Plain, rainwater and snowmelt percolating through leaf litter become acidified, a condition that the sandy soil through which the water flows is incapable of mitigating. Along shallow streams and in wet depressions created by human activities such as bog ore mining or turf cutting, this water acidity combined with inadequate drainage creates conditions

Figure 9-6. Pitch Pine Lowland forest near Shinn's Branch in Lebanon State Forest. The tall shrubs, here mostly highbush blueberry and sweet pepperbush, usually distinguish these areas from the dry pine forests on surrounding uplands.

favorable for heavy accumulations of peat. Such areas, which in their location and overall appearance often resemble some of the marshes along streams in northern New Jersey, are locally known as savannahs (Figure 9-7). But, because of their accumulation of peat, they are more accurately classified as mineral-poor fens.

These fens are often associated with Atlantic white cedar swamps, and in the natural course of wetland succession they will eventually become cedar swamps, and then hardwood swamps. They were much more extensive a century ago, when logging and bog ore mining had created openings in the forest. But while they last they have a rich and interesting flora, quite different from that of the Cedar Swamp or Pitch Pine Lowland forests. Like the bogs and fens of North Jersey, these South Jersey peatlands cover only a very small area of the state—something like 1,000 acres—but no discussion of New Jersey's vegetation would be complete without mentioning them.

As is true of plant habitats generally, no two of these savannahs are quite alike. But most of them are dominated by sedges, which frequently grow from a mat of sphagnum moss. Sedges are a very large group of plants, but a few species that are commonly present in these areas are woolgrass, twig rush, button sedge, cottongrass, common beak-rush,

Table 9-5. Some Typical Plant Species of the Pitch Pine Lowland Forest of the Outer Coastal Plain

Common name	Genus and species name
Dominant Tree	
Pitch pine	*Pinus rigida*
Other trees	
Atlantic white cedar	*Chamaecyparis thyoides*
Red maple	*Acer rubrum*
Sour gum	*Nyssa sylvatica*
Sweet bay magnolia	*Magnolia virginiana*
Very few others	
Shrubs and vines	
Highbush blueberry	*Vaccinium corymbosum*
Fetterbush	*Eubotrys racemosa*
Dangleberry	*Gaylussacia frondosa*
Black huckleberry	*Gaylussacia baccata*
Swamp azalea	*Rhododendron viscosum*
Maleberry	*Lyonia ligustrina*
Staggerbush	*Lyonia mariana*
Sheep laurel	*Kalmia angustifolia*
Leatherleaf	*Chamaedaphne calyculata*
Sand myrtle	*Leiophyllum buxifolium*
Sweet pepperbush	*Clethra alnifolia*
Winterberry	*Ilex verticillata*
Inkberry	*Ilex glabra*
Common greenbrier	*Smilax rotundifolia*
Glaucous greenbrier	*Smilax glauca*
Few others	
Herbs	
Bracken fern	*Pteridium aquilinum*
Swamp dewberry	*Rubus hispidus*
Turkeybeard	*Xerophyllum asphodeloides*
Wintergreen	*Gaultheria procumbens*
Sedge	*Carex* spp.
Cinnamon fern	*Osmunda cinnamomea*
Others	
Mosses	
Peat moss	*Sphagnum* spp.
Others	

Figure 9-7. A savannah along the headwaters of the Wading River, north of Chatsworth. Rushes and sedges dominate the area, and some small white cedars can be seen in the foreground.

and white beak-rush. Grasses, including rice cutgrass, blunt manna-grass, and beardgrass, and rushes, including Canada rush, bayonet rush, and brown-fruited rush, are also common.

These wetlands, like the bogs of North Jersey, are of great interest to botanists. They usually contain pitcher plants and several species of sundews and bladderworts. These are all carnivorous species that supplement the poor supplies of minerals they can get from their peat and sand substrate with animal food. Orchids of several species are not uncommon in some of these fens. Large cranberry is a common plant; its creeping stems readily colonize bare, damp sand and peat. The edges and islands within these savannahs typically have such shrubs as leatherleaf, sheep laurel, dwarf huckleberry, and dangleberry, as well as seedlings of Atlantic white cedar and pitch pine. About fifty species of plants in these fens are southern species at or near the northern limit of their range. Among these are false asphodel, golden crest, lance-leaved sabatia, bog asphodel, and coppery St. Johnswort. Table 9-6 lists some typical plant species of South Jersey fens.

These are fragile environments, and the best way to observe them is from a canoe on one of the Pine Barrens rivers. But glimpses also can be obtained from dry land. In Lebanon State Forest, where Glassworks Road crosses the south branch of Mount Misery Brook about 4 miles south of Route 70, one can get a good view of a cut-over cedar swamp from the bridge. This site is growing up to Atlantic white cedar, but for

Table 9-6. Some Typical Plant Species of South Jersey Fens

Common name	Genus and species name
Trees	
Atlantic white cedar	*Chamaecyparis thyoides*
Red maple	*Acer rubrum*
Pitch pine	*Pinus rigida*
Very few others	
Shrubs and vines	
Highbush blueberry	*Vaccinium corymbosum*
Dangleberry	*Gaylussacia frondosa*
Dwarf huckleberry	*Gaylussacia dumosa*
Sheep laurel	*Kalmia angustifolia*
Leatherleaf	*Chamaedaphne calyculata*
Large cranberry	*Vaccinium macrocarpon*
Few others	
Herbs	
Woolgrass	*Scirpus cyperinus*
Twig rush	*Cladium mariscoides*
Button sedge	*Carex bullata*
Cottongrass	*Eriophorum virginicum*
Common beak-rush	*Rhynchospora capitellata*
White beak-rush	*Rhynchospora alba*
Blunt manna-grass	*Glyceria obtusa*
Beardgrass	*Andropogon glomeratus*
Canada rush	*Juncus canadensis*
Bog asphodel	*Narthecium americanum*
Golden crest	*Lophiola aurea*
Lance-leaved sabatia	*Sabatia difformis*
Marsh St. Johnswort	*Triadenum virginicum*
Redroot	*Lachnanthes caroliniana*
Pipewort	*Eriocaulon* spp.
Golden club	*Orontium aquaticum*
Round-leaved sundew	*Drosera rotundifolia*
Spatulate-leaved sundew	*Drosera intermedia*
Thread-leaved sundew	*Drosera filiformis*
Calopogon	*Calopogon tuberosus*
Pitcher plant	*Sarracenia purpurea*
Orange milkwort	*Polygala lutea*
Cross-leaved milkwort	*Polygala cruciata*
Horned bladderwort	*Utricularia cornuta*

continued

Table 9-6 continued

Common name	Genus and species name
Herbs	
Cinnamon fern	*Osmunda cinnamomea*
Virginia chain fern	*Woodwardia virginica*
Curly-grass fern	*Schizaea pusilla*
Southern bog clubmoss	*Lycopodium appressum*
Many others	
Lichens and mosses	
Peat moss	*Sphagnum* spp.
Coastal plain ladder lichen	*Cladonia rappii*
Others	

the time being it has a savannahlike aspect, and many of the species noted above can be seen in it. A logging road runs east along the south side of the cut and affords a close look at some of the plants. Another interesting savannah area along the upper reaches of the Wading River can be seen from Route 563 in Burlington County, 3.3 miles south of Route 72 and just north of Chatsworth. On the east side of the road, a sedge-dominated wetland is growing up to young Atlantic white cedar. On the west side of the road appears an area dominated by leatherleaf.

A very well known place to see many typical plants of this habitat is at Webb's Mill, on the east side of Route 539 about 5 miles south of Route 70. Here a trail and rough boardwalk lead into a wet area south of Webb's Mill Branch, on the way passing through a young, rather dense growth of Atlantic white cedars with an understory of sweet pepperbush, with highbush blueberry, fetterbush, dangleberry, and other heaths. Three species of sundews—round-leaved, thread-leaved, and spatulate-leaved—can be seen in the wetland here, as can pitcher plants and several species of bladderworts. Hummocks provide places for such species as dwarf huckleberry, leatherleaf, large cranberry, sheep laurel, and some stunted Atlantic white cedars. Other plants easily found here in season are golden crest, marsh St. Johnswort, cross-leaved milkwort, coast sedge, cottongrass, and white beak-rush.

Human Influences on the Wetlands

As in North Jersey, human influences on wetlands in South Jersey have been considerable. Along the Delaware River, extensive areas of what were once marshes have been diked and covered with material dredged from the river channel. Water pollution, oil spills, and increased turbidity have had adverse effects on the vegetation of the marshes along

Figure 9-8. Commercial cranberry bogs along Route 563 south of Chatsworth.

the river and its tributaries; many plant species once common in this habitat are now rare. Agriculture has had a major impact on the wetland forests of the Coastal Plains, as it has in northern New Jersey. On the Inner Coastal Plain, most wetland forests have long since been cleared for farming; the woodlands that do remain are usually too wet to farm. Linear strips of forest that border fields almost inevitably conceal drainage ditches. Considerable acreage that is now used for growing crops would revert to wetland vegetation of a sort if tillage ceased and existing drain fields were blocked.

On the Outer Coastal Plain, since the middle of the nineteenth century, large areas that were once lowland forests have been given over to blueberry and cranberry cultivation (Figure 9-8). To create a commercial cranberry bog, a site must be carefully leveled and surrounded by dikes to permit controlled flooding to a set depth. The process involves the removal of all native vegetation. A system of dams and reservoirs is constructed, and ditches are made to divert natural drainage and control flooding. The area is then ready for the planting of selected cranberry varieties. Today, about 6,000 acres are devoted to this crop, an important one in the economy of the state.

Lumbering has also changed the composition of the wetland forests, particularly those of the Inner Coastal Plain. Most of the Atlantic white cedar swamps of South Jersey have been cut over half a dozen times, and some cedar cutting continues today. In many cases the result has been the replacement of Cedar Swamp forest by Hardwood Swamp forest. As already noted, this replacement is somewhat of a natural process; but since early settlers found Atlantic white cedars 6 feet in diameter, three times as large as any Atlantic white cedar living today, it is likely that cedar swamps have the potential for being much longer-lived than any are today. The extensive cedar swamps that once existed on the Inner Coastal Plain have largely disappeared, as have those of Cape May County, and those of other parts of the Outer Coastal Plain have been much reduced.

As already mentioned, natural lakes in South Jersey are few. Most of the many lakes that now exist in this part of the state are man-made, and these occupy the site of former natural wetlands. Some were originally created as cranberry bogs. Others, such as Batsto Lake, were built to provide a head of water for industry, particularly the iron industry that flourished in South Jersey from about 1700 to 1860. The iron industry is also responsible for some of the savannahs along South Jersey streams; they were once ore beds, from which bog ore, a low-grade iron ore that forms as a precipitate in stream beds, was removed in the eighteenth and early nineteenth centuries. The process left depressions that have since filled with peat.

As in North Jersey, various regulations are now in force in South Jersey to protect wetlands. In addition to these, the Pinelands Commission has regulations to protect wetlands within their million-acre jurisdiction. Large areas of wetlands in both the Inner and Outer Coastal Plains are now protected because they are in public ownership. However, even these publicly owned wetlands are potentially endangered. They depend on an adequate supply of unpolluted groundwater for their replenishment. As the population of the area increases, groundwater becomes more polluted, and the demand for water supplies from the groundwater aquifer increases. Excess pumping of water to meet these demands will destroy the wetland vegetation.

Summary

South Jersey, like North Jersey, has marshes, swamps, and peatlands, but these areas have vegetation different from their North Jersey counterparts. In addition, South Jersey has extensive salt marshes and tidal freshwater marshes, which are not common in North Jersey. Here as everywhere, wetland habitats have declined within historic times as a result of human activities. Natural change has also occurred, from marsh or fen to swamp forest, due to the natural processes of plant succession. Wetlands are now threatened by population growth and by needs for additional water supplies from the groundwater aquifer.

References and Source Material

Bernard, J. M. 1963. Lowland Forest of the Cape May Formation in Southern New Jersey. *Bulletin of the New Jersey Academy of Science* 8:1–12.

Forman, R. T., ed. 1979. *Pine Barrens: Ecosystem and Landscape.* New York: Academic Press.

Good, R. E., and N. F. Good. 1975. Vegetation and Production of the Woodbury Creek–Hessian Run Freshwater Tidal Marshes. *Bartonia* 43:38–45.

Harshberger, J. W. 1916. The Vegetation of the New Jersey Pine Barrens. Philadelphia, Pa.: Christopher Sower. Reprinted 1970 by Dover Publications, New York.

Johnson, C. W. 1985. *Bogs of the Northeast.* Hanover, N.H., and London: University Press of New England.

Leck, M. A., R. L. Simpson, D. F. Whigham, and C. F. Leck. 1988. Plants of the Hamilton Marshes: A Delaware River Freshwater Tidal Wetland. *Bartonia* 54:1–17.

Little, Silas. 1951. Observations on the Minor Vegetation of the Pine Barren Swamps in Southern New Jersey. *Bulletin of the Torrey Botanical Club* 78:153–160.

McCormick, J. 1970. The Pine Barrens: A Preliminary Ecological Inventory. New Jersey State Museum, Research Report No. 2, Trenton, N.J.

Roman, Charles, and R. E. Good. 1990. Ecology of White Cedar Swamps in the New Jersey Pinelands. In *Wetland Ecology and Management: Case Studies.* Norwell, Mass.: Kluwer Academic Press.

Rosenwinkel, E. R. 1964. Vegetational History of a New Jersey Tidal Marsh, Bog, and Vicinity. *Bulletin of the New Jersey Academy of Science* 9:1–20.

Stone, Witmer. 1910. The Plants of Southern New Jersey, with Especial Reference to the Flora of the Pine Barrens and the Geographic Distribution of the Species, in *Annual Report*, New Jersey State Museum, Trenton, N.J.

Tiner, R. W. 1985. Wetlands of New Jersey. Newton Center, Mass.: U.S. Fish and Wildlife Service, National Wetlands Inventory.

Chapter 10

✸ Pine Barrens of South Jersey

Located on the Outer Coastal Plain, the Pine Barrens is an island of mostly sandy, infertile soils bordered by the moister and more fertile uplands of the Inner Coastal Plain. Its distinctive flora, its wilderness, and its complete contrast with the urbanized surroundings make the Pine Barrens a precious resource. It has been internationally recognized as a unique landscape by the United Nations, which in 1983 designated the region as International Biosphere Reserve.

When measured as an ecosystem, the Pine Barrens totals about 1.4 million acres, or about 30 percent of the state. Under federal legislation, a land area of just over 1 million acres is designated as the New Jersey Pinelands National Reserve, and a slightly smaller area has been designated and protected as the Pinelands area by state legislation (Figure 10-1).

The Pine Barrens comprises an intricate mosaic of very acidic, sandy uplands dissected by slow-moving streams fed by a huge underlying aquifer of potable fresh water. The coarse, sandy soils, through which rainwater and snowmelt readily percolate, leaving little moisture behind, are very arid. They form a sharp contrast to the surrounding finer-textured soils of the Inner Coastal Plain, which retain adequate amounts of water for traditional agriculture.

This chapter describes the natural plant communities of dry upland Pine Barrens sites. But it must be kept in mind that wetlands occupy about 35 percent of the Pine Barrens. The vegetation of these wetland sites—the lowland forest swamps and marshlike savannahs—was described in the previous chapter.

History of the Pine Barrens Vegetation

The vegetation present today in the Pine Barrens has evolved over thousands of years and reflects the success of particular species in maintaining themselves in the various habitats that characterize the Pine Barrens. Upland plants must have tolerance for sandy soils with few nutrients and little water-retention capability; wetland vegetation must thrive in acidic waters with low levels of nutrients. Together with evolu-

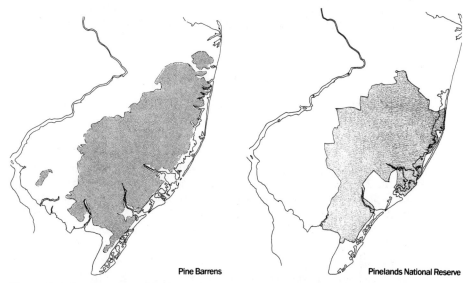

Pine Barrens   Pinelands National Reserve

Figure 10-1. A comparison of the boundaries of the Pine Barrens and the Pinelands National Reserve.

tionary selection for these habitat preferences, various past climatic events as well as fire have molded the present patterns of plant distribution in the Pine Barrens.

When the glacial ice started its final retreat from New Jersey about 18,000 years ago, sea level was still low and the coastline far to the east of its present location, making the coastal migratory path for both southern and northern plant species much wider than it is now. During the warm postglacial period, plants of southern coastal regions expanded their ranges northward, with some colonizing the Pine Barrens. To a lesser degree, range expansion from the southern Appalachians also proceeded northward, then east to the Pine Barrens. The climate then cooled again, and though there was general subsequent southward retreat of flora, many of the southern species continued to survive in the Barrens.

These elements are strongly reflected in the present-day flora. Over a hundred plants of southern affinity reach their northern edge of their range in the Barrens. Twelve plants found in the Pine Barrens are northern species at their southern range limit or their southernmost Coastal Plain range limit, and eight additional northern species or varieties of plants reach their southern range limit in Delaware. One plant, Knieskern's beak-rush, is known today only from southern New Jersey, as are particular varieties of grass-leaved blazing star, Pickering's morning glory, and sand myrtle. Bog asphodel, once found in the Coastal Plain of North and South Carolina as well as in the Pine Barrens, may now exist only in New Jersey. But only about twenty of the southern species, and only five of the northern species, are typical of the dry upland habitats discussed in this chapter.

Present Flora and Plant Communities

Because of the sandy, infertile soils and the frequent occurrence of fire, many plants cannot grow on the dry uplands. The botanical diversity in the upland forests of the Pine Barrens is rather low. This is true even though the region as a whole has a fairly rich flora. In 1910 Witmer Stone reported finding 565 species of plants in the uplands and lowlands of the Pine Barrens, 55 of which were not known to grow elsewhere in New Jersey. Since Stone made his study, additional plant species have been found, and in a study published in 1970 Jack McCormick estimated that a total of about 800 native Pine Barrens plant species, varieties, and forms existed.

Because of the particular nature of the soils—sandy and droughty— wildfires have always been a common phenomenon in the Pine Barrens. Caused by lightning and spread by high winds, fires have probably swept across the flat uplands since before prehistoric humans roamed the state. Only streams and wetlands served as natural firebreaks. Some believe that the Indians burned the Pine Barrens forests to improve hunting conditions; certainly ever since European colonization humans have accidentally or intentionally set fires here. Today, thousands of small wildfires still occur each year—for example, in spite of fire-control measures, on one weekend in 1963 more than 190,000 acres of woodland were burned. In the first 5 months of 1992, the state fire warden reported that 800 fires had ignited. Fire consumed almost 15,000 acres of Pine Barrens forests on one weekend of that year.

Some plant species are structurally more insulated from heat than others and are therefore less susceptible to fire damage. Also, some trees and shrubs are able to produce stem or root sprouts quickly after fire damage, while others have little or no resprouting capability. Seeds of some plants are destroyed by fire; the seeds of others germinate more quickly when heated by fire or when left on the relatively bare soils exposed by fire. The present flora of the Pine Barrens reflects the evolutionary success of particular species in maintaining themselves in the presence of frequent fire. All dominant species of upland trees and shrubs in the Pine Barrens are fire adapted, though to varying degrees.

Generally, fire on the uplands in the Pine Barrens favors the pitch pine and its less abundant evergreen associate, the shortleaf pine. Both have relatively thick bark and can send up new shoots from the base if the top of the tree is killed. Young pine seedlings, which cannot establish themselves where a thick accumulation of leaves and other litter exists on the forest floor, develop successfully when fire consumes the litter. Among the many species of oaks that are native to the Pine Barrens is wide varia-

Figure 10-2. Pine-dominated forest near McDonald's Branch in Lebanon State Forest. The trees grow rather far apart, allowing considerable light to reach the ground.

tion in resistance to fire damage. All have considerable ability to resprout after fire, but the smaller, so-called shrub oaks such as the blackjack, scrub, and dwarf chestnut oaks are able to survive more frequent fires than the taller species such as the black, white, chestnut, and scarlet oaks. Wetland species of trees, though less often exposed to fire, are more readily killed when fire does occur.

The occurrence of fire and especially its frequency determines to a great extent which one of three different plant communities prevails on upland sites in the Pine Barrens. These communities are the Pine-dominated forest, the Pine Plains or Dwarf Pine community, and the Oak-dominated forest.

Pine-Dominated Forest

The forest type usually associated with the Pine Barrens is one dominated by pine trees (Figure 10-2). This is true even though the natural tendency of the vegetation throughout most of the region, were fire to be excluded, is toward the development of a strongly oak-dominated forest. But when fire removes the litter on the forest floor, the exposed surface of the sandy soil creates an ideal condition for the establishment of pine seedlings. Once the pines grow beyond the seedling stage, they develop a relatively thick bark that makes them less susceptible to fire damage than oaks of comparable age. Also, the two principal pine species of the Barrens, unlike most pines, can send up new shoots from the base if the

Figure 10-3. A close view of the understory in the Pine-dominated forest. Black huckleberry and bracken fern are the dominant species here.

top is killed by fire. The result is that if fires occur, natural succession in the Pine Barrens tends to be held in the Pine-dominated forest stage.

Today, the Pine-dominated forest covers about 50 percent of the upland area of the Pine Barrens. The most abundant and most characteristic tree is the pitch pine, which in some places accounts for as much as 80 percent of the forest. It is not tall as trees go, usually reaching about 50 to 60 feet in height. The shortleaf pine, a southern species, occurs in the forest but is usually present in smaller numbers, although it can be locally abundant. It is not as fire resistant as pitch pine. Mixed with the pines one usually finds oak trees, including black, white, post, chestnut, scarlet, and blackjack oak in varying proportions.

The Pine-dominated forest of the Barrens is characteristically open, with trees growing sufficiently far apart from each other to allow considerable light to penetrate to the lower layers. The crowns of the trees are also thin, intercepting less of the light than other conifer-dominated forests do. For this reason the pine forest presents a striking visual contrast to the nearby white cedar swamps, which are shady and dark in their interiors.

Beneath the pine trees is usually a dense, low shrub layer (Figure 10-3) consisting largely of members of the heath family. Black huckleberry and early lowbush blueberry occur almost universally and are joined occasionally by staggerbush, dangleberry, mountain laurel, and sheep laurel. Mixed with the heaths are shrub oaks, including the dwarf chestnut oak, small specimens of blackjack oak, and scrub oak. In some places the latter species may be very abundant, making a dense understory as much as 10 to 15 feet tall.

Rather few species of herbs are present in the Pine-dominated forest. Bracken fern is often quite abundant, spreading from deeply buried underground stems, and Pennsylvania sedge may form a sparse lawn between the trees. Other species usually occur scattered throughout the forest. Little bluestem is one of the most common of these, but one may also find wild indigo, goat's rue, turkeybeard, black oatgrass, cow-wheat, rattlesnake weed, frostweed, golden heather, stemless lady's-slipper, woolly panic-grass, poverty-grass, stiff aster, and sweet goldenrod. But in general, the herbaceous plants are usually so few when compared with the overwhelming abundance of woody plants that they make only an incidental contribution to the vegetation. Some typical plant species of the Pine-dominated forest are listed in Table 10-1.

Pine-dominated forests of varying ages are easy to see from any roadway in the Barrens. But again, the state forests and parks are the most accessible places from which to view the forests more closely. In Lebanon State Forest, between Routes 70 and 72 in Burlington County, pitch pine dominates the area bordering Cooper Road and Woodmansie Road, and along the roads going north from there. Shortleaf pine can also be found here, particularly along Dakota Avenue and around Deep Hollow Pond, north of Route 70. Shortleaf pine usually has needles in bundles of two; bark that cracks into rather large, flat-topped plates; and relatively small cones. Pitch pine has needles in bundles of three, and thicker and rougher bark and larger cones. But the differences between these species are often rather subjective, especially when looking up into a tree canopy. Pitch pine usually has longer needles than shortleaf pine, but there is much overlap.

Along Route 206 south of Atsion in the Wharton State Forest is a botanically interesting area showing regrowth of an almost pure pitch pine forest from seed, following a very hot fire in 1983 that actually killed most of the mature pines in the area. Along this road, also, is much mature Pine-dominated forest. The Pine-dominated forest is favored by a fire frequency of about once every 20 years or somewhat less; but where fires have occurred more frequently, particularly as often as once every 10 years or less, the Pine Plains type of vegetation is favored.

Pine Plains (or Dwarf Pine Community)

Only two species of trees in the Barrens are able to recover from fires at intervals of 10 years or less. These are pitch pine and blackjack oak, both of which start growing again after each fire by sprouting from the root crown. The pitch pine and the blackjack oak also produce fruits from the new basal shoots only a few years after a fire. Rapid sprouting and early

Table 10-1. Some Typical Plant Species of the Pine-Dominated Forest of the Pine Barrens

Common name	Genus and species name
Dominant tree	
Pitch pine	*Pinus rigida*
Other trees	
Shortleaf pine	*Pinus echinata*
Black oak	*Quercus velutina*
Chestnut oak	*Quercus prinus*
White oak	*Quercus alba*
Scarlet oak	*Quercus coccinea*
Post oak	*Quercus stellata*
Sassafras	*Sassafras albidum*
Few others	
Shrubs and vines	
Scrub oak	*Quercus ilicifolia*
Blackjack oak	*Quercus marilandica*
Mountain laurel	*Kalmia latifolia*
Black huckleberry	*Gaylussacia baccata*
Early lowbush blueberry	*Vaccinium pallidum*
Staggerbush	*Lyonia mariana*
Dangleberry	*Gaylussacia frondosa*
Glaucous greenbrier	*Smilax glauca*
Few others	
Herbs	
Golden heather	*Hudsonia ericoides*
Bracken fern	*Pteridium aquilinum*
Little bluestem	*Schizachyrium scoparium*
Pennsylvania sedge	*Carex pensylvanica*
Wild indigo	*Baptisia tinctoria*
Goat's rue	*Tephrosia virginica*
Frostweed	*Helianthemum canadense*
Sweet goldenrod	*Solidago odora*
Pine Barrens sandwort	*Arenaria caroliniana*
Rattlesnake weed	*Hieracium venosum*
Ipecac spurge	*Euphorbia ipecacuanhae*
Stiff aster	*Aster linariifolius*
Others	

Table 10-1 continued

Common name	Genus and species name
Lichens and mosses	
White moss	*Leucobryum glaucum*
Juniper haircap	*Polytrichum juniperinum*
Broom moss	*Dicranum scoparium*
False reindeer lichen	*Cladina subtenuis*
Thorn lichen	*Cladonia uncialis*
Many others	

seed production make these species successful, but in the Pine Plains neither has the opportunity to grow to full tree stature before the recurrence of fire. Instead, they grow as low-spreading shrubs and reach an average height of only about 4 feet (Figure 10-4), making a truly "dwarf pine" forest.

In the understory here, as in the typical Pine-dominated forest, shrubs in the heath family, particularly black huckleberry and early lowbush blueberry, are most abundant. Mountain laurel is decidedly more abundant here than in the regular Pine-dominated forest, as are bearberry and sheep laurel. Other than the heaths, the shrubby growth includes sweet fern and scrub oak. The Pine Plains have much exposed ground between the tree sprouts and shrubs; this may be occupied by such low-growing plants as trailing arbutus, golden heather, and pyxie moss, as well as a variety of lichens and mosses. It is in the Pine Plains also that the broom crowberry, considered one of the most unusual plants in the Pine Barrens, occurs. Broom crowberry has a northern range centered in the maritime provinces of Canada; its presence in the Pine Plains, the only location of the species in New Jersey, represents the southern extreme of its range.

Until the 1950s the reasons for the dwarf growth of Pine Plains vegetation was not generally agreed on. Some felt that the stunted growth occurred only on particular types of soils; others suggested that strong winds might be responsible for the dwarfing; and still others proposed the presence or absence of certain soil elements or even insects as the inhibiting influence on plant growth. It is now generally agreed that the pines are genetically dwarfed; even when protected from fire, the typical "plains" race of the pitch pine will not reach the same height as typical pitch pines; will have a somewhat different, more shrubby shape; and will produce cones at an earlier age than usual. Moreover, many of these pines produce cones that will open only under the influence of heat. The blackjack oaks, however, are dwarfed primarily because they are fire-

Figure 10-4. Pine Plains community along Route 539 south of Warren Grove, in Ocean County. Most of the trees here are about 3 feet tall.

induced sucker growths from old, decaying rootstocks; that is, they are dwarfed because they are frequently burned.

It is estimated that the Pine Plains now occupy about 12,400 acres. At present the acreage is not continuous but consists of three sections, the West Plains, the East Plains, and the Spring Hill Plains. Most of the West (or Upper) Plains, approximately 6,000 acres in size, is located in Woodland Township of Burlington County. The East (or Lower) Plains, also about 6,000 acres in size, is mostly within Bass River Township of Burlington County. Spring Hill (or Little) Plains is a small area of only a few hundred acres located 1 mile south of the West Plains in Washington Township.

The Pine Plains can be seen from Route 72 or from Route 539. State Route 72 crosses the northern edge of the West Plains. From Route 72, about 1 mile west of its intersection with Route 539, an all-weather sand road runs south about 7 miles to Lake Oswego and Jenkins, south of Chatsworth. The first few miles of this road is in the West Plains. About a mile south of Route 72 the road crosses a hill, from which a good view can be obtained. Scattered clumps of broom crowberry can also be found here. Farther east, Route 539 runs along the eastern edge of the East Plains; there are various places to stop and view the area along the road south of the town of Warren Grove. Roughly the same plants will be seen along both roads.

Table 10-2 lists most of the plant species typical of this forest type.

Table 10-2. Some Typical Plant Species of the Pine Plains

Common name	Genus and species name
Dominant trees	
Pitch pine	*Pinus rigida*
Blackjack oak	*Quercus marilandica*
Other trees	
Very few	
Shrubs and vines	
Scrub oak	*Quercus ilicifolia*
Mountain laurel	*Kalmia latifolia*
Black huckleberry	*Gaylussacia baccata*
Early lowbush blueberry	*Vaccinium pallidum*
Staggerbush	*Lyonia mariana*
Sheep laurel	*Kalmia angustifolia*
Sweet fern	*Comptonia peregrina*
Bayberry	*Myrica pensylvanica*
Dangleberry	*Gaylussacia frondosa*
Bearberry	*Arctostaphylos uva-ursi*
Broom crowberry	*Corema conradii*
Few others	
Herbs	
Golden heather	*Hudsonia ericoides*
Bracken fern	*Pteridium aquilinum*
Pyxie moss	*Pyxidanthera barbulata*
Wintergreen	*Gaultheria procumbens*
Ipecac spurge	*Euphorbia ipecacuanhae*
Trailing arbutus	*Epigaea repens*
Few others	
Lichens and mosses	
White moss	*Leucobryum glaucum*
Juniper haircap	*Polytrichum juniperinum*
Awned haircap	*Polytrichum piliferum*
Broom moss	*Dicranum scoparium*
False reindeer lichen	*Cladina subtenuis*
Thorn lichen	*Cladonia uncialis*
Many others	

Figure 10-5. Oak-dominated forest of the Pine Barrens, along Shinn's Road in Lebanon State Forest. Black oak, white oak, and chestnut oak are the common species. As in the Pine-dominated forest, there is a low but dense shrub layer.

Oak-Dominated Forest

As already noted, in the absence of fires an Oak-dominated forest would develop on most of the uplands of the Pine Barrens. This is because the young seedlings of pine trees cannot establish themselves when substantial amounts of leaf litter have accumulated on the forest floor, but such conditions are ideal for the growth of oak seedlings. Thus, without fire, leaf litter accumulates and oak seedlings start to grow. As time goes by, old pines die and are replaced by oaks.

Oak-dominated forests (Figure 10-5) cover large areas in the Pine Barrens, and they grade into the Pine-dominated forests to form a series of oak–pine and pine–oak forest types. Five species of oaks commonly occur in this forest type—black oak, scarlet oak, chestnut oak, white oak, and post oak. The first four of these trees also occur in the uplands of North Jersey, but the post oak is a more southern species, and in New Jersey it is primarily a tree of the Pine Barrens. Of these, the black oak and the chestnut oak are generally the most common trees in the Oak-dominated forest, but other species may be locally important. Pitch pine and shortleaf pine, and in some places Virginia pine, often occur as scattered trees among the oaks. Sassafras may also be found. That the pitch pine and shortleaf pine are more tolerant to fire than oaks has already been noted, but the oaks also differ among themselves. On sites where fires occur at frequent intervals, the oaks may be represented by only the post oak and the blackjack oak, and where fires are very frequent only blackjack oak may be found.

The taller trees in the Oak-dominated forest are rather widely spaced but form a nearly closed canopy at a height of about 50 feet. As in the Pine-dominated forest, there is a rather low but often very dense shrub layer dominated by heath shrubs, including black huckleberry, early low-bush blueberry, and dangleberry, with some staggerbush, sheep laurel, bayberry, sweet fern, and others. Rather few herb species are found, and those that do occur are about the same species as appear in the Pine-dominated forest. Table 10-3 lists some typical plant species of the Oak-dominated forest.

These forests can be seen at many places in the Pine Barrens, but as usual the state forests and parks offer the best opportunity to stop and observe the forest close up. In Lebanon State Forest, the area around the park office, about a mile east of the intersection of Routes 72 and 70 in Burlington County, has an Oak-dominated forest, which also shows the effects of controlled burning to reduce leaf litter. A drive from here east toward Pakim Pond, on Shinn's road, will present many variations on Oak-dominated and Pine-dominated forest. Black, white, and chestnut oak trees are the most common large trees here, with a few post oaks and scarlet oaks, and pitch pines and shortleaf pines. One can see here many examples of oak trees with multiple trunks, often an indication that they originated as sprouts after a fire.

At Batsto. in Wharton State Forest, a short nature trail along Batsto Pond goes through an Oak-dominated forest and also a Hardwood Swamp and a Pitch Pine Lowland forest. Batsto, a partly restored iron-making-company town, is in southern Burlington County, off Route 542 about 9 miles west of the Garden State Parkway.

Other Successional Plant Communities of the Pine Barrens

Although the Pine-dominated forest and the Pine Plains vegetation may be considered successional stages in the Pine Barrens resulting from cutting and fire, one also finds old-field successional stages in the relatively few places where the land at one time has been cleared for cultivation and then allowed to return to natural vegetation. These follow a successional pattern similar to that of the mesic uplands of South Jersey, though with different plants. Horseweed and common ragweed are abundant as early invaders. Several species of panic-grass grow abundantly in the early stages of succession. Shrubs and tree seedlings ap-

Table 10-3. Some Typical Plant Species of the Oak-Dominated Forest of the Pine Barrens

Common name	Genus and species name
Dominant trees	
Black oak	*Quercus velutina*
Chestnut oak	*Quercus prinus*
White oak	*Quercus alba*
Post oak	*Quercus stellata*
Other trees	
Pitch pine	*Pinus rigida*
Shortleaf pine	*Pinus echinata*
Spanish oak	*Quercus falcata*
Scarlet oak	*Quercus coccinea*
Sassafras	*Sassafras albidum*
Few others	
Shrubs and vines	
Scrub oak	*Quercus ilicifolia*
Dwarf chestnut oak	*Quercus prinoides*
Mountain laurel	*Kalmia latifolia*
Black huckleberry	*Gaylussacia baccata*
Early lowbush blueberry	*Vaccinium pallidum*
Glaucous greenbrier	*Smilax glauca*
Bayberry	*Myrica pensylvanica*
Few others	
Herbs	
Bracken fern	*Pteridium aquilinum*
Little bluestem	*Schizachyrium scoparium*
Pennsylvania sedge	*Carex pensylvanica*
Goat's rue	*Tephrosia virginica*
Wild indigo	*Baptisia tinctoria*
Cow-wheat	*Melampyrum lineare*
Frostweed	*Helianthemum canadense*
Sweet goldenrod	*Solidago odora*
Black oatgrass	*Stipa avenacea*
Woolly panic-grass	*Panicum lanuginosum*
Rattlesnake weed	*Hieracium venosum*
Stiff aster	*Aster linariifolius*
Trailing arbutus	*Epigaea repens*
Others	

Table 10-3 continued

Common name	Genus and species name
Lichens and mosses	
White moss	*Leucobryum glaucum*
Juniper haircap	*Polytrichum juniperinum*
Broom moss	*Dicranum scoparium*
Thorn lichen	*Cladonia uncialis*
Many others	

pear, and soon an open woodland develops. Pitch pine is especially common as an early tree invader, but along with it there may be oaks, black cherry, and sassafras. An Oak-dominated forest, or depending on fire frequency, a Pine-dominated forest, will ultimately develop.

Human Influences on the Pine Barrens

The uses of timber from the Pine Barrens have been many. Lumber, tar, and pitch were taken to supply the early shipbuilding industry; oak, cedar, and some pine were used for home building in cities and towns outside the region. More pine provided fuelwood and charcoal needed to heat homes in early Philadelphia, New York, Newark, and Wilmington, as well as to supply the industries that flourished in the Pines during the century from 1760 to 1860. Although by the 1860s coal had generally replaced wood as a fuel, fuelwood continued to be, and still is, taken from the Pine Barrens. Today, pine is also used for pulpwood and some lumber. Because it is rot resistant, cedar continues to be the most valuable wood of the region; it is used for posts and poles and, in sawn form, for shingles, boat building, and a variety of other uses.

No area of the Pine Barrens has escaped being cut; state foresters estimate that since European settlement, the forests of the Pine Barrens have been cut over at least five times. The impacts of repeated cutting combined with those of frequent fire are reflected in the structural appearance and species composition of the present forests. Clearcutting in upland woods (as distinct from selective thinning), together with fire, favors pine, because pine seedlings develop best in open areas.

Fortunately, because the Pine Barrens soils for the most part are unsuited for traditional agriculture, the region has not been heavily populated. Though the state of New Jersey averages more than one thousand people per square mile, in some townships of the Pine Barrens there are less than 10 residents per square mile. It is still possible to drive for miles in the central Pine Barrens, even outside of state parks and forests, without seeing signs of human occupancy.

Management of the Pine Barrens Upland Forests

In their concern to find practical means of getting maximum economic value from the forests of the Pine Barrens, state foresters have adopted a technique called controlled burning, in which the upland forests are purposely burned at intervals. This is done in winter, when fire can be controlled and when trees are cold so that the heat from burning leaf litter is less apt to damage them. This practice eliminates combustible leaf litter and fallen branches, reduces shrub density, and exposes bare ground. It also creates the ideal open conditions for the establishment of pine seedlings and the maintenance of a pine forest, which is considered desirable because pine wood is more valuable than oak wood in this area. Another important benefit of burning in the cold season, from a management point of view, is that when warm, dry, windy weather comes—the "fire season"—less fuel in the form of forest litter remains to be burned. In this way destructive wildfires are minimized. Controlled burning can be used not only as a tool to perpetuate the Pine-dominated forest but also to convert oak forests to pine forests. Wild fires that do get started at any season are now usually rather quickly suppressed, thus changing the natural fire ecology of the region.

No species native to the upland forests of the Pine Barrens is eliminated by fire. This is as one would expect, since the vegetation in this area has evolved in an environment of which fire is a part. It is not clear, however, that the present-day fire regime of many small, rather cool fires, has the same effect on Pine Barrens ecology as fires in the past, which were probably hotter and larger but less frequent. Some plant species that are now rare might benefit from an occasional very hot fire. But it is clear that if fires were completely suppressed in the Pine Barrens the plant life of the area would be changed. Some of the specialized plants of the region would probably become increasingly rare or might even be eliminated entirely. Also, the Pine-dominated forest would largely be replaced by Oak-dominated forest. Much of the ecological uniqueness of the area would be lost. Human management of this area has become a virtual necessity to maintain it in its "natural" state.

During the 1970s, threats to the Pine Barrens spurred the enactment in 1979 of federal and state legislation to protect the region. As already noted, under federal legislation a land area of just over a million acres was designated as the New Jersey Pinelands National Reserve. Within this area, a slightly smaller area has been designated as the Pinelands area by state legislation. In the Pinelands area, land use is overseen by a state agency, the Pinelands Commission, which has developed a comprehensive master plan for the region. About 365,000 acres of the Pinelands are a preservation area in which only limited development and resource-related uses are permitted. The remainder of the Pinelands is divided into seven management areas with varying land uses permitted depending on the sensitivity of the natural resources. Most of the area that is within the Pinelands National Reserve but outside of the jurisdiction of the Pinelands Commission is coastal land that is protected by separate legislation.

Summary

The composition of the upland forests of southern New Jersey's Pine Barrens region is governed largely by fire frequency, with Pine-dominated forests existing on more frequently burned sites and Oak-dominated forests on sites that have been protected from fires. Fires have been a force in shaping this environment for a very long time. One proof of this is the local evolution of plant species and varieties, including a dwarf, closed-cone variety of pitch pine, that are well adapted to frequent fires. The flora of the Pine Barrens includes a number of southern species that are at or near the northeastern limit of their range, as well as some northern species that reach the southern limit of their range here. Such species are found in uplands as well as wetlands, even though the overall plant diversity in the upland forests, as opposed to the wetlands, is relatively low.

References and Source Material

Buell, M. F., and J. E. Cantlon. 1950. A Study of Two Communities of the New Jersey Pine Barrens and a Comparison of Methods. *Ecology* 31: 567–589.

Collins, B. R., and E. W. B. Russell, eds. 1988. Protecting the New Jersey Pinelands. New Brunswick, N.J.: Rutgers University Press.

Forman, R. T., ed. 1979. *Pine Barrens: Ecosystem and Landscape.* New York: Academic Press.

Harshberger, J. W. 1916. *The Vegetation of the New Jersey Pine Barrens.* Philadelphia, Pa.: Christopher Sower. Reprinted 1970 by Dover Publications, New York.

Little, Silas, Jr. 1946. The Effects of Forest Fires on the Stand History of the New Jersey Pine Region. Northeastern Forest Experiment Station, Forest Management Paper 2, Philadelphia, Pa.

McCormick, J. 1970. *The Pine Barrens: A Preliminary Ecological Inventory.* New Jersey State Museum, Research Report No. 2, Trenton, N.J. 100 pages.

McCormick, J., and M. F. Buell. 1957. Natural Vegetation of a Plowed Field in the New Jersey Pine Barrens. *Botanical Gazette* 118:261–264.

———. 1968. The Plains: Pygmy Forest of the New Jersey Pine Barrens. A Review and Annotated Bibliography. *New Jersey Academy of Science Bulletin* 13:20–34.

Stone, Witmer. 1910. The Plants of Southern New Jersey, with Especial Reference to the Flora of the Pine Barrens and the Geographic Distribution of the Species, in *Annual Report,* New Jersey State Museum, Trenton, N.J.

Vermeule, C. C., A. Hollick, J. B. Smith, and G. Pinchot. 1900. Report on Forests, in *Annual Report of the State Geologist for 1899,* Trenton, N.J.

Chapter 11

$ Uplands of South Jersey

Just as in North Jersey, the sites designated as uplands of South Jersey represent an idealized midpoint of soil moisture between the wettest habitats, such as marshes and swamps, and the driest habitats, such as the Pine Barrens and the coastal sand dunes. Unlike North Jersey, however, only a relatively small part of the Inner and Outer Coastal Plains can be classified as mesic uplands. Much of South Jersey is composed either of the drier soils, or of wetlands, the extremes of moisture conditions.

The mesic uplands of southern New Jersey occur primarily on the Inner Coastal Plain but extend also into the southern and northern sections of the Outer Coastal Plain, thereby encircling and grading into the drier region that includes the Pine Barrens. The topography of South Jersey does not have the extremes in relief found in North Jersey; elevations vary only from sea level to a high of 373 feet, at Beacon Hill in Monmouth County. Nor is the land underlain by the variety of rock found in the northern part of the state. Instead, the Coastal Plain consists mostly of sand, silt, gravel, and clays that are not cemented together in rock form. The soils of the mesic uplands are generally more fertile, more moist, and less sandy than those of the Pine Barrens; nevertheless, a wide variety of soil types exists. But as is true in the case of the North Jersey uplands, the same groups of plants appear to grow naturally on a wide spectrum of soil types, provided the ground moisture and fertility are about equivalent.

Botanically, the Inner Coastal Plain is a dividing area between the zone of primarily pine–oak forest of the Outer Coastal Plain and the deciduous forest of the Piedmont. It is also a transition zone between north and south; many species of northern affinity reach the southern limit of their range on the Inner Coastal Plain and are joined there by species of southern affinities. This has long been recognized by botanists. In 1910 Witmer Stone wrote that the boundary between the Piedmont and the Inner Coastal Plain marked a great change in plant life. He identified 1,373 native species of plants growing on the Inner and Outer Coastal Plains. Of this total, only 171 species were thought to be widely distributed over both the Inner and Outer Coastal Plains and the Piedmont. Another 727 species more or less common in the Piedmont were also found in the Inner Coastal Plain, but only 101 of these reached the Pine Barrens. The final 475 species were said to be restricted to the Inner and Outer Coastal Plains except for sporadic occurrences in the Piedmont, and then mostly in lowlands.

Today, on the mesic uplands of South Jersey, there exist two major forest types: the Mixed Oak forest and the Beech–Oak forest. In both, oaks of various species are abundant. As in North Jersey, a variety of successional plant communities have developed on lands that have been disturbed and then abandoned; and two long-lived successional forest types, the Virginia Pine forest and the Sweet Gum forest, are common.

Mixed Oak Forest

At the close of the last century the state geologist reported that the mesic upland forest of the Coastal Plain was a mixed one, mostly "oak and chestnut"; one such forest on the Navesink Highlands in the northeastern part of the Coastal Plain was reported to have as its principal trees the American chestnut and the five species of oak that are commonly found in the North Jersey upland forest—white, black, red, chestnut, and scarlet oaks. Unlike the typical Mixed Oak forest of North Jersey, however, the Navesink forest had a shrub cover of heath plants, primarily mountain laurel, blueberry, huckleberry, and swamp azalea. All are plants that are more typical of sandier or more acidic soils.

The forest composition just described from the Navesink Highlands is typical of the sandier areas of the South Jersey mesic uplands adjacent to the Pine Barrens, although just as in North Jersey, mature American chestnut has now disappeared from the southern upland forests. The upland forests located on the more fertile soil in the western and southwestern part of the Coastal Plain show a variation in composition, particularly in the area from western Monmouth County southward through western Burlington and Camden counties. Here, although the oaks, particularly the white and black oaks, are still the most abundant larger trees, they are joined by American beech, pignut and mockernut hickories, black walnut, tulip tree, and red maple (Figure 11-1). Spanish oak, or southern red oak, a species not found in North Jersey, is scattered throughout these woodlands.

Other trees that differentiate these forests from the Mixed Oak forests of northern New Jersey are persimmon, sweet gum, and Virginia pine, all more typical of southern areas, and American holly, which in New Jersey is also typical of forests on coastal sand dunes. Sugar maple and red oak, so common in mesic upland forests in North Jersey, are rare or absent in these forests. The understory in these Mixed Oak forests is typically dominated by flowering dogwood, ironwood, black cherry, and sassafras, rather than by the heath shrubs more typical of sandy soils. Vines are common and include Japanese honeysuckle, Virginia creeper, wild grapes of several species, and poison ivy. Spicebush, arrowwood,

Figure 11-1. South Jersey Mixed Oak forest, in Allaire State Park. The dense growth of shrubs and vines is often characteristic of these forests, particularly those on the more fertile soils.

American strawberry bush, and black haw are common shrubs in more moist locales. The most abundant herbs in this Mixed Oak forest are similar to those in the upland forest of North Jersey. Table 11-1 lists many plant species that are typical of the South Jersey upland Mixed Oak forest.

A very interesting example of this forest type occurs in the upland areas of Rancocas State Park (Figure 11-2) in Burlington County and can be seen from trails radiating from the Rancocas Nature Center. The forest has as its tree components black oak and white oak, with some chestnut oak, red maple, tulip tree, sweet gum, American holly, and Virginia pine. Sprouts of chestnut trees are common, and the heaths, particularly early lowbush blueberry, black huckleberry, and mountain laurel, form most of the shrub cover. The forest floor has a sparse cover of bracken fern, Pennsylvania sedge, and a few grasses.

Another good example of the Mixed Oak forest of South Jersey can be seen around the park office at the entrance to Allaire State Park in Monmouth County. The dominant trees here include white, chestnut, black, and scarlet oaks, with some Spanish oak and red maple. American holly and sassafras form a lower tree layer. There is a very dense shrub layer of sweet pepperbush, mountain laurel, and coralberry, with seedling hollies and sassafras. Common greenbrier forms dense tangles over and among the shrubs. There is little herbaceous plant life on the forest floor.

Table 11-1. Some Typical Plant Species of the Mixed Oak Forest of South Jersey

Common name	Genus and species name
Dominant trees	
White oak	*Quercus alba*
Chestnut oak	*Quercus prinus*
Black oak	*Quercus velutina*
Scarlet oak	*Quercus coccinea*
American holly	*Ilex opaca*
Sassafras	*Sassafras albidum*
Other trees	
Black cherry	*Prunus serotina*
Spanish oak	*Quercus falcata*
Sweet gum	*Liquidambar styraciflua*
Red maple	*Acer rubrum*
Virginia pine	*Pinus virginiana*
Persimmon	*Diospyros virginiana*
American beech	*Fagus grandifolia*
Others	
Shrubs and vines	
Early lowbush blueberry	*Vaccinium pallidum*
Black huckleberry	*Gaylussacia baccata*
Pinxter flower	*Rhododendron periclymenoides*
Mountain laurel	*Kalmia latifolia*
Downy juneberry	*Amelanchier arborea*
Sweet pepperbush	*Clethra alnifolia*
Bayberry	*Myrica pensylvanica*
Glaucous greenbrier	*Smilax glauca*
Common greenbrier	*Smilax rotundifolia*
Japanese honeysuckle	*Lonicera japonica*
Few others	
Herbs	
Bracken fern	*Pteridium aquilinum*
Rattlesnake weed	*Hieracium venosum*
Pennsylvania sedge	*Carex pensylvanica*
Cow-wheat	*Melampyrum lineare*
Spotted wintergreen	*Chimaphila maculata*
Stemless lady's-slipper	*Cypripedium acaule*
Few others	

Figure 11-2. American holly and sweet gum growing in a Mixed Oak forest at Rancocas State Park. These species are among those that differentiate the oak forests of southern New Jersey from superficially similar Mixed Oak forests of northern New Jersey.

Allaire State Park is located south of Farmingdale and can be reached from a marked exit on the Garden State Parkway.

The uplands of Cheesequake State Park are also covered with a Mixed Oak forest type. Near the Meadowview picnic area, the most common trees are chestnut oak and scarlet oak, followed by black oak and white oak. A few sassafras, American beech, and black cherry trees, and some sprouts of American chestnut can also be found. The shrub layer is very dense and low and is dominated by black huckleberry and late lowbush blueberry, mixed with scattered plants of early lowbush blueberry. Some taller shrubs of mountain laurel, downy juneberry, and highbush blueberry appear as well. There is little herbaceous flora, other than bracken fern, an occasional plant of glaucous greenbrier, and clumps of hairgrass and Pennsylvania sedge. In other parts of this park upland oak forests with red oak, American beech, pignut hickory, and black birch occur. Cheesequake State Park is also in Monmouth County, off Route 34 east of the town of Cheesequake.

Beech–Oak Forest

Writing in 1910, Witmer Stone noted that some woods near Camden were composed almost exclusively of American beech (Figure 11-3). Only remnants of these are left, and most are on private property and

Figure 11-3. A remnant of Beech–Oak forest growing on a well-drained slope near Mount Holly, in western Burlington County.

not accessible. Generally speaking, American beech in this area today is found in various admixtures with oak and other trees; and the Beech forests intergrade with Mixed Oak forests. Some typical plants of this forest type are listed in Table 11-2.

A typical Beech–Oak woodland of the Inner Coastal Plain can be seen from the roadside west of Chesterfield in Burlington County, on the right side of the road from Chesterfield to Arneytown, a few miles east of the intersection where Route 528 turns south to Jacobstown. In this privately owned forest American beech is abundant in all size classes, but there are also many tulip trees and black oaks. Shagbark hickory, pignut hickory, and red maple are also present. Ironwood and flowering dogwood are scattered in the forest. The shrub layer is moderately dense and consists mostly of arrowwood and maple-leaved viburnum, with some spicebush on what are perhaps slightly moister sections. Japanese honeysuckle, common and glaucous greenbriers, poison ivy, and dewberry and several other species of blackberry form a rather sparse layer on the forest floor. Beechdrops, an herb parasitic on the roots of American beech, is also common here.

At Mill Creek Park in Willingboro, Burlington County, American beech in places makes up as much as 50 percent of a forest that parallels the banks of Rancocas Creek. Beech is associated here with black, white,

Table 11-2. Some Typical Plant Species of the Beech–Oak Forest of South Jersey

Common name	Genus and species name
Dominant trees	
American beech	*Fagus grandifolia*
White oak	*Quercus alba*
Chestnut oak	*Quercus prinus*
Black oak	*Quercus velutina*
Tulip tree	*Liriodendron tulipifera*
American holly	*Ilex opaca*
Other trees	
Black cherry	*Prunus serotina*
Spanish oak	*Quercus falcata*
Sassafras	*Sassafras albidum*
Sweet gum	*Liquidambar styraciflua*
Red maple	*Acer rubrum*
Virginia pine	*Pinus virginiana*
Persimmon	*Diospyros virginiana*
Mockernut hickory	*Carya tomentosa*
Pignut hickory	*Carya glabra*
Others	
Shrubs and vines	
Maple-leaved viburnum	*Viburnum acerifolium*
Arrowwood	*Viburnum dentatum*
Black huckleberry	*Gaylussacia baccata*
Pinxter flower	*Rhododendron periclymenoides*
Mountain laurel	*Kalmia latifolia*
Early lowbush blueberry	*Vaccinium pallidum*
Sweet pepperbush	*Clethra alnifolia*
Bayberry	*Myrica pensylvanica*
Glaucous greenbrier	*Smilax glauca*
Common greenbrier	*Smilax rotundifolia*
Dewberry	*Rubus flagellaris*
Japanese honeysuckle	*Lonicera japonica*
Poison ivy	*Toxicodendron radicans*
Few others	
Herbs	
Rattlesnake weed	*Hieracium venosum*
Spotted wintergreen	*Chimaphila maculata*
Solomon's-seal	*Polygonatum biflorum*

Table 11-2 continued

Common name	Genus and species name
Herbs	
False Solomon's-seal	*Smilacina racemosa*
Canada mayflower	*Maianthemum canadense*
Beech drops	*Epifagus virginiana*
Stemless lady's-slipper	*Cypripedium acaule*
Pennsylvania sedge	*Carex pensylvanica*
Few others	

chestnut, scarlet, and Spanish oaks, with some willow oak on lower-lying areas. There is also some tulip tree, red maple, mockernut hickory, sweet gum, and sassafras. The shrub understory consists of arrowwood, with scattered mountain laurel, early lowbush blueberry, American holly, and seedlings of sassafras and black cherry; wet areas also have sweet bay magnolia. As in oak forests generally, the herbaceous flora is sparse, although there is some Japanese honeysuckle, eulalia grass, Pennsylvania sedge, hay-scented fern, and such wildflowers as Solomon's-seal, false Solomon's-seal, jack-in-the-pulpit, and a few asters and goldenrods. Mill Creek Park is on the south side of Beverly–Rancocas Road (route 626), about 3.5 miles west of I–295.

A third Beech-dominated forest in the Inner Coastal Plain can be found in Monmouth County, along the Stone Tavern–Roosevelt Road running south from Roosevelt into the Assunpink Wildlife Management Area. This forest is very close to the line between the Inner Coastal Plain and the Piedmont, and its composition has some features of Piedmont forests. As is true of the Beech–Oak forests in Burlington County described above, this forest is on a well-drained rise of ground above a stream. American beech is abundant here, but most of the trees are relatively small. The largest trees are black birch and tulip tree. There is also some black oak and red oak, and a few sweet gum and sassafras trees. The understory includes flowering dogwood, maple-leaved viburnum, arrowwood, spicebush, a few small black cherry trees, and common greenbrier, as well as seedlings of oaks and beech. On the forest floor is a sparse cover of poison ivy, Japanese honeysuckle, glaucous greenbrier, agrimony, partridgeberry, wild licorice, and other herbs and vines.

Virginia Pine Successional Forest

A forest type dominated by Virginia pine (Figure 11-4) occurs in areas of the Inner Coastal Plain west and south along the borders of the Pine Barrens. Virginia pine is a southern tree, reaching the northern limit of its range in Staten Island, New York. New Jersey's Virginia pine forests

Figure 11-4. A Virginia Pine forest in Smithville County Park near Mount Holly, in western Burlington County. The trees are about 25 years old. The ground cover is almost entirely hairgrass.

closely resemble forests in states south and west of New Jersey. The Inner Coastal Plain Virginia Pine forests develop on abandoned agricultural land and are themselves eventually replaced by the Mixed Oak forest.

One study found that when a seed source exists nearby, Virginia pine seedlings first appear in a field just 3 or 4 years after its abandonment. When these seedlings reach an age of about 6 or 7 years, they begin to produce cones. By the fifteenth year, the pines may cover over 99 percent of the ground and achieve a density of about 3,370 stems per acre. By this time, most of the herbaceous plants that existed in the original old field have disappeared. The Virginia pines begin to die as early as the twentieth year, and the number of stems per acre declines rapidly thereafter, but the canopy remains continuous. Broad-leaved deciduous trees, mostly saplings, become an important component of the Virginia Pine forest by the time the stand is 30 years old; some typical species include mockernut hickory, pignut hickory, sand hickory, white oak, Spanish oak, black oak, blackjack oak, and American holly. The original pines die off rapidly after about 60 years, but young pines persist in the understory of the developing deciduous forest until they too reach maturity and die. Understory shrubs include heath shrubs such as deerberry, early lowbush blueberry, and mountain laurel, with some dwarf chestnut oak. Herbaceous plants are sparse but include bracken fern, partridgeberry, spotted wintergreen, and poverty oatgrass. A few mosses and lichens can also be found. Table 11-3 lists some typical plant species of the Virginia Pine successional forest.

Virginia Pine forests of varying ages can be seen at many places in the Inner Coastal Plains. One can be seen in Ocean County on the east side of Route 539 at its intersection with the road that runs from New Egypt to Colliers Mills. The appearance of Virginia pine is quite different from that of pitch pine, the characteristic tree of the Pine Barrens. The needles of Virginia pine grow two in a cluster and are shorter than those of pitch pine. Also, each needle is twisted, giving the tree a unique appearance. The forest here is very dense and is composed almost entirely of Virginia pine, with only a few trees of chestnut oak, black oak, white oak, black cherry, and sassafras, and some shrubs of scrub oak, bayberry, and high-bush blueberry. The understory is likewise sparse and includes such plants as spotted wintergreen, common and glaucous greenbrier, and Pennsylvania sedge.

Virginia Pine forests are extremely common in western Cumberland County. They can be seen for miles along Route 646, which runs from Port Elizabeth to Cumberland. One stand, just north of Manumuskin Creek along the railroad track that runs south from Menantico Ponds, is over 90 percent Virginia pine, mixed with a few shortleaf pines, and only scattered individuals of other trees, including white, black, Spanish, and post oaks; American holly; and sand hickory. There are almost no understory shrubs, other than an occasional seedling of American holly or Virginia pine, or a straggling plant of early lowbush blueberry or black huckleberry, and there are even fewer herbaceous plants. But the ground is carpeted with lichens and mosses, including false reindeer lichen, thorn lichen, haircap mosses, and white moss.

Sweet Gum Successional Forest

Another type of successional forest found on the Inner Coastal Plain is dominated by the sweet gum tree. This tree is one of the most typical species of the Inner Coastal Plain forests and is found on both upland and wetland sites. Indeed, some of the locations where it grows best could be called either upland or wetland, depending on the technical definition of these terms. The branches of sweet gum trees growing close together have an upright growth form that, with their star-shaped leaves, makes them easy to recognize at a distance (Figure 9-4, 11-5).

One such Sweet Gum forest is located on private property in Burlington County just northwest of New Lisbon. It is on the west side of New Lisbon Road, about 0.5 miles south of the intersection of New Lisbon Road with Route 530, which goes from Pemberton to Browns Mills. The sweet gums here average about 10 inches in diameter and make up about 95 percent of the forest. The remaining trees are mostly red maple,

Table 11-3. Some Typical Plant Species of the Virginia Pine Successional Forest

Common name	Genus and species name
Dominant tree	
Virginia pine	*Pinus virginiana*
Other trees	
Shortleaf pine	*Pinus echinata*
Pitch pine	*Pinus rigida*
Black cherry	*Prunus serotina*
Spanish oak	*Quercus falcata*
Chestnut oak	*Quercus prinus*
Black oak	*Quercus velutina*
Post oak	*Quercus stellata*
American holly	*Ilex opaca*
Sassafras	*Sassafras albidum*
Mockernut hickory	*Carya tomentosa*
Pignut hickory	*Carya glabra*
Sand hickory	*Carya pallida*
Few others	
Shrubs and vines	
Black huckleberry	*Gaylussacia baccata*
Mountain laurel	*Kalmia latifolia*
Early lowbush blueberry	*Vaccinium pallidum*
Bayberry	*Myrica pensylvanica*
Scrub oak	*Quercus ilicifolia*
Glaucous greenbrier	*Smilax glauca*
Common greenbrier	*Smilax rotundifolia*
Few others	
Herbs	
Partridgeberry	*Mitchella repens*
Rattlesnake weed	*Hieracium venosum*
Spotted wintergreen	*Chimaphila maculata*
Pennsylvania sedge	*Carex pensylvanica*
Few others	
Lichens and mosses	
White moss	*Leucobryum glaucum*
Broom moss	*Dicranum scoparium*
Common haircap moss	*Polytrichum commune*
Juniper haircap moss	*Polytrichum juniperinum*
False reindeer lichen	*Cladina subtenuis*
Thorn lichen	*Cladonia uncialis*
Few others	

Figure 11-5. Sweet Gum successional forest near Pemberton, in western Burlington County.

with a few small trees of American holly, black cherry, and American beech. The shrub layer is sparse and includes spicebush, arrowwood, and a scattering of highbush blueberry and sweet pepperbush. On the ground is some Japanese honeysuckle, common greenbrier, swamp dewberry, field garlic, and tree clubmoss, with cinnamon fern and sensitive fern in damp spots. Poison ivy is common. This forest is on the edge of the Pine Barrens; if one continues south on New Lisbon Road the vegetation changes dramatically to a pine–oak forest in just a few miles.

Another fine example of an even-aged Sweet Gum successional forest can be seen from the red-marked nature trail at Allaire State Park, near the area known as the Brickfield. It parallels a wet swale with a good growth of tussock sedge. Mixed with the sweet gums, as is often the case in this type of forest, are a few red maples. The only other trees are a few small black cherries and an occasional river birch. There are few shrubs, and the species diversity is low; spicebush is most common, but coralberry and a few specimens of winterberry occur. The ground is thickly covered with eulalia grass, with some scattered enchanter's nightshade, woodreed, false nettle, field garlic, Japanese honeysuckle, and poison ivy.

Table 11-4 lists some plant species that are typical of the Sweet Gum forest.

Table 11-4. Some Typical Plant Species of the Sweet Gum Successional Forest

Common name	Genus and species name
Dominant tree	
Sweet gum	*Liquidambar styraciflua*
Other trees	
Red maple	*Acer rubrum*
Black cherry	*Prunus serotina*
American holly	*Ilex opaca*
Spanish oak	*Quercus falcata*
Persimmon	*Diospyros virginiana*
Others	
Shrubs and vines	
Arrowwood	*Viburnum dentatum*
Spicebush	*Lindera benzoin*
Highbush blueberry	*Vaccinium corymbosum*
Sweet pepperbush	*Clethra alnifolia*
Poison ivy	*Toxicodendron radicans*
Common greenbrier	*Smilax rotundifolia*
Japanese honeysuckle	*Lonicera japonica*
Swamp dewberry	*Rubus hispidus*
Others	
Herbs	
Field garlic	*Allium vineale*
Tree clubmoss	*Lycopodium obscurum*
Enchanter's nightshade	*Circaea lutetiana*
Eulalia grass	*Microstegium vimineum*
Few others	
Lichens and mosses	
White moss	*Leucobryum glaucum*
Common haircap moss	*Polytrichum commune*
Few others	

Other Successional Plant Communities of the South Jersey Uplands

Many examples of the natural changes that occur in vegetation with the passage of time have already been cited. The uplands of South Jersey are no exception, and if land is disturbed and left idle without human interference, various plant communities will occupy the land in succession.

As in North Jersey, on the uplands of South Jersey the first plants to occupy an abandoned field are the annual and biennial herbaceous plants. These are followed by longer-living perennial herbs. Next, a few seedlings of shrubs and trees develop into thickets and finally into a woodland. A study made on abandoned fields in the Inner Coastal Plain indicates that an annual called horseweed is the plant that most frequently invades a field left idle; with it in smaller numbers grow other herbs, including common ragweed, field chamomile, mouse-ear chickweed, prickly lettuce, sand spurry, and yellow foxtail. In fields left abandoned for 10 to 15 years, the most prominent plants are perennial herbs including early goldenrod, broomsedge, and king devil hawkweed, but shrubs such as blackberry, winged sumac, and silky dogwood are plentiful. Poison ivy is common. The first trees to grow in the field are black cherry, sweet gum, red maple, Virginia pine, and sassafras. With the passage of only 25 years, an idle field on the Inner Coastal Plain may be transformed into a woodland with trees as tall as 30 feet. Shrubs are not common in the woodland, though some spicebush and arrowwood can be found, and poison ivy and Japanese honeysuckle are abundant. Neither are herbs plentiful in the young woodland, though jewelweed, goldenrods of several species, bentgrass, and ground pine may be common. As more years pass, the woodland develops into a mature upland forest of one of the types described earlier. The change inevitably occurs, and for this reason it can be assumed that if left undisturbed, the whole of the South Jersey uplands, now so depleted of natural vegetation, would be covered with forest.

Human Influences on the Uplands Vegetation

The most fertile soils of South Jersey and those most suited for agriculture are on the Inner Coastal Plain, and this area was cleared and settled at a very early date. Descriptions of the South Jersey upland vegetation made earlier in this century comment on the exploitation of the natural vegetation of the Inner Coastal Plain. As early as 1900 the area was reported to be only 15 percent wooded, and the most recent map of forest distribution in the state shows little wooded acreage remaining in the area.

It is the Inner Coastal Plain of New Jersey that serves as the New Jersey transportation corridor for traffic between Washington, Philadelphia, and New York. It is the location for the Turnpike, for Interstate 295, and for major railroad lines. Historically, some areas of the Inner Coastal Plain not used for farming were dug for brick clay or for greensand marl, and even today some areas are being mined for glass sand or for gravel. The land not now being used for transportation facilities or for industrial or residential buildings has been cleared for the most part and is devoted to fruit, vegetable, dairy, and poultry farming. Thus, it is only the wetter lowlands that contain extensive tracts of natural vegetation.

The fragments of natural vegetation that do exist on the mesic uplands of South Jersey today reflect the influence of human activity, as do their counterparts in North Jersey. Virgin forest has disappeared, and the woodlands that remain have been cut over repeatedly since European settlement began. The chestnut blight eliminated American chestnut from the forests of the Inner Coastal Plain as it did from North Jersey's forests. And as elsewhere in New Jersey, introduced species such as Japanese honeysuckle, white mulberry, Asiatic bittersweet, eulalia grass, and others compete for space with the native vegetation.

Unlike northwestern New Jersey or the Pine Barrens, where some rather large areas of native forest have been preserved in state and county parks and wildlife management areas, only relatively small areas of the mesic uplands of South Jersey have been preserved as public open space.

Summary

Although South Jersey does not have the differences in elevation characteristic of North Jersey, there are still enough differences in soil moisture and climate to produce a considerable range of forest types, including several long-lived and distinctive successional forest types. Although little mature upland forest remains in southern New Jersey, the remnants that do exist suggest that the natural vegetation of this area is predominantly Mixed Oak or Beech–Oak forest. One outstanding characteristic of the vegetation of southern New Jersey, on both the Inner and Outer Coastal Plains, is the mingling of northern and southern, and of Piedmont and coastal, species of plants.

References and Source Material

Hanks, J. P. 1971. Secondary Succession and Soils on the Inner Coastal Plain of New Jersey. *Bulletin of the Torrey Botanical Club* 98:315–321.

McCormick, J., and J. W. Andresen. 1963. The Role of *Pinus Virginiana* in the Vegetation of Southern New Jersey. *New Jersey Nature News* [New Jersey Audubon Society] 110:1–12.

Stone, Witmer. 1910. The Plants of Southern New Jersey, with Especial Reference to the Flora of the Pine Barrens and the Geographic Distribution of the Species, in *Annual Report,* New Jersey State Museum, Trenton, N.J.

Vermeule, C. C., A. Hollick, J. B. Smith, and G. Pinchot. 1900. Reports on Forests, in *Annual Report of the State Geologist for 1899*, Trenton, N.J.

Chapter 12

℥ *Coastal Salt Marshes*

Marshland includes that part of tidal areas, estuaries, and river and pond edges that is covered with standing water most of the year or that is subject to flooding year round if only for a few days each month or for some part of each day. Factors that control the type of vegetation present in any marsh include the frequency, depth, and duration of flooding, and the nature of the substrate. Within the category of marshland, however, one more environmental condition controls the type of vegetation that grows in the habitat—the degree of water salinity. As noted previously, some plants, called halophytes, can successfully grow and reproduce in soil covered or saturated with salt water. Other plants, though able to flourish with their roots immersed in fresh water, will die if salt water invades their habitat. Only a very few plants can grow well in both fresh and salt water. For this reason a distinction is made between two types of marshland habitats—the saltwater marshes and the freshwater marshes.

The general location of salt marshes in New Jersey is relatively easy to predict, as they must follow the line of coastal tidal waters (Figure 12-1). However, the geology and topography of the coast determines the degree to which coastal marshes develop. Today, the real northern limit of salt marshland in New Jersey is in the Newark Bay area, a short distance up the Passaic and Hackensack rivers, although historically extensive salt marshes were found farther north along the Hudson River. Southward in New Jersey salt marshes are found around Raritan Bay and the streams that enter it, on the inner side of Sandy Hook, and along the shores of the Shrewsbury River.

The coastal area from Long Branch to Bay Head has little salt marsh because no offshore island stands in front of the mainland there. Marshes cannot form on the ever-shifting sand exposed to the full force of ocean waves. From Bay Head southward larger areas of salt marsh occur, both on the bay sides of the offshore islands and on mainland areas, particularly where streams empty into the bays that separate the mainland from the offshore islands. Around Barnegat and Tuckerton on the mainland are large stretches of salt marshes, and these continue to fringe the

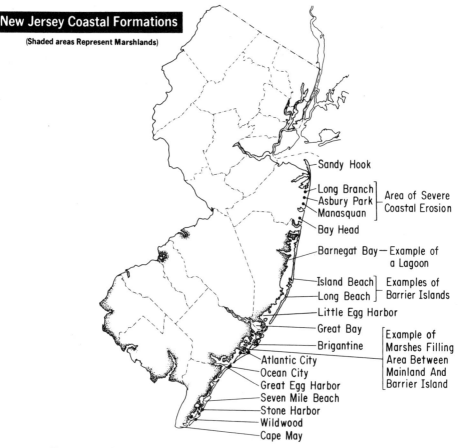

New Jersey Coastal Formations

(Shaded areas Represent Marshlands)

Sandy Hook

Long Branch ⎤
Asbury Park ⎬ Area of Severe
Manasquan ⎦ Coastal Erosion

Bay Head

Barnegat Bay — Example of
a Lagoon

Island Beach ⎤ Examples of
Long Beach ⎦ Barrier Islands

Little Egg Harbor

Great Bay

Brigantine

Atlantic City
Ocean City
Great Egg Harbor
Seven Mile Beach
Stone Harbor
Wildwood
Cape May

⎡ Example of
⎢ Marshes Filling
⎢ Area Between
⎢ Mainland And
⎣ Barrier Island

Figure 12-1. The location of New Jersey salt marshes.

mainland coast all the way to Cape May. From Atlantic City southward the area of tidal marshes grows wider, stretching from the coast of the mainland almost to the bay side of the offshore islands except for the open-water areas cleared for the inland waterway.

Salt marshes also occur along the southern coast of New Jersey in the Delaware Bay area from Cape May north. But from Salem County, on the southwestern coast, almost to Trenton, the marshland is mostly brackish, a somewhat arbitrary midpoint between the extremes of fresh and salt water. This is true also of other inland tidal marshes, where the sea water is diluted by freshwater streams or groundwater. Upstream, the saltwater marshes merge gradually with the freshwater tidal marshes described in Chapter 9. Altogether, New Jersey at present has about 325 square miles of salt or brackish marshes; of this, about 138 square miles edge Delaware Bay; about 17 square miles extend from Bergen and

Hudson counties south to Raritan Bay; and the remaining 170 square miles are along the southern coast of New Jersey in Monmouth, Ocean, Burlington, Atlantic, and Cape May counties.

Development and Change of Coastal Salt Marshes

In a book on the salt marshes of eastern North America, an oceanographer and his wife, John and Mildred Teal, describe the processes by which the salt marshes in stabilized coastline situations may develop and change through time. Shallow parts of a bay may develop into a salt marsh because of the natural encroachment of marsh vegetation into the bay water. Stems and roots of the marsh grasses that live at the water's edge slow the tidal currents and cause their sediments of sand and organic materials to be deposited around the plants. In addition, as marsh grasses die, their remains add to the deposits. As the fill accumulates, the roots of plants growing at the water's edge can extend outward. Thus, in a continuing process the edge of the marshland creeps farther and farther out into open water. Eventually, sediments and marsh grasses will fill the bays between the mainland and the offshore islands.

As the marshland extends itself out into the bay, the area of land covered by tidal water changes and the areas which originally were flooded are left farther and farther from the water's edge. Soon the tides no longer flood these areas, and if they receive freshwater drainage, the waters become brackish as the flooding becomes less frequent. If the land is never inundated by storm tides the site may evolve into a freshwater marsh or swamp. The extension of the marshland into a bay area and the change of saltwater marshes to freshwater marshes and, finally, to a swamp area are additional examples of the process of vegetation succession.

The events just described will occur only if the level of the ocean is relatively constant in relation to the level of the land. If this is not the case, salt marshes may be lost by erosion. At the time of the maximum glaciation the coastline of New Jersey probably extended about 80 miles east of its present line. But with the gradual rise in sea level because of the melting of glacial ice, the ocean has encroached landward. In this case the outer edges of the salt marshlands are eroded away. An example of this in New Jersey can be seen in the marshes around Tuckerton. Also, areas once covered by forests may now be salt marshes. Such is the case in parts of the Hackensack Meadows, where large stumps and logs, the remains of an Atlantic white cedar forest, lie buried under the present salt marsh. Ecologists have also found evidence that forest vegetation once existed in the salt marsh area of the Great Bay, where the lagoon separates Brigantine Island from the mainland. It is more common in New Jersey today, however, to find the rising sea level causing erosion of the outermost margins of the existing salt marshes than to find the

Figure 12-2. Salt marsh cordgrass grows best in the marshland zone closest to the water, where it receives tidal flooding twice each day. It is an upright, rather broad-leaved grass.

marshes expanding out into the bay. According to ecologist William Niering:

> Salt marshes constantly change their location and extent. After a single storm-caused flood, a river can discharge so much sediment that salt marshes at its mouth are deeply buried and destroyed. Sand dislodged from ocean beaches and carried through breaks in barrier islands can suffocate a salt marsh. Ancient marshes buried long ago can sometimes be found cropping out as coastal sand dunes migrate. Salt marshes are neither permanent nor especially stable; they are forever becoming something else. Some, inundated by rain or river flow, become freshwater swamps and eventually maritime forests; others are submerged under bay waters and become part of the marine environment.

Vegetation of the Salt Marshes

The salt marshes of New Jersey are dominated by two species of grasses, which are the most abundant plants in East Coast salt marshes from New England to the Carolinas. Both grasses have the same Latin genus name, *Spartina,* but their species names differ. One is *Spartina alterni-*

Figure 12-3. Salt-meadow grass, or salt hay, grows on the higher sections of the salt marsh. It is a fine-textured grass that is often formed by wind and water into "cowlicks" that make it easy to recognize at a distance.

flora, commonly called salt marsh cordgrass or thatch grass; the other of the two is *Spartina patens,* known as salt-meadow grass, or salt hay.

Salt marsh cordgrass (Figure 12-2) is a coarse, stiff, relatively broad-leaved grass, which in its tallest form (3 to 8 feet high) normally occupies the marshland zone closest to the water, the area that is flooded by high tides twice each day. In contrast, the more slender, delicate-appearing salt-meadow grass (Figure 12-3), which is usually no more than 2 feet tall, grows typically in the high marsh—the zone farther away from the water's edge, which is flooded only at the higher tides. Both grasses are green in summer and brown in winter, and both have special mechanisms for keeping salt out of the cell sap. These two grasses often form distinct zones on the tidal shores of New Jersey and other East Coast states. Table 12-1 lists many of the plant species that are typical of the salt marsh zones that are regularly flooded.

A third zone of vegetation occurs on still higher marshland, which is protected from daily tidal inflows and thus may be flooded only monthly at times of very high tides. Although salt-meadow grass is still found here, it is usually mixed with another grass, called spike grass, which looks something like salt-meadow grass but has wider leaves, grows taller, and has a rather plump spike of tiny flowers. Also common in this zone is a grasslike plant called black grass (really a rush), which grows only about 1 foot high; it occasionally occupies large areas. On the very

Table 12-1. Some Typical Plant Species of the Salt Marsh Zone Closest to the Water

Common name	Genus and species name
Herbs	
Salt marsh cordgrass	*Spartina alterniflora*
Salt-meadow grass	*Spartina patens*
Spike grass	*Distichlis spicata*
Black grass	*Juncus gerardi*
Perennial salt marsh aster	*Aster tenuifolius*
Sea lavender	*Limonium carolinianum*
Seaside mallow	*Kosteletzkya virginica*
Tall sea-blite	*Suaeda linearis*
Low sea-blite	*Suaeda maritima*
Slender glasswort	*Salicornia europaea*
Woody glasswort	*Salicornia virginica*
Orache	*Atriplex patula*
Salt marsh sand spurrey	*Spergularia maritima*
Salt marsh fleabane	*Pluchea odorata*
Few others	

highest part of the marsh (Figure 12-4) are additional salt marsh plants, some with rather showy flowers. These include annual and perennial salt marsh asters, sea lavender, salt marsh bulrush, big cordgrass, sea-pink, seaside mallow, and rose mallow. Along the edges grow seaside goldenrod, saltwort, sea blites, and two low shrubs, the groundsel bush and marsh elder. Many of the typical plant species of the high marsh are listed in Table 12-2.

Small shallow depressions called "pannes" (Figure 12-5) occur commonly on the high marsh; their conditions are very saline because they are flooded only infrequently and then remain dry for extended periods, during which time the water evaporates, leaving the salt behind. Few plants can adapt to these conditions; the most common are several species of glassworts. These have swollen stems that turn bright red in the fall, making the marsh almost as colorful as some of the inland forests. Another plant sometimes common in the pannes is salt marsh fleabane.

Finally, on the inland edge of the salt marshes, where the water tends to be less salty because of runoff from the land, some plants such as narrow-leaved cattail and phragmites, which are more typical of fresh-water wetlands, join those of the salt marsh.

Wide expanses of salt marsh can be seen from the Garden State Parkway south of exit 58, particularly where the highway crosses the Mullica River and Great Egg Harbor and then continues southward to Cape May. One of the best places on the Atlantic coast to see a salt marsh where one

Figure 12-4. The highest part of the marsh, which is flooded only occasionally, has the greatest diversity of plant species. Here marsh elder, phragmites, and other plants invade an area dominated by salt-meadow grass.

Figure 12-5. Pannes and shallow pools dot the marshes along Great Bay Boulevard, south of Tuckerton.

Table 12-2. Some Typical Plant Species of the High Marsh

Common name	Genus and species name
Shrubs and vines	
Marsh elder	*Iva frutescens*
Groundsel bush	*Baccharis halimifolia*
Bayberry	*Myrica pensylvanica*
Herbs	
Salt-meadow grass	*Spartina patens*
Spike grass	*Distichlis spicata*
Big cordgrass	*Spartina cynosuroides*
Salt marsh cordgrass	*Spartina alterniflora*
Black grass	*Juncus gerardi*
Perennial salt marsh aster	*Aster tenuifolius*
Sea lavender	*Limonium carolinianum*
Salt marsh bulrush	*Scirpus robustus*
Seaside goldenrod	*Solidago sempervirens*
Salt marsh cockspur grass	*Echinochloa walteri*
Beaked spike-rush	*Eleocharis rostellata*
Orache	*Atriplex patula*
Seaside gerardia	*Agalinis maritima*
Salt marsh sand spurrey	*Spergularia maritima*
Sea-pink	*Sabatia stellaris*
Others	

can walk on it and observe it closely is along Great Bay Boulevard south of Route 9 in Tuckerton, in Ocean County. In the high marsh here grow salt-meadow grass, spike grass, salt-marsh bulrush, narrow-leaved cattail, and big cordgrass. Salt marsh cordgrass grows along narrow creeks that are flooded at high tide. In autumn, sea-pink and perennial salt marsh aster can be found here. About 3 miles south of Route 9, just before the first bridge, an area on the right (west) side of the road has several large pannes, with three species of glasswort and other plants typical of this hypersaline habitat. Great Bay Boulevard ends at the shore of Great Bay.

Cheesequake State Park in Middlesex County also has salt marshes that are readily accessible. This park is off Route 34, east of the town of Cheesequake. A trail and boardwalk leads into the marsh from the Meadowview Picnic Area parking lot. The vegetation diversity here is somewhat less than that along Great Bay, but one can see the salt marsh cordgrass and salt-meadow grass, as well as spike grass, black rush, orache, perennial salt marsh aster, slender glasswort, phragmites, marsh elder, and groundsel bush. The salt marsh here is bordered by a shrub thicket of bayberry, with some highbush blueberry, seaside goldenrod, switchgrass, and a few small sour gums that mark the transition from salt marsh to freshwater swamp forest.

On the Delaware Bay side of New Jersey, salt marshes can be seen in many places, including most of the wildlife management areas along the bay in Salem and Cumberland counties. At the Mad Horse Creek Wildlife Management Area southeast of Canton in Salem County, Stow Creek Road runs through areas dominated by phragmites at first, but then emerges into a typical salt marsh with salt marsh cordgrass, salt-meadow grass, and most of the typical associated plants. Large stands of big cordgrass can be seen here. The road ends in a parking lot from which one can walk and explore the area. As is often the case, there are several forested islands in this marsh; most have trees such as Spanish oak, black oak, white oak, American holly, black cherry, and sour gum, and a shrub understory of arrowwood, highbush blueberry, winged sumac, and common greenbrier. One island—aptly named Pine Island—has a grove of loblolly pines, a southern species that is here at its northern natural limit of range.

Vegetation of Brackish Marshes

As already noted, brackish waters fall between the extremes of fresh and salt water in salt content. Marshes with such water can be found along streams and in other inland areas of tidal marshes, where seawater is at least occasionally diluted by freshwater streams or groundwater. They vary from waters that are only slightly less salty than sea water to water with such a slight trace of salt that it cannot be tasted by most people. Large rivers, such as the Delaware, the Raritan, and the Mullica, become increasingly fresher upstream from the river mouth as salt water is diluted by the river's freshwater discharge. Since river discharge varies widely during different seasons of the year, and since ocean tides vary in amplitude, the salinity of such waters also varies seasonally, and even daily. In dry seasons, when freshwater runoff is minimal, the salinity of the water in these brackish marshes approaches that of the ocean; in wet seasons, the water may be virtually fresh. As one would expect, a variety of vegetation types develop in brackish marshes because of differences in salinity and duration and frequency of flooding. Generally, brackish marshes are areas of transition, where some plants more typical of the freshwater wetlands join those of the salt marsh, and some of the more specialized halophytes such as the glassworts disappear. In the Hackensack Meadows, the dominant plant of brackish marshes is phragmites, with salt marsh cordgrass along the edges of tidal creeks. Farther south in New Jersey, big cordgrass, Olney's three-square, narrow-leaved cattail, and rose mallow are more typical of this habitat. A few plant species that are typical of moderately saline brackish marshes are listed in Table 12-3.

Table 12-3. Some Typical Plant Species of Brackish Tidal Marshes of Moderate Salinity

Common name	Genus and species name
Shrubs	
Marsh elder	*Iva frutescens*
Groundsel bush	*Baccharis halimifolia*
Indigo bush	*Amorpha fruticosa*
Few others	
Herbs	
Phragmites	*Phragmites australis*
Narrow-leaved cattail	*Typha angustifolia*
Rose mallow	*Hibiscus moscheutos*
Water hemp	*Amaranthus cannabinus*
Salt marsh cordgrass	*Spartina alterniflora*
Big cordgrass	*Spartina cynosuroides*
Annual salt marsh aster	*Aster subulatus*
Salt marsh bulrush	*Scirpus robustus*
Three-square	*Scirpus pungens*
Olney's three-square	*Scirpus americanus*
Others	

Human Influences on the Coastal Salt Marsh Vegetation

Only in recent years has public interest in preservation of coastal salt marshes become widespread. Yet for centuries, humans have been destroying the natural tidal and freshwater marshlands by drainage, by filling, and by pollution, without consideration of the consequences. Why the change in attitude?

It is not simply a will to preserve the beauty of marshlands that has stimulated public interest, although to many people natural beauty is itself a value to be cherished. More important is the growing recognition that these wetlands perform functions indispensable to humans. The first of these functions, and perhaps the most important, is the unique role that these lands play in human food supply.

The U.S. Bureau of Sport Fisheries and Wildlife has estimated that two out of every three species of useful Atlantic fish depend in some way upon the tidal marshlands for their survival. The marshes provide the shelter that acts as "nursery areas" for the young of many species. Without the marshes, the fish, clams, shrimp, oysters, and other shellfish on which we depend could not exist. In addition, the marshes furnish homes for a multitude of land-inhabiting animals—raccoons, otters, mink, muskrats, and rabbits among others. Ducks, pheasants, geese, and many other waterfowl and shorebirds use the marshes for nesting or migratory resting places. The fascinating world of marsh life and the food-chain relationships so important to humans are described in the book by the Teals mentioned earlier and in another book entitled *The Life of the Marsh,* by William Niering.

Other functions performed by marshland are related to flood control and water storage. Coastal and estuary marshlands take the brunt of storm waves, thereby protecting the inner uplands from flooding and erosion. These important benefits need not be accompanied by offsetting disadvantages to humans; mosquitoes can be controlled by artificial change in water levels during their breeding season or by insecticides not damaging to other life.

The marshland in New Jersey, like that of other states, has suffered severely from human actions. Of the 12,541 square miles of salt marsh that once existed along the eastern edge of the United States, it is estimated that 50 percent have been destroyed, and this just in the last 2 centuries. One has only to travel through the Newark Bay area to observe the actions that have caused such destruction—drainage; fill-in; development of the land for industry, housing, or highways; pollution from industries, oil spills, or urban sewage. As a result of the massive interference with the ecosystem, the variety of plant and animal life in the Hackensack Meadows has been severely depleted.

Today marshes farther south in New Jersey have been filled for development of seashore houses or for industrial use. Little marshland in the state remains unpolluted, and Raritan Bay oysters, once well known in New York restaurants, no longer appear on menus. Most of the oysters have vanished from the bay, and those remaining are unsafe to eat.

Summary

Extensive areas of salt marsh fringe the shores of New Jersey. The vegetation of the salt marshes differs from that of freshwater marshes because of the varying tolerance of different plant species to water salinity. Within salt marshes, as is true of freshwater marshes, zones of vegetation occur because different plants are best adapted to particular conditions of flooding. Brackish marshes occupy a position intermediate in salinity and location between salt marshes and freshwater marshes.

Natural changes occur in salt marshes as plants at the water's edge gradually encroach upon the water. The plants of the marshland extend outward, and other types of vegetation move in to occupy the original sites, which no longer are continually flooded. This is another example of succession in vegetation.

Marshlands not only serve people as a peaceful refuge from the turmoil of urbanized life but also serve as habitats for a multitude of living organisms. As barriers to storm waves and water storage areas, these wetlands also serve other functions important to people. For these reasons, it is unfortunate that we in New Jersey as in other areas continue to despoil the dwindling supply of marshland.

References and Source Material

Ferren, W. R., Jr., R. E. Good, R. Walker, and J. Arsenault. 1981. Vegetation and Flora of Hog Island, a Brackish Wetland in the Mullica River, New Jersey. *Bartonia* 48:1–10.

Good, R. E. 1965. Salt Marsh Vegetation, Cape May, New Jersey. *Bulletin of the New Jersey Academy of Science* 10:1–11.

Niering, William A. 1966. *The Life of the Marsh.* New York: McGraw-Hill.

Stone, Witmer. 1910. The Plants of Southern New Jersey, with Especial Reference to the Flora of the Pine Barrens and the Geographic Distribution of the Species, in *Annual Report,* New Jersey State Museum, Trenton, N.J.

Teal, John, and Mildred Teal. 1969. *Life and Death of a Salt Marsh.* Boston, Mass.: Little, Brown.

Tiner, R. W. 1985. Wetlands of New Jersey. Newton Center, Mass.: U.S. Fish and Wildlife Service, National Wetlands Inventory.

Chapter 13

❧ Coastal Sand Dunes

The ocean coast of New Jersey extends about 125 miles from the tip of Sandy Hook in the north to Cape May in the south. Opposing forces have long been at work shaping this coastal area. Since the melting of the glaciers some 12,000 to 18,000 years ago the land has risen slightly, a reaction to the removal of the tremendous weight of glacial ice. But concurrently, sea levels have risen as the ice has melted. Thus, although the ocean now covers areas that in glacial times had been dry land, the present coast of New Jersey still shows features typical of coastal land that has been uplifted relatively recently. These features include barrier islands, spits, and hooks.

Barrier islands are offshore sand ridges that parallel the shore and rise only slightly above high tide. Spits and hooks are ridges of sand attached to land at the down-current end. These formations, built from sand by combinations of waves and currents, are not static. The contour of the shore changes noticeably from year to year and even from day to day. Spits tend to elongate as sand is added to them by along-shore currents. Barrier islands are eroded on the seaward side by wave action and eventually are pushed so far back that they merge with the mainland and are no longer recognizable. Altogether, it is estimated that the New Jersey barrier islands are retreating toward the mainland at an average rate of about 2 feet per year. This process has occurred on the northern coast of New Jersey, from Sandy Hook south to Manasquan, and barrier islands that once existed in this area have disappeared.

The sand dunes of New Jersey occur primarily on the barrier islands and on Sandy Hook, though a few dunes appear on the mainland, even as far inland as the Pine Barrens. A dune is a windblown pile of sand, but when fully developed a dune formation has a particular topography that is well illustrated in New Jersey. Mature sand dune formations consist of more-or-less parallel and continuous ridges of sand with intervening troughs or depressions. From the standpoint of vegetation, it is necessary to distinguish between the dune ridges and the hollows between the ridges. This is so because particular environmental conditions that influence vegetation, including variations in the amounts of salt spray, sand movement, soil moisture, and soil salinity, are associated with differences in height. These environmental gradients are reflected in the vegetation of the sand dunes.

Four general types of vegetation more or less typify the plants of the New Jersey sand dunes; these are the Dunegrass, the Beach Heather, the Shrub Thicket, and the Dune Woodland communities. Although these communities are treated as though they are distinct, it should be remembered that in nature gradations occur among them, particularly among the last three.

Dunegrass Community

The dunes nearest the ocean are called primary dunes, and the particular dune ridge that lies immediately parallel to the water is called the primary foredune. Only the beach, an ever-shifting ribbon of sand and pebbles, separates the primary foredune and the ocean. Normal high tides cover all but the highest part of the beach. Wind-borne salt spray and sand movement are most intense on the ocean-facing primary foredunes, which also has the least amount of soil moisture.

Most plants are highly intolerant of salt spray, which may kill both plant foliage and new plant growth. Few plants grow on the beach separating the primary dunes from the ocean, and those few occur in sparse numbers. In New Jersey the two most common beach plants are sea rocket, an annual plant that flowers throughout most of the summer, and dusty miller, an introduced biennial with gray-green dissected leaves.

On the primary foredune, only about 10 percent of the sand is covered with plants, but it is here that the first recognizable plant community occurs. This is the Dunegrass community, named for the most abundant plant (Figure 13-1). Dunegrass, also called beachgrass or marram grass, is a perennial plant with an extensive network of roots that help bind the sand, thus protecting the dune from damage. In addition, the dunegrass helps build up dunes by trapping windblown sand among its foliage and underground structures. Interestingly, there is a mutually constructive relationship between the accumulation of sand and the growth of dunegrass. The healthier dunegrass is, the more effective it is in trapping sand carried by the wind. At the same time, the healthiest growth of the grass is dependent upon a substantial rate of accumulation of sand.

In this community the dunegrass accounts for most of the rather sparse plant cover on the primary foredune. Growing with it in smaller numbers are sea rocket, dusty miller, saltwort, seaside spurge, seaside goldenrod, beach pea, sandbur, and cocklebur. In some places in New Jersey, these plants are joined by an Asiatic sedge, *Carex kobomugi,* and by sea-beach panic-grass; both these plants, like dunegrass, have extensive, spreading root systems that bind the dune surface and trap sand. Table 13-1 lists some typical plant species of the Dunegrass community,

Figure 13-1. Dunegrass community on the primary dunes at Island Beach State Park. Dunegrass here grows with seaside goldenrod, the basal leaves of which are visible in the foreground.

Table 13-1. Some Typical Plant Species of the Dunegrass Community

Common name	Genus and species name
Herbs	
Dunegrass	*Ammophila breviligulata*
Sea rocket	*Cakile edentula*
Seaside spurge	*Euphorbia polygonifolia*
Sandbur	*Cenchrus tribuloides*
Long-spined sandbur	*Cenchrus longispinus*
Sandgrass	*Triplasis purpurea*
Sea-beach panic-grass	*Panicum amarum*
Seaside goldenrod	*Solidago sempervirens*
Saltwort	*Salsola kali*
Sedge	*Carex kobomugi*
Cocklebur	*Xanthium strumarium*
Beach pea	*Lathyrus japonicus*
Dusty miller	*Artemisia stelleriana*

which grows throughout the primary dune zone as well as on dunes farther back from the beach.

The Dunegrass community can be seen in many places on New Jersey's shore; even in areas where development has largely destroyed the other plant communities of the coastal sand dunes, the primary dunes themselves have often been left intact. In fact, dunegrass is often planted as a means of stabilizing dunes to protect beach property. However, the best places to see the Dunegrass community are the relatively unspoiled state parks and recreation areas. Island Beach State Park has excellent examples. This park can be reached from Highway 37 east of Garden State Parkway exit 82. Sandy Hook National Recreation Area, in Monmouth County, is another good location at which to view this plant community.

Beach Heather Community

Immediately behind the ridge of primary foredunes are flattened areas, hollows, and smaller dunes, an area referred to as the primary backdunes. At Island Beach State Park the ocean beach is about 150 feet wide and the zone of the primary dunes, including the foredune and the backdunes, is about 450 feet wide. Additional dunes lie to the rear of the primary dune area and are referred to as secondary dunes. Each of these also has a foredune ridge and associated backdunes.

In these more protected areas of the primary and secondary dune zones, the low-growing beach heather occurs in great abundance, often covering large areas (Figure 13-2). Beach heather is much less tolerant of salt spray than the plants of the Dunegrass community and does not compete with them on the exposed dunes. Rather, it tends to grow in the backdune areas at an average elevation of about 9 feet above sea level. This habitat is less exposed to salt spray and sand movement than is the primary foredune, but it is very dry. Several of the plant species here, including the beach heather, show adaptations to dry conditions, including reduced leaf surface, prostrate growth habit, and leaf surfaces covered with hairs or a waxy covering to reduce water loss.

Branches of the beach heather spread across the dune, but the plant usually grows no more than 1 foot tall. In areas occupied by the Beach Heather community less bare, sandy area remains than in the Dunegrass community. The beach heather itself forms most of the plant cover here, but growing with it in sparse numbers are many of the plants of the Dunegrass community. In addition, one finds such plants as sea-beach three-awn, switchgrass, little bluestem, sandgrass, beach pinweed, prickly pear, and several species of sedges. Horizontal networks of poison ivy and Virginia creeper spread across the sand. Several species of lichens add to the botanical diversity. Some typical plant species of the Beach Heather community are listed in Table 13-2.

Figure 13-2. Beach heather often covers the ground in the protected area between the primary and secondary dune zones. The Shrub Thicket community can be seen in the background.

Again, examples of this community can best be seen in places like Island Beach and Sandy Hook, although isolated remnants can be found on most of the barrier islands in New Jersey south of Manasquan.

Shrub Thicket Community

Inland from the ocean there is a decreasing amount of salt spray combined with an increase in soil moisture, conditions that make for more varied natural plant cover including communities of woody plants. These occur mostly in the zone of the secondary dunes, and even there, where the salt spray is the highest, woody plants attain only low growth, forming more or less a thicket (Figure 13-3). The most common plants in this Shrub Thicket community include bayberry, beach plum, shadbush, and highbush blueberry, with some low-growing red cedar, black cherry, scrub oak, winged sumac, and American holly. In some places, extensive tangles of poison ivy and Virginia creeper make the thickets impassable. On the driest sites, the herb cover in the Shrub Thicket community is sparse, with dunegrass, seaside goldenrod, and switchgrass most common, along with other plants more typical of the Dunegrass

Table 13-2. Some Typical Plant Species of the Beach Heather Community

Common name	Genus and species name
Vines	
Virginia creeper	*Parthenocissus quinquefolia*
Poison ivy	*Toxicodendron radicans*
Herbs	
Beach heather	*Hudsonia tomentosa*
Sea rocket	*Cakile edentula*
Seaside spurge	*Euphorbia polygonifolia*
Sandbur	*Cenchrus tribuloides*
Long-spined sandbur	*Cenchrus longispinus*
Sandgrass	*Triplasis purpurea*
Sea-beach panic-grass	*Panicum amarum*
Switchgrass	*Panicum virgatum*
Dunegrass	*Ammophila breviligulata*
Sea-beach three-awn	*Aristida tuberculosa*
Little bluestem	*Schizachyrium scoparium*
Seaside goldenrod	*Solidago sempervirens*
Sedge	*Carex kobomugi*
Cocklebur	*Xanthium strumarium*
Beach pea	*Lathyrus japonicus*
Dusty miller	*Artemisia stelleriana*
Prickly pear	*Opuntia humifusa*
Gray's cyperus	*Cyperus grayii*
Beach pinweed	*Lechea maritima*
Trailing wild bean	*Strophostyles helvola*
Others	
Lichens and mosses	
Thorn lichen	*Cladonia uncialis*
Coastal reindeer lichen	*Cladina submitis*
Others	

and of the Beach Heather communities. On moister sites, several species of ferns, beardgrass, and phragmites can be found. Table 13-3 lists some plant species of the Shrub Thicket community.

The height of the Shrub Thicket vegetation varies from 1 to 15 feet depending upon the amount of salt spray reaching the area—the taller heights being farther away from salt spray exposure. Isolated trees and shrubs in this area, if growing exposed to wind from the ocean, may take on a molded one-sided form with branches on the lee side growing vigorously while those on the windward side remain short, being killed back annually by wind-borne deposits of salt (Figure 13-4). Salt spray

Figure 13-3. Shrub Thicket community at Island Beach State Park, with bayberry, beach plum, and red cedar. Beach heather grows on the sand in the foreground.

Figure 13-4. An exposed thicket of bayberry and beach plum at Island Beach State Park, showing the effects of wind and salt spray on the form of the plants.

Table 13-3. Some Typical Plant Species of the Shrub Thicket Community

Common name	Genus and species name
Trees	
Red cedar	*Juniperus virginiana*
Black cherry	*Prunus serotina*
American holly	*Ilex opaca*
Shrubs and vines	
Scrub oak	*Quercus ilicifolia*
Bayberry	*Myrica pensylvanica*
Beach plum	*Prunus maritima*
Shadbush	*Amelanchier canadensis*
Highbush blueberry	*Vaccinium corymbosum*
Winged sumac	*Rhus copallina*
Virginia creeper	*Parthenocissus quinquefolia*
Poison ivy	*Toxicodendron radicans*
Herbs	
Common greenbrier	*Smilax rotundifolia*
Seaside spurge	*Euphorbia polygonifolia*
Sandbur	*Cenchrus tribuloides*
Long-spined sandbur	*Cenchrus longispinus*
Sandgrass	*Triplasis purpurea*
Dunegrass	*Ammophila breviligulata*
Switchgrass	*Panicum virgatum*
Sea-beach three-awn	*Aristida tuberculosa*
Little bluestem	*Schizachyrium scoparium*
Dusty miller	*Artemisia stelleriana*
Prickly pear	*Opuntia humifusa*
Beach pinweed	*Lechea maritima*

also inhibits height, resulting in flattened tops as the plants reach the level of the main windstream that crosses the barrier island.

Again, examples of this community can best be seen in places like Island Beach and Sandy Hook, although isolated remnants can be found on most of New Jersey's barrier islands. At Sandy Hook, the paved road that runs north from parking lot L to the Battery Gunnison area goes through this habitat. At Island Beach, many of the trails that lead east to the beach in the natural area will give good views of the Shrub Thicket community, and a short, self-guiding trail at the Aeolium Visitor Center goes through this habitat. At Higbee Beach Wildlife Management Area in Cape May County, some good examples of the Shrub Thicket community on dunes that face Delaware Bay can be found. Higbee Beach is

Figure 13-5. Dune Woodlands in a protected area at Island Beach State Park are dominated by red cedar, with some black cherry and sassafras. The trees here are about 30 feet tall.

just south of the Cape May Canal and is reachable by taking New England Road west from Route 9 to the end of the road.

Dune Woodland Community

In moister and more protected hollows of the secondary sand dunes, beyond the reach of heavy salt spray, are the Dune Woodlands (Figure 13-5), which are quite different from most mainland forests. At Sandy Hook the Dune Woodland is well known for its very large American holly trees, some of which are more than 18 inches in diameter. Although the composition of the Dune Woodland community varies from site to site, the most common trees on the Sandy Hook dunes include American holly, black cherry, red cedar, red maple, pitch pine, hackberry, and sassafras. In places, poison ivy, Virginia creeper, common greenbrier, and American bittersweet grow abundantly and reach up to the treetops, making a dense forest.

The Dune Woodlands south of Sandy Hook are slightly different, for although more or less the same species occur, the proportions of abundance by species may change. For example, the woodlands at Island Beach are dominated mostly by red cedar, but in one small area pitch

Table 13-4. Some Typical Plant Species of the Dune Woodland

Common name	Genus and species name
Trees	
Red cedar	*Juniperus virginiana*
Black cherry	*Prunus serotina*
American holly	*Ilex opaca*
Red maple	*Acer rubrum*
Hackberry	*Celtis occidentalis*
Sassafras	*Sassafras albidum*
Pitch pine	*Pinus rigida*
Shrubs and vines	
Scrub oak	*Quercus ilicifolia*
Bayberry	*Myrica pensylvanica*
Beach plum	*Prunus maritima*
Shadbush	*Amelanchier canadensis*
Highbush blueberry	*Vaccinium corymbosum*
Winged sumac	*Rhus copallina*
Common greenbrier	*Smilax rotundifolia*
Virginia creeper	*Parthenocissus quinquefolia*
Poison ivy	*Toxicodendron radicans*
Others	
Herbs	
Switchgrass	*Panicum virgatum*
Sea-beach three-awn	*Aristida tuberculosa*
Little bluestem	*Schizachyrium scoparium*
Others	

pine is abundant. In the red cedar woodland the associated trees include the American holly, black cherry, sassafras, willow oak, and shadbush, while the lower-growing shrubs include bayberry, highbush blueberry, and sweet pepperbush. Vines include common greenbrier, poison ivy, and Virginia creeper.

Some typical plant species of this community are listed in Table 13-4.

The pine woodland at Island Beach is more open, and pitch pines growing between 15 and 30 feet high make up about half of the forest canopy trees. Atlantic white cedar is common, and scattered specimens of American holly, blackjack oak, Spanish oak, white oak, and willow oak are found. Highbush blueberry and sheep laurel form much of the shrub cover in this woodland, but also present are some scrub oak, dangleberry, inkberry, bayberry, and greenbrier. Herbs are not common except in moist depressions, where a few sedges, along with sphagnum mosses, can be found.

The existing woodland at the Stone Harbor Sanctuary in Cape May County is a lower-growing forest composed chiefly of red cedar, American holly, and black cherry trees. At Higbee Beach Wildlife Management Area, hackberry and mockernut hickory are major components of the forest. Unfortunately, few other dune woodlands remain in New Jersey. In 1910 Witmer Stone reported both red cedar and pitch pine woodlands with compositions similar to those at Island Beach today on a tract of land south of Atlantic City. At the time of his report Five-mile and Seven-mile beaches were thickly wooded, though he remarked that the forests were rapidly being leveled. From descriptions left to us, it appears that the former plant cover on these sites was also similar to that of Island Beach, except that an additional tree, the sweet bay magnolia, was present.

Human Influences on the Vegetation of the Sand Dunes

As early as 1910, John Harshberger, a botanist who studied natural vegetation in New Jersey, wrote:

> The development of the Atlantic sea coast from Maine to Virginia, and especially of the coastal lands of New Jersey, as places of summer resort has rendered a botanical survey of the shoreline an imperative necessity. With the rise of towns and cities and the building of railroads, the primitive condition of the sea beaches has been remarkably changed. Dunes have been leveled, marshes have been filled in, old drainage areas have been removed, new soil has been brought in to cover the sand formations to prevent their drifting, and these alterations have not failed to produce corresponding changes in the vegetation. New plants, weeds and the like, able, as well as the native plants, to withstand the saline conditions of air and soil, have been introduced with the coming of man as a permanent inhabitant; the old vegetation has been gradually removed, or, no longer able to grow under the altered conditions, has given place to the emigrants distributed by the aid of humans.

Dr. Harshberger's fears were well founded and at present only in state park and sanctuary areas is the full variety of dune vegetation well preserved. The Beach Heather and the Shrub Thicket communities, which grew best on sites suitable for development, are particularly uncommon today. It is now generally recognized that dunes are not just piles of sand; the buried network of living and dead parts of the dunegrass form a strengthening skeleton that can bind a dune together. In most shore communities sad experience has taught that the dunes should be protected from foot traffic. In many cases however, the area of dunes protected is a narrow strip, consisting only of the primary foredune, that has been planted with dunegrass and has few if any other species. Although this may serve in the short run to protect the developed areas behind the dune from the effects of wind and surf, it is little substitute for a complete dune system.

Summary

The natural vegetation of sand dunes is determined primarily by variations in soil moisture, salt spray, dune sand movement, and soil salinity. The ocean-facing primary dunes have the least soil moisture and the highest amount of salt spray and sand movement. Dunegrass lives successfully under these rigorous environmental conditions and while doing so serves to stabilize and to build up the accumulation of sand in the dunes. Beach Heather communities occupy more protected areas of the primary sand dune. Taller-growing shrub thickets and dune woodlands occur only in the more protected areas of the inland or secondary dunes. Human disturbance of the natural dune vegetation results in the removal of the natural protective barriers for coastal land.

References and Source Material

Chrysler, M. A. 1930. The Origin and Development of the Vegetation of Sandy Hook. *Bulletin of the Torrey Botanical Club* 57:163–176.

Harshberger, J. W. 1910. *An Ecological Study of the New Jersey Strand Flora.* Proceedings of the Academy of Natural Sciences, Philadelphia, Pa.

———. 1916. *The Vegetation of the New Jersey Pine Barrens.* Philadelphia, Pa.: Christopher Sower. Reprinted 1970 by Dover Publications, New York.

Martin, W. E. 1959. The Vegetation of Island Beach State Park, New Jersey. *Ecological Monographs* 29:1–46.

———. 1960. An Unspoiled Bit of Atlantic Coast. *Journal of the American Museum of Natural History* 69:8–19.

Small, J. A. The Vegetation of the Seacoast of New Jersey. *New Jersey Nature News* [New Jersey Audubon Society] 16:51–58.

Small, J. A., and W. E. Martin. 1958. A Partially Annotated Catalogue of Vascular Plants Reported from Island Beach State Park, New Jersey. *Bulletin of the Torrey Botanical Club* 85:368–377.

Stone, Witmer. 1910. The Plants of Southern New Jersey, with Especial Reference to the Flora of the Pine Barrens and the Geographic Distribution of the Species, in *Annual Report*, New Jersey State Museum, Trenton, N.J.

Part IV

The Future

Chapter 14

❦ New Jersey's Landscape of Tomorrow

Against almost overwhelming odds, New Jersey has retained a rich array of the natural habitats and plant communities described in the previous chapters. That such a small, densely populated, and heavily trafficked state has any natural vegetation at all probably comes as a surprise to those acquainted only with that part of New Jersey seen en route from New York to Philadelphia.

But what about the future? What will New Jersey's landscape be in 2050? How much of the present diversity of habitats and natural plant communities will remain? These and related questions are explored in this chapter.

New Jersey's Major Environmental Issues

Currently much is being said and written about the disastrous impact that continued environmental degradation will have on the human species—a subject that only a few decades ago received little public thought. It was in 1972 that a book entitled *Limits to Growth* brought international attention to the world's environmental crisis. Written by a group of scientists, educators, economists, humanists, industrialists, and public officials, the authors predicted a dire outcome for humankind given continuation of the then-current rates of population increase, industrial growth, use of nonrenewable resources, consumption of food, and environmental pollution—five interrelated factors. The predictions stirred up much controversy. Some of the assumptions used in the models were criticized, and so the authors revised the report. But the revision still supported the original's pessimistic outlook for the human species. *Limits to Growth* generated a stream of literature that attempted to predict the ultimate outcomes from present environmental trends; many reinforced the findings of the earlier work.

Concerned about the deterioration of the global environment, in 1992 the United Nations convened an international conference in Rio de Janeiro to discuss critical environmental problems and actions needed to solve them. Earth Summit, as the conference was called, was attended by more than one hundred leaders of nations and thousands of environmentalists. Although many were disappointed by the outcome, the conference did move the international community closer to agreement on global environmental issues.

We share with others the feeling of urgency about seeking solutions to global environmental problems but intentionally focus this discussion on issues that particularly concern the future of New Jersey's landscape and natural vegetation.

Population growth: How much and where?
Economic growth: How much and where?
Our polluting lifestyles: Will they change?
Land-use planning and regulation: Will they be improved?

Population Growth: How Much and Where?

Perhaps the least debated yet most destructive influence on New Jersey's natural landscape has come, and will come, from population growth. In 1991 the United Nations Population Fund again revised upward its projection for world population growth. It now estimates that the global population, which doubled in the last fifty years, will reach six billion before the turn of the century and will then double again in the coming 50 years. By 2025 the United Nations forecasts that there will be 8.5 billion people on earth, and this will increase to 10 billion individuals by 2050, about twice today's world's population.

Population growth rates vary by region and nation. Although the populations of the less developed nations are growing more rapidly than those of the more developed countries, even the United States in 1992 amended its forecasts in anticipation of greater than expected population growth. Now at 253 million, the U.S. Census Bureau predicts a population of 275 million in this country by the year 2000, and 383 million by the year 2050. This means that the number of individuals in the United States will increase by more than 50 percent in the 6 decades 1990 to 2050. Three factors—fertility rates, net immigration, and longevity—account for the upward revision in population forecasts.

New Jersey, already the most densely populated state, will share in the nation's future population growth. Projections made by the N.J. Department of Labor's Economic and Demographic Model forecast a state population of 8.5 million by the year 2000, almost 10 percent higher than the 1990 population. By the year 2030 it is expected that New Jersey will be home to more than 9.6 million people, which is about 23 percent more than the current population (Figure 14-1). By the year 2030 the population density, already the highest in the nation, will average 1,279 people per square mile.

According to the N.J. Department of Labor's forecasts, the trend of the last 2 decades, that of population dispersal to rural areas (described in Chapter 4), will continue in future years. Those counties projected to have the highest population growth rates from 1990 to 2030 are Atlantic

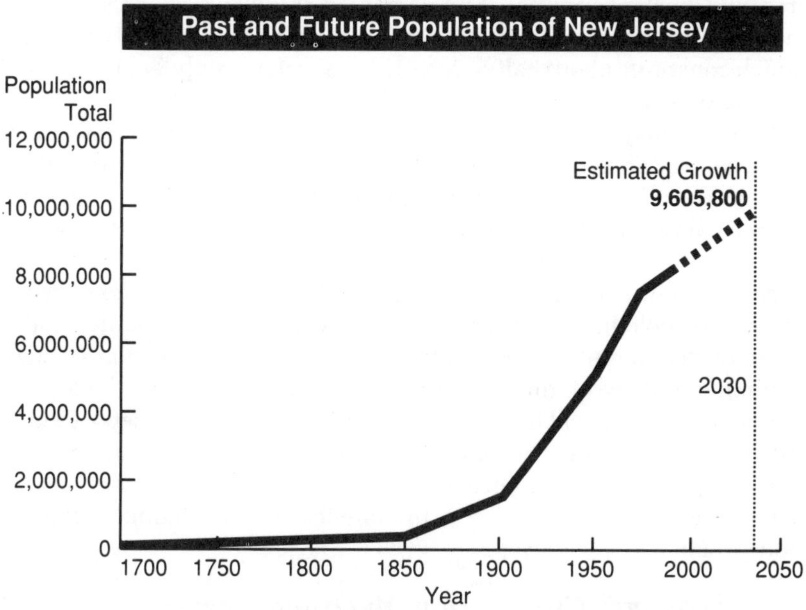

Past and Future Population of New Jersey

Figure 14-1. Official estimates of population growth project a figure of 9.6 million residents in New Jersey by the year 2030. This would mean about 23 percent more people in the state than in 1990. (SOURCE: N.J. State Planning Department.)

(63 percent), Ocean (55 percent), Sussex (42 percent), Hunterdon (42 percent), Cape May (40 percent) and Somerset (40 percent). In contrast, the older, urbanized counties are projected to have minimum growth in the next 40 years—Essex and Union are forecasted to have a growth rate of 2 percent, and Hudson, 4 percent.

Accommodating the projected population growth in New Jersey will require ever-more unexploited land for housing and infrastructure. Additional sprawling development into rural counties means more loss of open space—farmland and forested areas—and increased traffic congestion. The hopes are that effective implementation of the 1992 State Development and Redevelopment Plan, to be discussed later in this chapter, will contain the location and pattern of heretofore-uncontrolled population dispersal. Nevertheless, the basic issue still remains: How many more people (and automobiles) can the finite land, water, and other resources of the state support?

Already, some areas of the state are experiencing shortages in potable water. Cape May, for example, which is forecast to have a sizable population increase, is having problems with its water supply; salt water is intruding into the underground freshwater supplies because of excessive pumping to meet current demands. To supply the needs of other counties running out of water, demands are now being made to pump water from the Pinelands aquifer. If implemented, this would endanger its precious ecosystems. And the water resources in the New Jersey Highlands, which constitute about half of New Jersey's water supply, are threatened by development.

Unfortunately, there is no easy answer to the question of how many more people can fit on the planet Earth, or even in the 7,509 square miles that make up New Jersey, without causing irreversible damage to environmental resources upon which human life depends. Scientists do not know what the "optimum" limits of population are for humans, but experiments with some animal species have revealed that they experience severe psychological disturbances when forced to live together under overcrowded conditions. As an initial step and as a function of state planning, more work must be done on the impacts that the forecasted population growth will have on the environment of New Jersey—specifically on land and water resources, the atmosphere, and natural ecosystems. Only when this has been done can the citizens of the state together with public officials truly assess the implications of unlimited population growth.

Economic Growth: How Much and Where?

Economic growth is interwoven with population growth in several ways. Expansion of service and support industries is needed to accommodate increased numbers of people. Utilities must be expanded to meet additional demands for electricity, for example. There is also continuing pressure to create greater employment opportunities within the state, and economic growth is widely hailed as a virtue. State and local public officials as well as private business groups, particularly land developers, builders, and realtors, are continually trying to lure new industry and commerce to New Jersey, which in turn will attract new residents.

Past industrial growth has left New Jersey a legacy of environmental problems: rivers and streams polluted by industrial discharges, atmospheric contaminants from industrial emissions, and the dubious distinction of being first among states in the number of toxic waste "Superfund" sites, 109 in need of cleanup (Figure 14-2). According to the N.J. Department of Environmental Protection and Energy, more than 500,000 tons of soil have been contaminated with petroleum in just the past 5 years.

The years 1980 to 1990 saw an economic boom in New Jersey. It was a decade of unprecedented growth, and much of it took place in areas away from older industrial centers. Industry seeking less expensive land and relatively lower taxes located corporate office complexes and high-technology industries in more rural areas, particularly in the northern and central parts of the state. New interstate highways spawned huge amounts of speculative office building along their corridors. Even older Route 1 did not escape the development boom: in the 1980s more square footage of office space was built along 13 square miles of the Route 1 corridor in central New Jersey than existed in downtown Indianapolis, the thirteenth largest city in the country.

Because of the siting of new economic development in more rural areas, thousands of workers are required to commute by auto from suburb to suburb instead of traveling by public transport. This, accompanied by the increase in population, has created an enormous amount of traffic congestion across the state; and by 1990 the traffic was creating rush-hour nightmares in many areas.

As the nation moved into a recession in the early 1990s, New Jersey's economic boom collapsed. Many of the recently constructed office buildings were left vacant or only partially filled. The unemployment rate, which had dropped below 4 percent in 1986, began to climb. One reason for the increase is that New Jersey is amply endowed with banks, insurance companies, and other financial services that had expanded rapidly in the 1980s but retrenched even faster in the 1990s, shedding thousands of workers. A second reason is that the bases of manufacturing in the state, including chemical and pharmaceutical companies and auto plants, were badly hurt by the national recession. By April 1993 the unemployment rate in New Jersey reached 9.1 percent, the worst among the nation's largest industrial states.

As happens at times of recession, public officials and members of the private sector are now sounding the call to "create more jobs" and to "make New Jersey more competitive." They seek short-term relief from policies and regulations intended to protect the quality of the environment in the long term. Yet some economists question whether employment can return to the 1989 peak, believing that it represented a "bubble" economy, one of economic excesses. In addition, Stephen Meyer, a professor at the Massachusetts Institute of Technology, has reported that in the last 2 decades U.S. economic growth has not been stifled and jobs have not been sacrificed at the "altar of environmentalism . . . and that based on the evidence there is no reason to expect that loosening environmental standards will have any effect on the pace of economic growth"; furthermore, "if stringent environmental policies have negative economic effects, they are so marginal and transient that they are completely lost in the noise of much more powerful domestic and international economic influences."

The issue is to what extent must future economic growth be channeled in location and even restrained so as to ensure both a good life for every citizen and the preservation of a healthy environment. At the 1992 Earth Summit in Rio it was agreed that we should seek as national and global goals a "sustainable economy," defined as one that meets the needs and aspirations of the present without compromising the ability of future generations to meet their own needs; one that develops economies while protecting the environment and natural resources. After footdragging by

Figure 14-2. Pollution in New Jersey.

Air pollution in the Newark industrial area.

Water pollution in a stream on the Inner Coastal Plain. (Photo by the N.J. Department of Environmental Protection.)

Soil erosion on an agricultural field held for future development. (Photo by the U.S. Soil Conservation Service.)

the previous administration, President Clinton supported this goal in 1993. Time will tell if true sustainability, at any scale, can actually be attained.

Our Polluting Lifestyles: Will They Change?

New Jersey residents share with their fellow Americans an international stigma of being major despoilers of the environment because of their lifestyles. Statistics support the accusation: although the United States has less than 5 percent of the world's population, it uses nearly 30 percent of the world's energy and material resources, it emits 25 percent of the world's carbon dioxide (CO_2), and produces 20 percent of its waste. The deleterious impact of lifestyle on New Jersey's environment is illustrated in three areas: solid-waste accumulations, nonpoint source pollution, and atmospheric pollution.

Reducing Solid Waste In the small state of New Jersey, about 14 to 15 million tons of industrial and household garbage are generated each year. On a per capita basis, this may be no more than that of other states, but because of its high population and small land area, 20 percent of New Jersey's solid waste must be sent to other states for disposal. Another 45 percent is recycled, and the remaining 35 percent is landfilled or incinerated within the state. In 1982, the last year for which full data are available, about 450,000 tons of hazardous waste were produced in the state; and while solid and hazardous waste has been piling up above ground, contaminants have been seeping into the ground.

Future population and economic growth will generate more waste; at the same time, additional landfill space is in short supply and more states are refusing to accept New Jersey's waste products. For the protection of New Jersey's environment, changes in individual lifestyles are essential to waste source reduction and recycling.

Waste source reduction means selecting durable and reusable products that have the least amount of packaging and fewest toxic components in both the product and packaging materials. Plastics, which are made from petroleum in a manufacturing process that produces toxic wastes, create havoc in landfills, and despite claims are not yet biodegradable. Millions of birds and marine creatures die each year by ingesting or becoming entangled in plastic debris.

Residents of New Jersey must be willing to accept more responsibility for reducing their contributions to the waste stream and for increasing the amount of household waste materials—paper, cardboard, glass, plastic, aluminum, and batteries, for example—they recycle. A state goal is to raise by the end of 1995 the amount of recycled household waste to 50 percent from the present 20 percent. Finally, to avoid further pollution of our water, more care must be taken to remove hazardous household waste materials from the regular solid waste stream for handling by defined special disposal programs.

Reducing Nonpoint Source Pollution In recent years through federal and state legislation steady progress has been made in reducing industrial and municipal point source pollution, that is, waste and toxic substances that enter the environment through a well-identified source or location, by a pipe or ditch, for example. But the state's water quality is still being adversely affected by nonpoint source pollution (sometimes called "people pollution"). This type of pollution does not originate from a single, identifiable source as does point source pollution; instead, it comes from scattered or diffuse sources, the origins of which are often hard to determine. Examples of nonpoint source pollution are pollutants such as pesticides on lawns, fertilizers on croplands, and motor oil or pet wastes on streets that are washed every time it rains into local streams or rivers either directly or through storm drains and sewers that empty into the waterways.

A statewide evaluation made in 1987 found runoff from agriculture, roadways, and urban/suburban surfaces the most common forms of nonpoint source pollution in New Jersey. Other nonpoint sources are construction sites, from which silt is washed into storm water runoff, and defective septic systems.

To reduce the amount of residential nonsource point pollution, the N.J. Department of Environmental Protection and Energy suggests changes in behavioral patterns: avoid the overuse of pesticides and fertilizers, do not pour toxic household products down household or storm drains, do not discard motor oils or paint materials on the ground or down storm drains, and dispose of pet wastes in the garbage rather than litter the street. Some of us might find these instructions a nuisance to follow, but unless New Jerseyans are willing to change their habits, the quality of the state's waterways will continue to decline.

Reducing Atmospheric Pollution   Chapter 3 referred to the impacts of poor air quality on natural vegetation. Atmospheric pollutants can also be very harmful to humans. Exposure to excessive ground-level ozone is particularly dangerous for people who suffer from respiratory diseases such as asthma and emphysema, but even healthy people can suffer adverse affects when exposed to elevated levels of ozone. Carbon monoxide is especially harmful for people who suffer from cardiac problems. By the 1990s the air quality in New Jersey was the worst in the country except for that in the Southern California–Los Angeles area. Every county in the state failed to meet the federal ozone health standards set by the Clean Air Act of 1963 and its subsequent amendments (1970 and 1977); in eighteen of New Jersey's twenty-one counties the ozone levels were classified as severe.

The most painful change in lifestyles that faces the residents of New Jersey concerns their use of automobiles, because motor vehicles cause more than half the emissions that produce ground-level ozone in New Jersey and 90 percent of the carbon monoxide. They also generate other air pollutants, including 25 percent of the emissions of carbon dioxide, the primary greenhouse gas contributing to global warming. Each year the number of registered vehicles in the state has increased, and during the last 10 years total vehicle miles traveled have increased by 15 percent. Because of the recent sprawl of business development away from established urban and inner suburban centers where mass transit systems exist, the automobile rather than mass transit has become the prime means of getting to work (Figure 14-3). More than 70 percent of employed New Jerseyans now drive to work in a car in which the driver is the sole occupant. At the same time, the spread of residential development to more rural areas has increased household use of the automobile.

The federal Clean Air Act of 1990 was designed to put more teeth in the original legislation by setting dates by which states must comply with the federal health standards for air quality. To comply with these standards, technological improvements must be made in automobiles and gasoline to reduce emission pollutants. But much more is needed. Auto dependency must be reduced in New Jersey.

A 1991 Eagleton Poll at Rutgers revealed that although residents of New Jersey are concerned about the harmful effects of air pollution on the health of family members, they greatly underestimate how polluted the air in New Jersey and particularly in their area really is. They also do

Figure 14-3. Typical traffic congestion on New Jersey highways; the automobile is the major source of ozone pollution throughout the state. (Photo © 1993 by Bob Stovall.)

not understand the cause of harmful air pollution, wrongly blaming industry rather than their own automobile travel—the single biggest cause of ground-level ozone pollution.

To meet the federal clean air standards large businesses are now taking steps to reduce the number of single-occupancy vehicles operating during peak hours. The long-term key to improving air quality, however, is to direct future economic and residential growth in a manner that will decrease automobile dependency. Growth must be channeled toward urban and older suburban areas where mass transit already exists and in clusters along corridors where bus service can be effectively provided. This, of course, is also a fundamental key to protecting New Jersey's landscape and natural vegetation.

Land-Use Planning and Regulation: Will They Be Improved?

For most of its history, New Jersey has had a strong tradition of home rule. Divided into twenty-one counties, the state is further subdivided into 567 municipalities (or townships). Under the Municipal Land Use Law of 1975, each municipality retains the right to plan and zone its own land use. Legally, local master plans must give consideration to land uses in neighboring communities and to county guidelines. Practically, however, they often do not. Though the enactment of a state income tax in the late 1970s lightened the property tax burden, a high percentage of state, county, and local expenditures are still supported by local assessments on property. Eager to obtain more and more ratables, municipal officials are often quick to respond positively to pressure for development from large landowners and developers. But often the reality has been that expansion of municipal services, such as schools, to handle new development has required more funds than those obtained through the new ratables.

As long as New Jersey, and other states as well, appeared to have an inexhaustible amount of land, there was no overwhelming reason to replace or curtail local home rule or even to place restrictions on the rights of individuals to acquire and to develop land without consideration for the effects of land use on the public. The situation has changed. What worked for many years began to break down in the 1950s, when the post–World War II population expansion invaded New Jersey suburban areas. As population growth continued to explode in the next decades (Figure 14-1), local officials approved more and more office parks, residential developments, and shopping malls. Hundreds of thousands of farmland acres and other areas of open space were replaced by buildings and pavement; water and air quality deteriorated.

Uncoordinated local land-use decision making in New Jersey has had disastrous environmental consequences. For example, filling in a floodplain in one area has caused severe flooding in other areas, and developments sited on floodplains (as well as those on coastal sand dunes) have been damaged by storm waters; the use of septic tanks for the disposal of sewage for one residential development has endangered the water supplies of other areas; the dumping of pollutants into streams by one community has fouled the water supplies of other communities; and large developments approved by one municipality have caused traffic congestion in the wider surrounding region.

Starting in the 1960s there was growing realization that 567 political units acting independently are unable to cope effectively with environmental problems that transcend municipal boundaries. This was evident in the attempts of the fourteen municipalities to control individually the parts of the Hackensack Meadows lying within their borders and those of fifty-four other municipalities in South Jersey who share the precious Pine Barrens resources. The New Jersey legislature in 1968 created the Hackensack Meadowlands Development Commission and charged it with the responsibility to develop an integrated plan for the whole area. Powerful authority for comprehensive regional land-use planning and regulation was granted in 1979 to the Pinelands Commission, which was charged with overseeing and regulating almost 1 million acres in South Jersey. Less powerful was the regional authority given to regulate the use of coastal wetlands and shores under the 1973 Coastal Area Facility Review Act (CAFRA).

Despite the successes of these regional authorities and the pressing needs for coordinated local planning (elimination of traffic congestion, for one), New Jersey legislators, pressured by builders and real-estate interests, were reluctant for many years to create a strong state-planning activity. Finally, in January 1986, they passed the New Jersey State Planning Act, which established a planning process and a State Planning Commission to "conserve" its [New Jersey's] natural resources, revitalize its urban centers, protect the quality of its environment, and provide needed housing and adequate public services at a reasonable cost while promoting beneficial economic growth, development and renewal" (NJSA 52:18A–196, et seq.).

Surmounting intense pressure from groups who profit from the sprawl development that has characterized New Jersey, a growth-management plan, entitled the New Jersey State Development and Redevelopment Plan, was adopted on June 12, 1992. Although it is not as strong as environmentalists wanted, if effectively implemented, the plan will be a useful instrument in guiding the location of future growth in the state so as to minimize further sprawl development. It should also serve as a much-needed vehicle to coordinate municipal planning activities.

In addition to effective land-use planning at the state level, there is a need for implementing legislation to encourage more regional planning and management action in New Jersey, particularly to protect watersheds and natural resources that overlap municipal boundaries, such as the Great Swamp Wildlife Refuge, the Delaware estuary, and the New Jersey Highlands, an area of unusual scenic beauty and diversity and a source of drinking water for half the state's residents.

Finally, protection of our landscape and natural vegetation assumes the enactment of legislation, state and federal, to establish environmental standards and to regulate human actions so that these standards are not violated—for example, standards that control disposal of industrial and municipal effluents into waterways, toxic wastes in landfills, and incinerator wastes in the atmosphere. New Jersey has been among the leaders in protecting water, air, and land by regulatory legislation. It was the first state in the country to pass air pollution control legislation (1954), and since then it has developed a complex of laws and regulations protecting the state's resources, including recent legislation protecting freshwater wetlands.

Passage of environmental legislation, however, has always been hotly contested by development, real-estate, and related interests. Once enacted, opponents have nibbled away at regulatory agencies to weaken the regulations. Such is the case of the 1988 Freshwater Wetlands Act legislation; continued lobbying efforts by builders and real-estate interests diluted the original strength of the law. The lesson is that environmental organizations aided by volunteers must continually monitor the actions of state legislators and state agencies to ensure, first, passage of legislation that will protect the environment and, second, effective implementation of the enacted laws and agency regulations.

That this is also true on the national level was illustrated by the attempt of the Bush administration in 1991 to weaken the 1989 federal rules defining wetlands (Chapter 5) so that developers could more easily win approval for their projects. If this effort had been successful, protection for an estimated 30 million acres of wetlands in the nation would have been eliminated. New Jersey itself would have lost more than 50 percent of its wetland protection under the proposal, as state regulations are linked to the federal definition of wetlands.

The Future—a Biologically Impoverished Landscape?

How New Jerseyans face up to the four issues just discussed—population growth and dispersal, economic growth and dispersal, polluting lifestyles, and needs for improved land-use planning and regulation—will determine the state's future landscape. Continuing the current rates of environmental deterioration and sprawl development will result in a biologically impoverished landscape (Figure 14-4).

Biodiversity

The phrase "biologically impoverished" denotes a loss in the variety (or diversity) of living organisms. In ecological parlance, the word "biodiversity," short for "biological diversity," is used to describe the degree of variety of living organisms in a region, a landscape, an ecosystem, or a community type. High biodiversity indicates a large variety of organisms and a low diversity, a biologically impoverished system.

In measuring biodiversity, emphasis is usually on the number of species present, although the variety of organisms at all levels may be considered: the full array of families, genera, and species, including genetic variants belonging to the same species. Scientists feel that the loss of genetically distinct populations within species is as important as the loss of an entire species. Genetic diversity may add to a species' ability to adapt to changing environmental conditions and ultimately to survive.

Worldwide there is concern about the decline of global biodiversity; plant and animal species have been disappearing at an accelerated rate. Because the total number of living species is not known, no precise estimate can be made about the rate of extinction. But well-known biologist Edward O. Wilson suggests that a fifth or more of the present species of plants and animals could vanish or be doomed to early extinction by the year 2020 unless better efforts are made to save them. The bleak reality is that the assembly of life that took billions of years to evolve is now being destroyed by human actions.

The decline of biodiversity has been caused primarily by the destruction of natural habitats and the alteration of conditions in others: the pollution of waters, soils, and air; changes in hydrology and fire regimes; and introduction of exotic (non-native species) plants that outcompete native species. Also, the populations of some species have been over-exploited for human use.

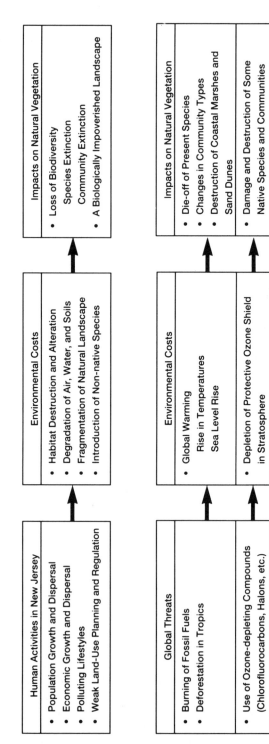

Threats to the Natural Vegetation of New Jersey

Human Activities in New Jersey
• Population Growth and Dispersal
• Economic Growth and Dispersal
• Polluting Lifestyles
• Weak Land-Use Planning and Regulation

Environmental Costs
• Habitat Destruction and Alteration
• Degradation of Air, Water, and Soils
• Fragmentation of Natural Landscape
• Introduction of Non-native Species

Impacts on Natural Vegetation
• Loss of Biodiversity
Species Extinction
Community Extinction
• A Biologically Impoverished Landscape

Global Threats
• Burning of Fossil Fuels
• Deforestation in Tropics
• Use of Ozone-depleting Compounds (Chlorofluorocarbons, Halons, etc.)

Environmental Costs
• Global Warming
Rise in Temperatures
Sea Level Rise
• Depletion of Protective Ozone Shield in Stratosphere

Impacts on Natural Vegetation
• Die-off of Present Species
• Changes in Community Types
• Destruction of Coastal Marshes and Sand Dunes
• Damage and Destruction of Some Native Species and Communities

Figure 14-4. Human activities within New Jersey and global actions that threaten the landscape and natural vegetation of the state.

A global treaty to reduce the loss in biodiversity particularly by defor-estation was introduced at the 1992 Earth Summit conference in Rio and finally signed by the United States in 1993. In 1993 the U.S. Interior Department also established a biological survey unit with responsibility to establish a nationwide biodiversity data bank and program to ensure better protection for the country's natural plant and animal species.

At the state level, in 1993 the Department of Natural Lands Manage-ment reported that thirty-four plant species had been lost in this century and estimated that 11 percent of New Jersey's native plant species were endangered, meaning that their survival is in jeopardy. Such plant spe-cies are officially classified under the state's 1989 Endangered Species List Act (NJSA 13:1B-15.151 et seq.). Three of these plants are found no where else in the world.

Fragmentation of New Jersey's Landscape

One legacy of the leapfrogging development across rural areas in recent decades is a fragmented landscape, one in which only patches (rem-nants) of natural vegetation remain as islands surrounded by develop-ment or agriculture (Figure 14-5). The microclimate of a remnant will be different from that of an undissected landscape: its solar radiation, wind exposure, and surface water pathways, for example. These changes can have important influences on the plants within the isolated island especially at or near the edges, between the remnant and the surround-ing area. Ecologists have found that usually there is a loss of native spe-cies in a fragmented landscape, patch vegetation being less diverse than the original whole. Smaller and more isolated remnants in particular are less able to maintain their biodiversity.

The extent of fragmentation in New Jersey's landscape can be ob-served when driving around the state or, even better, by flying over it. Aerial photography provided a group of Rutgers researchers with a means to compare the landscape of the Pinelands at two points in time. Between 1972 and 1988 the Pinelands landscape became more frag-mented; the number of forest patches increased and the size of the patches decreased dramatically. Looking at the evidence of fragmenta-tion in another way, David Moore, executive director of the New Jersey Conservation Foundation, observes that there is an increase in the par-celization of New Jersey's land, the process by which the landscape is subdivided into smaller and smaller pieces as it changes from a rural to suburban character. Statistics prepared by the U.S. Forest Service sup-port this: the average parcel of land in the Highlands region was 22 acres in 1972; by 1988 it had dropped to 12.8 acres.

The immediate local impacts of such fragmentation may be readily apparent in the extinction of a rare species or the disappearance of a particular vegetation type, but the total, long-term impact may not be quite so easy to see for some time. The complexity of ecosystem pro-cesses and the spatial and temporal heterogeneity of patterns of biologi-

Figure 14-5. Fragmentation of natural vegetation in New Jersey.

A patch of about 65 acres of fragmented forest near Mercerville, Mercer County. Forest is now surrounded on three sides by development and soon will be completely isolated by new development on the fourth side. (Photo by the N.J. Bureau of Forest Management.)

Forest along a ridge of the Watchung Mountains on the Piedmont is fragmented by houses. (Photo by the N.J. Bureau of Forest Management.)

Houses sited in the midst of the Pine Barrens in South Jersey are endangered by fires, a natural element of this ecosystem. (Photo by the N.J. Bureau of Forest Management.)

cal distribution often obscure single small changes. But in the aggregate, small changes can have dramatic effects on the continued viability of natural communities, particularly those that reflect the essential character of the New Jersey landscape.

The Value of Biodiversity

The benefits of protecting biodiversity have sometimes been clouded by controversy over protection on an endangered species, such as the spotted owl in the Pacific Northwest. Lost in the disputes is consideration of the benefits of protecting the habitat of the endangered species; in the owl's case, the old-growth forests that were in existence before European settlers came into the area represent a precious resource that future generations should be able to enjoy.

Certainly, the most pleasant landscape in which to live is one that encompasses a diversity of landforms and plant communities—marshes, swamps, and forests of different ages and composition. Natural diversity has even greater values than those of aesthetics, however. Through the years natural species of plants have been an invaluable source of medicines and food. Aspirin, the most widely used pharmaceutical in the world, was derived from an acid in a plant, and throughout the world a quarter of all medicinal prescriptions have as their origin chemical compounds from plants or microorganisms, or synthetic derivatives of those compounds. Mayapple (Figure 7-4), a common herb in North Jersey Mixed Oak forests, is the source of compounds used to treat certain types of cancer.

About 30,000 native plants have edible parts and 20 species provide 90 percent of the food consumed by humans. The value of protecting native species was illustrated in the 1970s, when a wild species of maize was found in Mexico. This species is resistant to disease and is unique in possessing perennial growth. By transferring its genes into domestic corn, food production can be increased enormously.

Ecologists are not yet completely clear about the relationship between diversity and stability in communities of plants and animals. They know however, that in growing agricultural crops, uniformity in plant culture can be unstable. Extensive areas of land covered with just one crop have been completely devastated either by a single species of insect or by one plant fungus disease. In areas of mixed plant growth, such as occurs in a natural forest, this normally does not happen. But it leaves open the question of if species composing a particular ecosystem start to go extinct, at what point will the ecosystem functioning be so disrupted that the functional interactions break down? As Edward Wilson suggests, it may be reckless to suppose that biodiversity can be diminished indefinitely without threatening the health of the biosphere and humanity itself.

Global Threats to New Jersey's Landscape

Of all human impacts on the earth's resources, global changes in the atmosphere, particularly greenhouse warming and depletion of upper-level ozone, could cause the most far-reaching transformation of our planet and, in particular, the landscape of New Jersey.

Global Warming

That the problem of global warming is real and imminent was reflected by President Clinton's promise in 1993 to reverse former President Bush's stand at the 1992 Earth Summit Conference by committing the United States to a specific timetable for curtailing the release of carbon dioxide and other greenhouse gases. He stated, "We must take the lead in addressing the challenges of global warming that could make our planet and its climate less hospitable and more hostile to human life."

A group of international scientists convened by the United Nations predicted that if humans continue to pour greenhouse gases (see Chapter 3) into the air at the present rate, the average surface temperature of the globe will rise by 3 to 8 degrees Fahrenheit sometime in the twenty-first century. But all agree that there is a long way to go before truly precise predictions can be made about the magnitude and rapidity of such changes.

Global warming as predicted could bring enormous change to New Jersey's landscape as well as to human society. The natural vegetation of the state could be substantially altered by the increasing temperatures, rising sea level, and changing patterns of precipitation and storms.

Trees and other plants in our natural communities respond individually to various ecological elements such as temperature, and different species have different dispersal abilities. In response to rises in temperature, for example, particular species of forest trees will migrate in different directions at different rates and at different times. For this reason, predicting the exact response of the community types now found in New Jersey to global warming is difficult. But based on the work done by scientists, several types of changes can be expected.

As the climate continues to warm, seedlings of particular tree species sensitive to temperature changes will disappear within a few decades, while more adult trees may last for four or five decades. As their temperature tolerance limits are exceeded, trees will also experience increased susceptibility to disease. Loss of trees in the canopy will affect the survival of understory plants that depend on the light, nutrient, and microclimate conditions produced by the canopy dominants. The migrating (dispersal) ability of some species may be too slow to adjust to so large and rapid a temperature rise, with the result that they will be much reduced in numbers or even become extinct. The composition of New Jersey's community types will be changed as individual species shift their ranges.

Ecologist Margaret Davis of the University of Minnesota studied in the laboratory the response of four tree species common in upland North Jersey forests to predicted levels of carbon dioxide and resulting global warming: hemlock, sugar maple, yellow birch, and beech, the latter also an important component of the South Jersey upland community. If temperatures rise as predicted, none of these species will survive in New Jersey. Rather, New Jersey's plant communities may in the future be more reflective of those new found in southeastern United States.

Global warming will cause rises in sea levels because of the melting of glacial ice, which will flow into the oceans. Predictions made for the Environmental Protection Agency suggest that sea levels along the middle Atlantic coast could rise in the next century by 2½ to 5 feet. This compares with a rise of about 16 inches in the last century along the New Jersey coast. The changes in sea levels will cause erosion of beaches and shifting of barrier islands toward the mainland. Salt water will move inland; some of the aquifers would become salty, as would the Delaware River, a source of drinking water for a large population. Finally, if the predicted sea-level changes take place, New Jersey would lose many of its coastal marshes, a very valuable habitat (Chapter 12). Without human interference the marshes normally would move inland as sea level rises. But existing development along the coastline would prevent most of the marshes from doing so because, unfortunately, the state has no legislation that prevents development on what should be tomorrow's marsh.

Changes in precipitation patterns will occur with global warming, particularly in the interior of continents. The global redistribution of water would subject some areas to flooding, and in others drought would devastate crops and natural vegetation. Forecasts thus far suggest that New Jersey may experience higher precipitation than at present.

Scientific studies also suggest that by pouring more energy into the climate system, global warming will cause more frequent and more destructive storms and weather extremes, such as prolonged heat waves, changes that would have impacts on the natural vegetation.

Depletion of Upper-Level Ozone

The harmful effects of excessive ozone at ground levels to vegetation as well as to humans are discussed in Chapter 3. In contrast to this "bad" ozone, a layer of "good" ozone about 18 to 30 miles above earth in the stratosphere envelops the globe and acts as a protective shield against ultraviolet radiation from the sun.

In 1974 two scientists from the University of California warned that a new group of organic compounds, called chlorofluorocarbons (CFCs), could damage the protective ozone shield in the stratosphere. Molecules from CFC compounds rise to the stratosphere and decompose, releasing chlorine atoms. The chlorine molecules catalyze a reaction with ozone molecules, converting them to oxygen molecules, which do not shield out ultraviolet radiation. The warning from the scientists was ignored, and even ridiculed, until 1985, when a British Antartica Survey team discovered evidence that a hole was appearing each winter in the ozone layer over Antarctica, a finding that was reinforced by other scientists. In 1988 the National Aeronautics and Space Administration reported that the ozone layer over the entire globe was eroding through unevenly.

The news about ozone depletion shocked industrial and national leaders. Ultraviolet radiation causes skin cancers and cataracts in humans, and it can be more broadly injurious to plants and to certain animals. In the case of plants, radiation inhibits their ability to carry out photosynthesis, reduces leaf size and water-use efficiency, and adversely affects plant growth generally. Very significant could be radiation's impact on marine ecosystems: phytoplankton, the tiny surface ocean plants that play a crucial role in the global food chain (all animals depend upon them directly or indirectly), could be killed by relatively small increases in radiation.

In 1987, a landmark international agreement, the Montreal Protocol on Substances That Deplete the Ozone Layer, called for a stepped phase-out of CFCs, which had been used as propellants for aerosol sprays and cleaning agents and in the manufacture of a host of common products from refrigerators and air conditioners to foam mattresses. As news about the rate of ozone depletion worsened, the Montreal Protocol was amended in 1990 and 1992 to hasten the phaseout of CFCs and other substances such as the halons. The United States and other countries also took more stringent individual actions to ban the harmful chemical compounds.

By April 1993 scientists reported that in the first 3 months of the year amount of upper-level ozone had plummeted to new lows, down 10 to 20 percent from the normal ranges in the heavily populated middle latitudes of the Northern Hemisphere, including the United States and Europe. In hindsight, we must decry the fact that the 1974 warning from the scientists was unheeded and that more than 10 years passed before actions were taken to stop the causes of ozone depletion.

A Pressing Need: Securing More Open Space

The need to take action to protect land as open space is particularly critical in New Jersey because of the limited amount of land relative to the state's present and projected future population. Since 1970 half of New Jersey's farmland and hundreds of thousands acres of forests and other open space have been claimed by development. Still, remaining unspoiled areas encompassing diverse scenic, biological, and water resources are threatened. Though the recession of the early 1990s slowed residential and office construction, land investment for future development continued.

From 1961 to 1992 voters of the state approved eight Green Acres bond issues totaling over $1 billion for acquisition and protection of open space, including environmentally sensitive lands, farmland, and historic and cultural sites. But in 1993 the New Jersey Green Acres Department reported that there was still not enough open land to provide adequate recreational opportunities for present and future populations. By applying so-called balanced guidelines that delineate open-space needs on municipal, county, state, and federal levels, it was estimated that an additional 272,000 acres should be dedicated as open space.

But providing recreational opportunities and a pleasant landscape in which to live represents only part of the worth of open space. Many tangible physical values accrue from the protection of the habitats and vegetation types described in earlier chapters. The plants making up the vegetation of New Jersey, like those elsewhere in the world, perform three essential, priceless, and exclusive functions without which humans could not exist: they absorb carbon dioxide (CO_2) from the atmosphere; they convert nonliving material to food; and, as a byproduct of this activity, they release oxygen to the earth's atmosphere. A forest ecosystem plays a particularly important role in absorption of atmospheric CO_2, the key greenhouse gas. New Jersey's natural forest cover on the uplands and slopes also prevents land erosion and loss of soil nutrients, increases the rate at which rainwater infiltrates into the ground, and serves as a habitat to a variety of wildlife: birds, mammals, and other organisms. As a protective windbreak, a wooded area can reduce wind velocity by 20 to 60 percent and cause cooling of air to temperatures significantly lower than those in open areas. Trees and lower-growing shrubs reduce noise pollution by acting as barriers to sound. It is estimated that each 100-foot width of woodland vegetation can absorb about 6 to 8 decibels of sound intensity, giving nearby residents much-needed relief from highway noise.

The value of wetlands has gained widespread attention in recent decades. Coastal and inland marshes provide feeding, spawning, and nursery grounds and shelter for a variety of fish, birds, and other animals. The names for Great Egg and Little Egg harbors were derived from the fact that each year thousands of waterfowl used to nest along the shores. Much of this habitat has been destroyed.

Areas of wetlands are important as protection against flooding and erosion of higher land. Coastal marshes protect the landward bay areas against high tides and damage from storm waves and act as water storage facilities to absorb incoming floodwaters. A rise of only inches in an area as small as 10 acres means more than a million gallons of water, which a marshland can store, preventing damaging flooding.

In the same way, if left undeveloped, inland wetlands, such as floodplain forests bordering rivers and streams, serve as protection against flood damage from swollen rivers (Figure 14-6). Floods tend to occur in inland New Jersey in spring, when the rapid melting of snow accumulations in the northern part of the state adds abnormally large volumes of water to upland river sources. At other times of the year, very heavy and concentrated rainfall may add more water to rivers than the stream basins can contain. Natural floodplains absorb floodwaters that overflow river banks and, by so doing, help protect adjacent and downstream property from floodwaters. In places where the floodplains have been cleared, filled in, and developed, such as in the Passaic River Basin, the floodwaters are more likely to overrun downstream and settled areas, causing extensive property damage. The risks of denying rivers their floodplains was well illustrated to the nation by the destruction caused by the 1993 flooding of the Mississippi River.

In addition to acting as a mechanism for flood control, wetland areas also serve as a source for the replenishment of groundwater supplies. Although some of the water that floods wetlands is lost to the air either by evaporation or by plant transpiration, a sizable amount often sinks into the ground and becomes part of the underground water supply. Where water is in short supply, as in New Jersey, the maintenance of large reservoirs of groundwater is extremely critical. Wetlands also have a certain self-cleaning ability and improve water quality by removing and retaining chemical and organic wastes and nutrients, such as nitro-

Figure 14-6. The floodplain of the Millstone River on April 6, 1967, when torrential rains caused the water to overflow its banks. This has happened many times since, and if this floodplain had been developed, the flooding would have caused severe property damage.

gen and phosphorous—the components of fertilizers—and by reducing sediment loads.

The 1992 State Development and Redevelopment Plan contains detailed guidelines (Policies) to aid municipal, county, and state officials in designating within each Planning Area those environmentally sensitive habitats and sites that should be protected from development. In addition, one of the five land-use Planning Areas, the Environmentally Sensitive Planning Area, provides special protection for large, contiguous land areas with valuable ecosystems and wildlife habitats. The State Planning Commission also identifies the need to coordinate its efforts with planning work in "Areas of Critical State Concern" already having statutory protection (the Hackensack Meadowlands, Pinelands, and CAFRA coastal area) and further suggests that additional areas of critical state concern, examples given, be included in subsequent plan revisions.

The priorities assigned by the state plan to protection of critical natural resources reflect the conservation priorities of the state's leading environmental organizations. In 1993 the Regional Plan Association echoed the same priorities in proposing a system of protected open space in the tristate area. In all, the first emphasis is on the need to protect in the form of regional reserves the few remaining large rural areas that encompass valuable scenic, ecological, and watershed resources and that are now threatened by development; in New Jersey such areas include the Highlands, Delaware River valley and bayshore, and Pinelands (which needs to complete its acquisition program).

A second priority is to conserve greenways, undeveloped corridors that provide links between larger tracts of public land. These connecting links may be along streams and rivers or even run through urban areas; if wide enough, greenways serve as migratory corridors, permitting species to change geographic distributions, thereby offsetting in part impacts of fragmentation. Examples of New Jersey greenways are the Delaware and Raritan Canal Greenway and the Arthur Kill Greenway.

Other conservation priorities include protection of migratory bird corridors, areas that have been well documented by the New Jersey Audubon Society; addition of buffer land to protect existing critical sites such as the Great Swamp Refuge; and protection of critical environmental sites such as undisturbed high-quality scenic areas, wildlife habitats, habitats for rare community types or species, headwaters, and aquifer recharge areas.

Tomorrow—Bleak or Bright?

The symptoms of environmental stress are widespread and growing. Some scientists paint a grim picture of the future destiny for Planet Earth and the human species, though others, quite optimistic about the future, have confidence that the environmental challenges can be met by the application of new technology. Between these extremes, many believe that environmental catastrophe can still be avoided if we make fundamental changes in lifestyles and synthesize our economic and environmental goals and policies. Whether enough people will make the needed changes in time remains to be seen.

It is easier to have hope for New Jersey. The 1992 State Development and Redevelopment Plan combined with the 1990 federal amendments to the Clean Air Act provides a framework for channeling growth and development so as to be more compatible with the protection of valuable natural resources. More is needed, however. The citizens of New Jersey must share a consensus that the goals and policies of the state plan be implemented to ensure a safe and pleasant environment for future generations. Then municipal and county officials and state agencies must be prodded and monitored to ensure that their land-use and infrastructure-planning activities are in accordance with the plan.

Finally, ours is a small state; bonded by a common interest of making New Jersey a better place to live and work, is it not possible to forge a better working partnership of environmental organizations, industry including development interests, and government officials? By agreeing on areas that should be conserved and those that have prime development value, such a consortium could be a powerful influence in shaping a healthier and more pleasing landscape for New Jersey.

References and Source Material

Botkin, Daniel B., et al., ed. 1989. *Changing the Global Environment: Perspectives on Human Involvement.* San Diego, Calif.: Academic Press.

Brown, L. R., ed. 1993. *The State of the World, 1993.* New York: Norton.

Davis, Margaret B., and Catherine Zabinski. 1992. Changes in Geographical Range Resulting from Greenhouse Warming Effects on Biodiversity in Forests. In *Global Warming and Biological Diversity,* 297–308. New Haven, Conn.: Yale University Press.

Kareiva, Peter, Joel G. Kingsolver, and Raymond B. Huey, eds. 1993. *Biotic Interactions and Global Change.* Sunderland, Mass.: Sinauer Associates.

Meadows, D. H., et al. 1972. *the Limits to Growth.* New York: Universe Books.

Meyer, Stephen M. 1992 and 1993. *Environmentalism and Economic Prosperity.* Report and update. Massachusetts Institute of Technology, Department of Political Science, Cambridge, Mass.

Meyerson, Lee A., ed. 1986. The Effect of Sea Level Rise on the Middle Atlantic Coast. *Bulletin of the New Jersey Academy of Science* 31:2.

New Jersey State Planning Commission. 1992. *Communities of Place: The New Jersey State Development and Redevelopment Plan.* Trenton, N.J.: Office of State Planning.

Peters, Robert L., and Thomas E. Lovejoy. 1992. *Global Warming and Biological Diversity.* New Haven, Conn.: Yale University Press.

Stokes, R. S., et al. 1989. *The Common Wealth of New Jersey: Outdoor Recreation Resources Plan Summary.* Trenton, N.J.: New Jersey Department of Environmental Protection.

United Nations Population Fund. 1991. *The State of World Population, 1991.* New York: UNFPA.

Wilson, Edward O. 1992. *The Diversity of Life.* Cambridge, Mass.: Harvard University Press, Belknap.

Wilson, Edward O., and Frances Peter, ed. 1988. *Biodiversity.* Washington, D.C.: National Academy Press.

Appendix I

Locations at Which Particular Vegetation Types Can Be Seen

The following is a tabulation of a few locations, many of them not already noted in the text, at which good examples of particular vegetation types can be found. Most of these are state or county parks, national wildlife refuges (NWRs), or wildlife management areas (WMAs), which are readily located on maps and are accessible to the public. For many of them, maps, trail guides, and other interpretive materials to enhance a visit are available.

A complete list of all the locations in New Jersey at which native vegetation could be seen would be endless. Some widespread habitats, such as salt marshes, Pine Barrens, or Mixed-Oak forests, can be seen at almost any undeveloped site, public or private, in those parts of the state in which they occur.

References

Brown, Michael P. 1992. *New Jersey Parks, Forests, and Natural Areas: A Guide.* New Brunswick, N.J.: Rutgers University Press.

N.J. Department of Environmental Protection and Energy. 1992. *Guide to New Jersey's Wildlife Management Areas.* Trenton: N.J. Department of Environmental Protection and Energy.

	Greenbrook Sanctuary, Bergen County	Campgaw Mountain County Reservation, Bergen County	Mahlon Dickerson Reservation, Morris County	Norvin Green State Forest, Passaic County	Abram S. Hewitt State Forest, Passaic County	Wawayanda State Park, Sussex & Passaic Counties	Worthington State Forest, Warren County	Delaware Water Gap NRA, Warren & Sussex Counties	Voorhees State Park, Hunterdon County	High Point State Park, Sussex County
Ch. 6 Chestnut Oak forest	•		•	•	•	•		•	•	•
Ch. 6 Pitch Pine–Scrub Oak forest					•	•		•		•
Ch. 6 Plant succession on rock			•		•	•				•
Ch. 7 North Jersey Mixed Oak forest	•	•	•	•	•	•	•	•	•	•
Ch. 7 Sugar Maple–Mixed Hardwood forest				•		•	•	•		•
Ch. 7 Hemlock–Mixed Hardwood forest	•				•	•		•		•
Ch. 8 North Jersey freshwater marshes						•				•
Ch. 8 North Jersey swamps and floodplains										
Ch. 8 North Jersey bogs and fens						•		•		•
Ch. 9 South Jersey freshwater marshes										
Ch. 9 South Jersey Cedar Swamp										
Ch. 9 South Jersey Hardwood Swamp										
Ch. 9 Pitch Pine Lowland										
Ch. 9 South Jersey fens										
Ch. 10 Pine-dominated forest										
Ch. 10 Oak-dominated forest										
Ch. 10 Pine Plains community										
Ch. 11 South Jersey Mixed Oak forest										
Ch. 11 South Jersey Beech–Oak forest										
Ch. 11 Virginia Pine forest										
Ch. 11 Sweet Gum forest										
Ch. 12 Salt marsh										
Ch. 13 Dunegrass community										
Ch. 13 Beach Heather community										
Ch. 13 Shrub Thicket										
Ch. 13 Dune Woodland										

	Stokes State Forest, Sussex County	Merrill Creek Reservoir, Warren County	Watchung Reservation, Union County	De Korte State Park, Bergen County	Great Swamp NWR, Morris County	Black River WMA, Morris County	Lord Stirling Envir. Center, Somerset County	Morris County Outdoor Educ. Ctr., Morris County	Whittingham WMA, Sussex County	Johnson Park, Middlesex County
Ch. 6 Chestnut Oak forest	•	•								
Ch. 6 Pitch Pine–Scrub Oak forest	•									
Ch. 6 Plant succession on rock	•									
Ch. 7 North Jersey Mixed Oak forest	•	•	•			•			•	
Ch. 7 Sugar Maple–Mixed Hardwood forest	•	•							•	
Ch. 7 Hemlock–Mixed Hardwood forest	•		•						•	
Ch. 8 North Jersey freshwater marshes				•	•	•			•	
Ch. 8 North Jersey swamps and floodplains					•		•	•		•
Ch. 8 North Jersey bogs and fens										
Ch. 9 South Jersey freshwater marshes										
Ch. 9 South Jersey Cedar Swamp										
Ch. 9 South Jersey Hardwood Swamp										
Ch. 9 Pitch Pine Lowland										
Ch. 9 South Jersey fens										
Ch. 10 Pine-dominated forest										
Ch. 10 Oak-dominated forest										
Ch. 10 Pine Plains community										
Ch. 11 South Jersey Mixed Oak forest										
Ch. 11 South Jersey Beech–Oak forest										
Ch. 11 Virginia Pine forest										
Ch. 11 Sweet Gum forest										
Ch. 12 Salt marsh										
Ch. 13 Dunegrass community										
Ch. 13 Beach Heather community										
Ch. 13 Shrub Thicket										
Ch. 13 Dune Woodland										

	Belleplain State Forest, Cape May County	Assunpink WMA, Monmouth County	Glassboro WMA, Gloucester County	Medford WMA, Burlington County	Dennis Creek WMA, Cape May County	Great Bay WMA, Ocean County	Brigantine NWR, Atlantic County	Sandy Hook State Park, Monmouth County	Island Beach State Park, Ocean County	Higbee Beach WMA, Cape May County
Ch. 6 Chestnut Oak forest										
Ch. 6 Pitch Pine–Scrub Oak forest										
Ch. 6 Plant succession on rock										
Ch. 7 North Jersey Mixed Oak forest										
Ch. 7 Sugar Maple–Mixed Hardwood forest										
Ch. 7 Hemlock–Mixed Hardwood forest										
Ch. 8 North Jersey freshwater marshes										
Ch. 8 North Jersey swamps and floodplains										
Ch. 8 North Jersey bogs and fens										
Ch. 9 South Jersey freshwater marshes							•			
Ch. 9 South Jersey Cedar Swamp	•		•				•			
Ch. 9 South Jersey Hardwood Swamp	•	•	•	•			•			
Ch. 9 Pitch Pine Lowland										
Ch. 9 South Jersey fens										
Ch. 10 Pine-dominated forest										
Ch. 10 Oak-dominated forest										
Ch. 10 Pine Plains community										
Ch. 11 South Jersey Mixed Oak forest	•	•	•	•			•			
Ch. 11 South Jersey Beech–Oak forest		•								
Ch. 11 Virginia Pine forest	•									
Ch. 11 Sweet Gum forest		•	•	•						
Ch. 12 Salt marsh					•	•	•			
Ch. 13 Dunegrass community								•	•	
Ch. 13 Beach Heather community								•	•	•
Ch. 13 Shrub Thicket								•	•	•
Ch. 13 Dune Woodland								•	•	•

Appendix II

References for Plant Identification

Trees

Brockman, C. Frank. 1986. *Trees of North America.* Racine, Wis.: Western Publishing. 280 pages.

A handy reference to over 600 species of native and naturalized trees of all of North America. The book is well illustrated with color paintings of leaves, twigs, and fruit, with range maps and brief descriptions on the pages facing the illustrations. The arrangement of species is by family.

Little, Elbert. 1980. *The Audubon Society Field Guide to North American Trees.* New York: Knopf. 714 pages.

This book identifies 364 native and naturalized trees of eastern North America, north of subtropical Florida. It is illustrated with photographs of leaves and bark for all species, with additional photographs of flowers, fruit, and autumn foliage for some species. The arrangement of the illustrations is by leaf shape; the arrangement of the text is by family.

Petrides, George A. 1988. *A Field Guide to Eastern Trees.* Boston, Mass.: Houghton Mifflin. 272 pages.

This field guide identifies 455 species of native or naturalized trees of eastern North America, including southern Florida. It is illustrated with paintings of leaves, fruit, and twigs. The text includes fine points of identification, uses of wood, range maps, and descriptions of habitat and growth. The arrangement of species is by leaf shape and branching pattern.

Trees and Shrubs

Harlow, William M. 1959. *Fruit Key and Twig Key to Trees and Shrubs.* New York: Dover. 56 pages.

This is a handy guide for the winter identification of woody plants. It provides keys and descriptions for both fruit and twig features of the common woody plants of eastern North America. It is illustrated with black-and-white photos.

Petrides, George A. 1958. *A Field Guide to Trees and Shrubs.* Boston, Mass.: Houghton Mifflin. 431 pages.

If a plant has a woody stem and is native or naturalized in northeastern or north central North America, it is likely to be in this book, which includes

645 species of trees, shrubs, and woody vines. It is illustrated with line drawings. The text includes fine points of identification, uses of wood, range maps, and descriptions of habitat and growth.

Wildflowers

Newcomb, Lawrence. 1977. *Newcomb's Wildflower Guide.* Boston, Mass.: Little, Brown. 490 pages.

This field guide identifies almost 1,400 species of flowering herbs, shrubs, and vines of northeastern North America. It is illustrated with line drawings, some of them in color. The arrangement of species within the book is by flower and plant structure, and leaf shape, which, incidentally, makes it possible to identify some plants that are not in bloom.

Peterson, Roger Tory, and Margaret McKenny. 1968. *A Field Guide to Wild Flowers.* Boston, Mass.: Houghton Mifflin. 420 pages.

This book identifies 1,293 species of herbs and a few flowering shrubs and vines that grow in northeastern North America. The plant descriptions, though very brief, include ranges, habitat, approximate flowering period, and some identification tips. The book is illustrated with line drawings and a few color paintings. The arrangement of species is by flower color.

Ferns

Cobb, Boughton. 1956. *Field Guide to the Ferns.* Boston, Mass.: Houghton Mifflin. 281 pages.

This book identifies all the ferns and "fern allies" of the northeastern United States. It is illustrated with line drawings.

Montgomery, James, and David Fairbrothers. 1992. *New Jersey Ferns and Fern-allies.* New Brunswick, N.J.: Rutgers University Press. 293 pages.

This up-to-date work includes keys, descriptions, and maps showing the distribution of all New Jersey pteridophytes, including hybrids. It is illustrated with line drawings.

Grasses

Brown, Lauren. 1979. *Grasses: An Identification Guide.* Boston, Mass.: Houghton Mifflin. 240 pages.

A nontechnical guide to 135 common grasses and grasslike plants of the northeastern United States. Identification is by overall structure, shape, and size of the plants rather than by details of flower structure. The book is illustrated with line drawings.

Hitchcock, A. S. 1935. *Manual of the Grasses of the United States.* Washington, D.C.: U.S. Government Printing Office. 1,051 pages.

This is the classic text for identification of grasses; though somewhat dated and quite technical it is still useful. It provides a complete description and illustration of all the grasses growing naturally throughout the United States.

Mosses, Lichens, Fungi

Conard, Henry S. 1979. *How to Know the Mosses and Liverworts,* 2d ed. Dubuque, Iowa: Wm. C. Brown. 302 pages.

This book provides a good introduction to the study of mosses and liverworts. It includes a description of the life cycle and structure of these plants, and keys—often using microscopic characters—for their identification. It is illustrated with small line drawings.

Hale, Mason E. 1979. *How to Know the Lichens,* 2d ed. Dubuque, Iowa: Wm. C. Brown. 246 pages.

A good introduction to the study of lichens. This book includes a description of the life cycle and structure of these organisms, and keys for the identification of most of the common foliose and fruticose lichens of North America.

Lincoff, Gary. 1981. *The Audubon Society Field Guide to North American Mushrooms.* New York: Knopf. 926 pages.

This book identifies over 800 species of mushrooms and other fungi of North America. It is illustrated with color photographs of 703 species. The text includes information about ranges, habitat, and fine points of identification.

Other References

Fernald, Merritt L. 1950. *Gray's Manual of Botany,* 8th Ed. New York: Van Nostrand. 1,632 pages.

The standard technical manual for the identification of all the vascular plants of the northeastern United States and adjacent Canada, this book covers over 8,000 species, varieties, and forms of native and introduced plants. It is sparingly illustrated with small line drawings. Although somewhat out of date, this book remains useful for its detailed coverage.

Gleason, Henry A., and Arthur Cronquist. 1991. *Manual of Vascular Plants of Northeastern United States and Adjacent Canada,* 2d ed. New York: New York Botanical Garden. 910 pages.

This is the most recent technical manual covering our area, and it has incorporated many taxonomic changes made in the last 30 years. The text is somewhat abbreviated, and there are no illustrations. The area dealt with is the same as that of *Gray's Manual.*

Appendix III

Plant Names

Appendix III contains a cross reference between the common names of all the plants mentioned in the text and their scientific names. Part A lists the common names in alphabetical order, and then gives the scientific name for each. Part B lists the scientific names in alphabetical order, and then gives the common name. The purpose of this appendix is to facilitate reference to these plants in technical manuals, and to make comparisons possible between this book and other books, which may use different common names.

Simply described, a plant species is a particular type of plant that maintains its identity because it generally does not interbreed with other plant species. The scientific name for a plant consists of two latinized words, the first classifying a plant by its genus category (like the surname of a person) and the second identifying each specific type of plant within a genus by its species name (like the first name of a person). All known plants have a scientific name.

Many plants do not have a generally accepted common name in English, so botanists usually use the scientific names when referring to plant species. For the sake of consistency in compiling plant checklists and popular field guides, however, artificial names have often been constructed for these plants. Many such artificial names are more or less free translations of the scientific name, such as "Pennsylvania sedge" for *Carex pensylvanica*. On the other hand, some widely distributed plants are known by more than one common name. For example, jewelweed, *Impatiens capensis*, is also called spotted touch-me-not and spotted snapweed. The common names of plants used in this book have been taken from a variety of sources, but only one common name is used throughout for any one species.

In some cases, a widely used English name is not specific and can refer to a number of species within a particular genus. For example, the common name "hickory" refers to half a dozen trees in the genus *Carya*. Wherever a common name used in this book does refer to more than one species, the corresponding scientific name is listed as the genus name followed by the abbreviation "spp.," indicating that several species exist within that genus.

At any given time, there is only one acceptable scientific name, worldwide, for any particular plant species. Plant taxonomy is an ongoing science, however, and botanists do not always agree on the scientific names of plants, which are subject to change. The scientific names used in the following list conform to the nomenclature given in Gleason and Cronquist's *Manual of Vascular Plants* (1991).

Part A: Plant Common Names to Scientific Names

Common name	Genus and species name
Coniferous Trees	
American larch	*Larix laricina*
Atlantic white cedar	*Chamaecyparis thyoides*
Black spruce	*Picea mariana*
Eastern hemlock	*Tsuga canadensis*
Loblolly pine	*Pinus taeda*
Pitch pine	*Pinus rigida*
Red cedar	*Juniperus virginiana*
Shortleaf pine	*Pinus echinata*
Virginia pine	*Pinus virginiana*
White pine	*Pinus strobus*
Deciduous trees	
Ailanthus	*Ailanthus altissima*
American beech	*Fagus grandifolia*
American chestnut	*Castanea dentata*
American elm	*Ulmus americana*
American holly	*Ilex opaca*
American mountain ash	*Sorbus americana*
Balsam poplar	*Populus balsamifera*
Basket oak	*Quercus michauxii*
Basswood	*Tilia americana*
Big-toothed aspen	*Populus grandidentata*
Black birch	*Betula lenta*
Black cherry	*Prunus serotina*
Blackjack oak	*Quercus marilandica*
Black locust	*Robinia pseudoacacia*
Black oak	*Quercus velutina*
Black walnut	*Juglans nigra*
Black willow	*Salix nigra*
Box elder	*Acer negundo*
Chestnut oak	*Quercus prinus*
Downy juneberry	*Amelanchier arborea*
Flowering dogwood	*Cornus florida*
Gray birch	*Betula populifolia*
Hackberry	*Celtis occidentalis*
Hawthorn	*Crataegus* spp.
Honey locust	*Gleditsia triacanthos*
Hop hornbeam	*Ostrya virginiana*
Ironwood	*Carpinus caroliniana*

Part A: Plant Common Names to Scientific Names

Common name	Genus and species name
Mockernut hickory	*Carya tomentosa*
Norway maple	*Acer platanoides*
Paper birch	*Betula papyrifera*
Persimmon	*Diospyros virginiana*
Pignut hickory	*Carya glabra*
Pin oak	*Quercus palustris*
Post oak	*Quercus stellata*
Red maple	*Acer rubrum*
Red oak	*Quercus rubra*
River birch	*Betula nigra*
Sand hickory	*Carya pallida*
Sassafras	*Sassafras albidum*
Scarlet oak	*Quercus coccinea*
Shadbush	*Amelanchier canadensis*
Shagbark hickory	*Carya ovata*
Silver maple	*Acer saccharinum*
Smooth juneberry	*Amelanchier laevis*
Sour gum	*Nyssa sylvatica*
Spanish oak	*Quercus falcata*
Striped maple	*Acer pensylvanicum*
Sugar maple	*Acer saccharum*
Swamp white oak	*Quercus bicolor*
Sweet bay magnolia	*Magnolia virginiana*
Sweet cherry	*Prunus avium*
Sweet gum	*Liquidambar styraciflua*
Sweet pignut hickory	*Carya ovalis*
Sycamore	*Platanus occidentalis*
Trembling aspen	*Populus tremuloides*
Tulip tree	*Liriodendron tulipifera*
Water oak	*Quercus nigra*
White ash	*Fraxinus americana*
White mulberry	*Morus alba*
White oak	*Quercus alba*
Willow	*Salix* spp.
Willow oak	*Quercus phellos*
Yellow birch	*Betula alleghaniensis*

Part A: Plant Common Names to Scientific Names

Common name	Genus and species name
Shrubs	
Alder	*Alnus* spp.
American hazel	*Corylus americana*
American strawberry-bush	*Euonymus americanus*
Arrowwood	*Viburnum dentatum*
Bayberry	*Myrica pensylvanica*
Beach plum	*Prunus maritima*
Beaked hazel	*Corylus cornuta*
Bearberry	*Arctostaphylos uva-ursi*
Blackberry	*Rubus* spp.
Black chokeberry	*Aronia melanocarpa*
Black haw	*Viburnum prunifolium*
Black huckleberry	*Gaylussacia baccata*
Blueberry	*Vaccinium* spp.
Bog laurel	*Kalmia polifolia*
Bog rosemary	*Andromeda glaucophylla*
Broom crowberry	*Corema conradii*
Bush honeysuckle	*Diervilla lonicera*
Buttonbush	*Cephalanthus occidentalis*
Common elder	*Sambucus canadensis*
Coralberry	*Symphoricarpos orbiculatus*
Dangleberry	*Gaylussacia frondosa*
Deerberry	*Vaccinium stamineum*
Dewberry	*Rubus flagellaris*
Dwarf chestnut oak	*Quercus prinoides*
Dwarf huckleberry	*Gaylussacia dumosa*
Early lowbush blueberry	*Vaccinium pallidum*
Fetterbush	*Eubotrys racemosa*
Gray dogwood	*Cornus racemosa*
Great rhododendron	*Rhododendron maximum*
Groundsel bush	*Baccharis halimifolia*
Highbush blueberry	*Vaccinium corymbosum*
Huckleberry	*Gaylussacia* spp.
Indigo bush	*Amorpha fruticosa*
Inkberry	*Ilex glabra*
Japanese barberry	*Berberis thunbergii*
Large cranberry	*Vaccinium macrocarpon*
Late lowbush blueberry	*Vaccinium angustifolium*
Leatherleaf	*Chamaedaphne calyculata*
Maleberry	*Lyonia ligustrina*

Part A: Plant Common Names to Scientific Names

Common name	Genus and species name
Maple-leaved viburnum	*Viburnum acerifolium*
Marsh elder	*Iva frutescens*
Mountain holly	*Nemopanthus mucronata*
Mountain laurel	*Kalmia latifolia*
Multiflora rose	*Rosa multiflora*
Naked witherod	*Viburnum nudum*
Nannyberry	*Viburnum lentago*
Pinxter flower	*Rhododendron periclymenoides*
Sand myrtle	*Leiophyllum buxifolium*
Scrub oak	*Quercus ilicifolia*
Sheep laurel	*Kalmia angustifolia*
Shrubby cinquefoil	*Potentilla fruticosa*
Silky dogwood	*Cornus amomum*
Small cranberry	*Vaccinium oxycoccus*
Smooth alder	*Alnus serrulata*
Smooth sumac	*Rhus glabra*
Speckled alder	*Alnus incana*
Spicebush	*Lindera benzoin*
Staggerbush	*Lyonia mariana*
Staghorn sumac	*Rhus typhina*
Swamp azalea	*Rhododendron viscosum*
Swamp dewberry	*Rubus hispidus*
Sweet fern	*Comptonia peregrina*
Sweet pepperbush	*Clethra alnifolia*
Wax myrtle	*Myrica cerifera*
Winged sumac	*Rhus copallina*
Winterberry	*Ilex verticillata*
Witch hazel	*Hamamelis virginiana*

Vines

American bittersweet	*Celastrus scandens*
Asiatic bittersweet	*Celastrus orbiculatus*
Common greenbrier	*Smilax rotundifolia*
Glaucous greenbrier	*Smilax glauca*
Japanese honeysuckle	*Lonicera japonica*
Poison ivy	*Toxicodendron radicans*
Virginia creeper	*Parthenocissus quinquefolia*
Wild grape	*Vitis* spp.

Part A: Plant Common Names to Scientific Names

Common name	Genus and species name
Herbs	
Agrimony	*Agrimonia* spp.
Annual salt marsh aster	*Aster subulatus*
Arrow arum	*Peltandra virginica*
Arrowhead	*Sagittaria latifolia*
Arrow-leaved tearthumb	*Polygonum sagittatum*
Aster	*Aster* spp.
Bayonet rush	*Juncus militaris*
Beach heather	*Hudsonia tomentosa*
Beach pea	*Lathyrus japonicus*
Beach pinweed	*Lechea maritima*
Bead lily	*Clintonia borealis*
Beardgrass	*Andropogon glomeratus*
Beechdrops	*Epifagus virginiana*
Bentgrass	*Agrostis* spp.
Big bluestem	*Andropogon gerardi*
Big cordgrass	*Spartina cynosuroides*
Black-eyed susan	*Rudbeckia hirta*
Black grass	*Juncus gerardi*
Black oatgrass	*Stipa avenacea*
Black snakeroot	*Cimifuga racemosa*
Bladderwort	*Utricularia* spp.
Blue flag	*Iris versicolor*
Bluejoint	*Calamagrostis canadensis*
Blunt manna-grass	*Glyceria obtusa*
Bog asphodel	*Narthecium americanum*
Bristly sarsaparilla	*Aralia hispida*
Broad-leaved cattail	*Typha latifolia*
Broomsedge	*Andropogon virginicus*
Brown-fruited rush	*Juncus pelocarpus*
Bulrush	*Scirpus* spp.
Bunchberry	*Cornus canadensis*
Bur-reed	*Sparganium* spp.
Butter-and-eggs	*Linaria vulgaris*
Button sedge	*Carex bullata*
Canada bluegrass	*Poa compressa*
Canada mayflower	*Maianthemum canadense*
Canada rush	*Juncus canadensis*
Canada thistle	*Cirsium arvense*
Chicory	*Cichorium intybus*

Part A: Plant Common Names to Scientific Names

Common name	Genus and species name
Coast sedge	*Carex exilis*
Cocklebur	*Xanthium strumarium*
Collins sedge	*Carex collinsii*
Columbine	*Aquilegia canadensis*
Common beak-rush	*Rhynchospora capitellata*
Common cinquefoil	*Potentilla simplex*
Common mullein	*Verbascum thapsus*
Common rush	*Juncus effusus*
Common ragweed	*Ambrosia artemisiifolia*
Common St. Johnswort	*Hypericum perforatum*
Coppery St. Johnswort	*Hypericum denticulatum*
Cottongrass	*Eriophorum virginicum*
Cow-wheat	*Melampyrum lineare*
Cross-leaved milkwort	*Polygala cruciata*
Dandelion	*Taraxacum officinale*
Duckweed	*Lemna* spp.
Dunegrass	*Ammophila breviligulata*
Dusty miller	*Artemisia stelleriana*
Early goldenrod	*Solidago juncea*
Enchanter's nightshade	*Circaea lutetiana*
English plantain	*Plantago lanceolata*
Eulalia grass	*Microstegium vimineum*
False asphodel	*Tofieldia racemosa*
False nettle	*Boehmeria cylindrica*
False Solomon's-seal	*Smilacina racemosa*
Fanwort	*Cabomba caroliniana*
Field chamomile	*Anthemis arvensis*
Field garlic	*Allium vineale*
Fringed gentian	*Gentianopsis crinita*
Frostweed	*Helianthemum canadense*
Garlic mustard	*Alliaria petiolata*
Glasswort	*Salicornia* spp.
Goat's-rue	*Tephrosia virginica*
Golden crest	*Lophiola aurea*
Golden heather	*Hudsonia ericoides*
Goldenrod	*Solidago* spp.
Goldthread	*Coptis trifolia*
Grass-leaved blazing star	*Liatris graminifolia*
Grass-leaved goldenrod	*Euthamia graminifolia*
Grass-of-Parnassus	*Parnassia glauca*

Part A: Plant Common Names to Scientific Names

Common name	Genus and species name
Gray goldenrod	*Solidago nemoralis*
Hairgrass	*Deschampsia flexuosa*
Halberd-leaved tearthumb	*Polygonum arifolium*
Hawkweed	*Hieracium* spp.
Hoary mountain-mint	*Pycnanthemum incanum*
Hog peanut	*Amphicarpa bracteata*
Horseweed	*Conyza canadensis*
Jack-in-the-pulpit	*Arisaema triphyllum*
Jewelweed	*Impatiens capensis*
Joe-pye weed	*Eupatorium* spp.
Kentucky bluegrass	*Poa pratensis*
King devil hawkweed	*Hieracium caespitosum*
Kneiskern's beak-rush	*Rhynchospora kneiskernii*
Lance-leaved sabatia	*Sabatia difformis*
Little bluestem	*Schizachyrium scoparium*
Lizard's-tail	*Saururus cernuus*
Long sedge	*Carex folliculata*
Manna-grass	*Glyceria striata*
Marsh marigold	*Caltha palustris*
Marsh St. Johnswort	*Triadenum virginicum*
Mayapple	*Podophyllum peltatum*
Mouse-ear chickweed	*Cerastium vulgatum*
Narrow-leaved cattail	*Typha angustifolia*
Nodding beggar-ticks	*Bidens cernua*
Olney's three-square	*Scirpus americanus*
Orache	*Atriplex patula*
Orchard grass	*Dactylis glomerata*
Ox-eye daisy	*Chrysanthemum leucanthemum*
Pale corydalis	*Corydalis sempervirens*
Partridgeberry	*Mitchella repens*
Pennsylvania sedge	*Carex pensylvanica*
Perennial salt marsh aster	*Aster tenuifolius*
Phragmites	*Phragmites australis*
Pickerelweed	*Pontederia cordata*
Pickering's morning glory	*Stylisma pickeringii*
Pilewort	*Erechtites hieracifolia*
Pitcher plant	*Sarracenia purpurea*
Pokeweed	*Phytolacca americana*
Poverty oatgrass	*Danthonia spicata*
Prickly lettuce	*Lactuca serriola*

Part A: Plant Common Names to Scientific Names

Common name	Genus and species name
Prickly pear	*Opuntia humifusa*
Primrose-leaved violet	*Viola primulifolia*
Purple loosestrife	*Lythrum salicaria*
Pyxie moss	*Pyxidanthera barbulata*
Rattlesnake weed	*Hieracium venosum*
Red clover	*Trifolium pratense*
Red trillium	*Trillium erectum*
Rice cutgrass	*Leersia oryzoides*
Rose mallow	*Hibiscus moscheutos*
Round-leaved sundew	*Drosera rotundifolia*
Rue anemone	*Anemonella thalictroides*
Salt marsh bulrush	*Scirpus robustus*
Salt marsh cordgrass	*Spartina alterniflora*
Salt marsh fleabane	*Pluchea odorata*
Salt-meadow grass	*Spartina patens*
Saltwort	*Salsola kali*
Sandbur	*Cenchrus tribuloides*
Sandgrass	*Triplasis purpurea*
Sand spurry	*Spergularia rubra*
Sea-beach panic-grass	*Panicum amarum*
Sea-beach three-awn	*Aristida tuberculosa*
Sea blite	*Suaeda* spp.
Sea lavender	*Limonium carolinianum*
Sea-pink	*Sabatia stellaris*
Sea rocket	*Cakile edentula*
Seaside goldenrod	*Solidago sempervirens*
Seaside mallow	*Kosteletzkya virginica*
Seaside spurge	*Euphorbia polygonifolia*
Skunk cabbage	*Symplocarpus foetidus*
Slender glasswort	*Salicornia europaea*
Slender spike grass	*Chasmanthium laxum*
Smartweed	*Polygonum* spp.
Smooth crabgrass	*Digitaria ischaemum*
Sneezeweed	*Helenium autumnale*
Solomon's-seal	*Polygonatum biflorum*
Spatterdock	*Nuphar advena*
Spatulate-leaved sundew	*Drosera intermedia*
Spike grass	*Distichlis spicata*
Spike-rush	*Eleocharis* spp.
Spotted wintergreen	*Chimaphila maculata*

Part A: Plant Common Names to Scientific Names

Common name	Genus and species name
Spring beauty	*Claytonia virginica*
Starved panic-grass	*Panicum depauperatum*
Stemless lady's-slipper	*Cypripedium acaule*
Stiff aster	*Aster linariifolius*
Sundew	*Drosera* spp.
Swamp loosestrife	*Decodon verticillatus*
Swamp milkweed	*Asclepias incarnata*
Sweet flag	*Acorus calamus*
Sweet goldenrod	*Solidago odora*
Switchgrass	*Panicum virgatum*
Thread-leaved sundew	*Drosera filiformis*
Three-leaved false Solomon's-seal	*Smilacina trifolia*
Tickseed-sunflower	*Bidens* spp.
Trailing arbutus	*Epigaea repens*
Trout lily	*Erythronium americanum*
Tufted loosestrife	*Lysimachia thyrsiflora*
Turkeybeard	*Xerophyllum asphodeloides*
Tussock sedge	*Carex stricta*
Twig rush	*Cladium mariscoides*
Virginia bluebell	*Mertensia virginica*
Water hemp	*Amaranthus cannabinus*
Water lily	*Nymphaea odorata*
Water meal	*Wolffia* spp.
White baneberry	*Actaea pachypoda*
White beak-rush	*Rhynchospora alba*
White clover	*Trifolium repens*
Wild calla	*Calla palustris*
Wild carrot	*Daucus carota*
Wild ginger	*Asarum canadense*
Wild indigo	*Baptisia tinctoria*
Wild licorice	*Galium circaezans*
Wild parsnip	*Pastinaca sativa*
Wild radish	*Raphanus raphanistrum*
Wild rice	*Zizania aquatica*
Wild sarsaparilla	*Aralia nudicaulis*
Wild strawberry	*Fragaria virginiana*
Wintergreen	*Gaultheria procumbens*
Wintercress	*Barbarea vulgaris*
Wood anemone	*Anemone quinquefolia*
Woodreed	*Cinna arundinacea*

Part A: Plant Common Names to Scientific Names

Common name	Genus and species name
Woolgrass	*Scirpus cyperinus*
Woolly panic-grass	*Panicum lanuginosum*
Yarrow	*Achillea millefolium*
Yellow foxtail	*Setaria glauca*
Yellow water crowfoot	*Ranunculus flabellaris*

Ferns and fern allies

Bog fern	*Thelypteris simulata*
Bracken fern	*Pteridium aquilinum*
Christmas fern	*Polystichum acrostichoides*
Cinnamon fern	*Osmunda cinnamomea*
Common polypody	*Polypodium virginianum*
Curly-grass fern	*Schizaea pusilla*
Ground pine	*Lycopodium* spp.
Hay-scented fern	*Dennstaedtia punctilobula*
Interrupted fern	*Osmunda claytoni*
Marsh fern	*Thelypteris palustris*
Netted chain fern	*Woodwardia areolata*
New York fern	*Thelypteris noveboracensis*
Royal fern	*Osmunda regalis*
Sensitive fern	*Onoclea sensibilis*
Spinulose woodfern	*Dryopteris carthusiana*
Tree clubmoss	*Lycopodium obscurum*
Virginia chain fern	*Woodwardia virginica*

Lichens and mosses

Awned haircap moss	*Polytrichum piliferum*
Blistered rock tripe	*Lasallia papulosa*
Coastal plain ladder lichen	*Cladonia rappii*
Dimelaena	*Dimelaena oreina*
False reindeer lichen	*Cladina subtenuis*
Juniper haircap moss	*Polytrichum juniperinum*
Haircap moss	*Polytrichum* spp.
Ohio haircap moss	*Polytrichum ohioense*
Peat moss	*Sphagnum* spp.
Rock lichen	*Xanthoparmelia conspersa*
Rock moss	*Dicranum* spp.
Smooth rock tripe	*Umbilicaria mammulata*
Thread moss	*Bryum* spp.
Thorn lichen	*Cladonia uncialis*
White moss	*Leucobryum glaucum*

Part B: Plant Scientific Names to Common Names

Genus and species name	Common name
Coniferous Trees	
Chamaecyparis thyoides	Atlantic white cedar
Juniperus virginiana	Red cedar
Larix laricina	American larch
Picea mariana	Black spruce
Pinus echinata	Shortleaf pine
Pinus rigida	Pitch pine
Pinus strobus	White pine
Pinus taeda	Loblolly pine
Pinus virginiana	Virginia pine
Tsuga canadensis	Eastern hemlock
Deciduous Trees	
Acer negundo	Box elder
Acer pensylvanicum	Striped maple
Acer platanoides	Norway maple
Acer rubrum	Red maple
Acer saccharinum	Silver maple
Acer saccharum	Sugar maple
Ailanthus altissima	Ailanthus
Amelanchier arborea	Downy juneberry
Amelanchier canadensis	Shadbush
Amelanchier laevis	Smooth juneberry
Betula alleghaniensis	Yellow birch
Betula lenta	Black birch
Betula nigra	River birch
Betula papyrifera	Paper birch
Betula populifolia	Gray birch
Carpinus caroliniana	Ironwood
Carya glabra	Pignut hickory
Carya ovalis	Sweet pignut hickory
Carya ovata	Shagbark hickory
Carya pallida	Sand hickory
Carya tomentosa	Mockernut hickory
Castanea dentata	American chestnut
Celtis occidentalis	Hackberry
Cornus florida	Flowering dogwood
Crataegus spp.	Hawthorn
Diospyros virginiana	Persimmon
Fagus grandifolia	American beech

Part B: Plant Scientific Names to Common Names

Genus and species name	Common name
Fraxinus americana	White ash
Gleditsia triacanthos	Honey locust
Ilex opaca	American holly
Juglans nigra	Black walnut
Liquidambar styraciflua	Sweet gum
Liriodendron tulipifera	Tulip tree
Magnolia virginiana	Sweet bay magnolia
Morus alba	White mulberry
Nyssa sylvatica	Sour gum
Ostrya virginiana	Hop hornbeam
Platanus occidentalis	Sycamore
Populus balsamifera	Balsam poplar
Populus grandidentata	Big-toothed aspen
Populus tremuloides	Trembling aspen
Prunus avium	Sweet cherry
Prunus serotina	Black cherry
Quercus alba	White oak
Quercus bicolor	Swamp white oak
Quercus coccinea	Scarlet oak
Quercus falcata	Spanish oak
Quercus marilandica	Blackjack oak
Quercus michauxii	Basket oak
Quercus nigra	Water oak
Quercus palustris	Pin oak
Quercus phellos	Willow oak
Quercus prinus	Chestnut oak
Quercus rubra	Red oak
Quercus stellata	Post oak
Quercus velutina	Black oak
Robinia pseudoacacia	Black locust
Salix spp.	Willow
Salix nigra	Black willow
Sassafras albidum	Sassafras
Sorbus americana	American mountain ash
Tilia americana	Basswood
Ulmus americana	American elm

Part B: Plant Scientific Names to Common Names

Genus and species name	Common name
Shrubs	
Alnus spp.	Alder
Alnus incana	Speckled alder
Alnus serrulata	Smooth alder
Amorpha fruticosa	Indigo bush
Andromeda glaucophylla	Bog rosemary
Arctostaphylos uva-ursi	Bearberry
Aronia melanocarpa	Black chokeberry
Baccharis halimifolia	Groundsel bush
Berberis thunbergii	Japanese barberry
Cephalanthus occidentalis	Buttonbush
Chamaedaphne calyculata	Leatherleaf
Clethra alnifolia	Sweet pepperbush
Comptonia peregrina	Sweet fern
Corema conradii	Broom crowberry
Cornus amomum	Silky dogwood
Cornus racemosa	Gray dogwood
Corylus americana	American hazel
Corylus cornuta	Beaked hazel
Diervilla lonicera	Bush honeysuckle
Eubotrys racemosa	Fetterbush
Euonymus americanus	American strawberry-bush
Gaylussacia spp.	Huckleberry
Gaylussacia baccata	Black huckleberry
Gaylussacia dumosa	Dwarf huckleberry
Gaylussacia frondosa	Dangleberry
Hamamelis virginiana	Witch hazel
Ilex glabra	Inkberry
Ilex verticillata	Winterberry
Iva frutescens	Marsh elder
Kalmia angustifolia	Sheep laurel
Kalmia latifolia	Mountain laurel
Kalmia polifolia	Bog laurel
Leiophyllum buxifolium	Sand myrtle
Lindera benzoin	Spicebush
Lyonia ligustrina	Maleberry
Lyonia mariana	Staggerbush
Myrica cerifera	Wax myrtle
Myrica pensylvanica	Bayberry
Nemopanthus mucronata	Mountain holly

Part B: Plant Scientific Names to Common Names

Genus and species name	Common name
Potentilla fruticosa	Shrubby cinquefoil
Prunus maritima	Beach plum
Quercus ilicifolia	Scrub oak
Quercus prinoides	Dwarf chestnut oak
Rhododendron maximum	Great rhododendron
Rhododendron periclymenoides	Pinxter flower
Rhododendron viscosum	Swamp azalea
Rhus copallina	Winged sumac
Rhus glabra	Smooth sumac
Rhus typhina	Staghorn sumac
Rosa multiflora	Multiflora rose
Rubus spp.	Blackberry, raspberry
Rubus flagellaris	Dewberry
Rubus hispidus	Swamp dewberry
Sambucus canadensis	Common elder
Symphoricarpos orbiculatus	Coralberry
Vaccinium spp.	Blueberry, cranberry
Vaccinium angustifolium	Late lowbush blueberry
Vaccinium corymbosum	Highbush blueberry
Vaccinium macrocarpon	Large cranberry
Vaccinium oxycoccus	Small cranberry
Vaccinium pallidum	Early lowbush blueberry
Vaccinium stamineum	Deerberry
Viburnum acerifolium	Maple-leaved viburnum
Viburnum dentatum	Arrowwood
Viburnum lentago	Nannyberry
Viburnum nudum	Naked witherod
Viburnum prunifolium	Black haw

Vines

Celastrus orbiculatus	Asiatic bittersweet
Celastrus scandens	American bittersweet
Lonicera japonica	Japanese honeysuckle
Parthenocissus quinquefolia	Virginia creeper
Smilax glauca	Glaucous greenbrier
Smilax rotundifolia	Common greenbrier
Toxicodendron radicans	Poison ivy
Vitis spp.	Wild grape

Part B: Plant Scientific Names to Common Names

Genus and species name	Common name
Herbs	
Achillea millefolium	Yarrow
Acorus calamus	Sweet flag
Actaea pachypoda	White baneberry
Agrimonia spp.	Agrimony
Agrostis spp.	Bentgrass
Alliaria petiolata	Garlic mustard
Allium vineale	Field garlic
Amaranthus cannabinus	Water hemp
Ambrosia artemisiifolia	Common ragweed
Ammophila breviligulata	Dunegrass
Amphicarpa bracteata	Hog peanut
Andropogon gerardi	Big bluestem
Andropogon glomeratus	Beardgrass
Andropogon virginicus	Broomsedge
Anemone quinquefolia	Wood anemone
Anemonella thalictroides	Rue anemone
Anthemis arvensis	Field chamomile
Aquilegia canadensis	Columbine
Aralia hispida	Bristly sarsaparilla
Aralia nudicaulis	Wild sarsaparilla
Arisaema triphyllum	Jack-in-the-pulpit
Aristida tuberculosa	Sea-beach three-awn
Artemisia stelleriana	Dusty miller
Asarum canadense	Wild ginger
Asclepias incarnata	Swamp milkweed
Aster spp.	Aster
Aster linariifolius	Stiff aster
Aster subulatus	Annual salt marsh aster
Aster tenuifolius	Perennial salt marsh aster
Atriplex patula	Orache
Baptisia tinctoria	Wild indigo
Barbarea vulgaris	Wintercress
Bidens spp.	Tickseed-sunflower
Bidens cernua	Nodding beggar-ticks
Boehmeria cylindrica	False nettle
Cabomba caroliniana	Fanwort
Cakile edentula	Sea rocket
Calamagrostis canadensis	Bluejoint
Calla palustris	Wild calla

Part B: Plant Scientific Names to Common Names

Genus and species name	Common name
Caltha palustris	Marsh marigold
Carex bullata	Button sedge
Carex collinsii	Collins sedge
Carex exilis	Coast sedge
Carex folliculata	Long sedge
Carex pensylvanica	Pennsylvania sedge
Carex stricta	Tussock sedge
Cenchrus tribuloides	Sandbur
Cerastium vulgatum	Mouse-ear chickweed
Chasmanthium laxum	Slender spike grass
Chimaphila maculata	Spotted wintergreen
Chrysanthemum leucanthemum	Ox-eye daisy
Cichorium intybus	Chicory
Cimifuga racemosa	Black snakeroot
Cinna arundinacea	Woodreed
Circaea lutetiana	Enchanter's nightshade
Cirsium arvense	Canada thistle
Cladium mariscoides	Twig rush
Claytonia virginica	Spring beauty
Clintonia borealis	Bead lily
Conyza canadensis	Horseweed
Coptis trifolia	Goldthread
Cornus canadensis	Bunchberry
Corydalis sempervirens	Pale corydalis
Cypripedium acaule	Stemless lady's-slipper
Dactylis glomerata	Orchard grass
Danthonia spicata	Poverty oatgrass
Daucus carota	Wild carrot
Decodon verticillatus	Swamp loosestrife
Deschampsia flexuosa	Hairgrass
Digitaria ischaemum	Smooth crabgrass
Distichlis spicata	Spike grass
Drosera spp.	Sundew
Drosera filiformis	Thread-leaved sundew
Drosera intermedia	Spatulate-leaved sundew
Drosera rotundifolia	Round-leaved sundew
Eleocharis spp.	Spike-rush
Epifagus virginiana	Beechdrops
Epigaea repens	Trailing arbutus
Erechtites hieracifolia	Pilewort

Part B: Plant Scientific Names to Common Names

Genus and species name	Common name
Eriophorum virginicum	Cottongrass
Erythronium americanum	Trout lily
Eupatorium spp.	Joe-pye weed, boneset
Euphorbia polygonifolia	Seaside spurge
Euthamia graminifolia	Grass-leaved goldenrod
Fragaria virginiana	Wild strawberry
Galium circaezans	Wild licorice
Gaultheria procumbens	Wintergreen
Gentianopsis crinita	Fringed gentian
Glyceria obtusa	Blunt manna-grass
Glyceria striata	Manna-grass
Helenium autumnale	Sneezeweed
Helianthemum canadense	Frostweed
Hibiscus moscheutos	Rose mallow
Hieracium spp.	Hawkweed
Hieracium caespitosum	King devil hawkweed
Hieracium venosum	Rattlesnake weed
Hudsonia ericoides	Golden heather
Hudsonia tomentosa	Beach heather
Hypericum denticulatum	Coppery St. Johnswort
Hypericum perforatum	Common St. Johnswort
Impatiens capensis	Jewelweed
Iris versicolor	Blue flag
Juncus canadensis	Canada rush
Juncus effusus	Common rush
Juncus gerardi	Black grass
Juncus militaris	Bayonet rush
Juncus pelocarpus	Brown-fruited rush
Kosteletzkya virginica	Seaside mallow
Lactuca serriola	Prickly lettuce
Lathyrus japonicus	Beach pea
Lechea maritima	Beach pinweed
Leersia oryzoides	Rice cutgrass
Lemna spp.	Duckweed
Liatris graminifolia	Grass-leaved blazing star
Limonium carolinianum	Sea lavender
Linaria vulgaris	Butter-and-eggs
Lophiola aurea	Golden crest
Lysimachia thyrsiflora	Tufted loosestrife
Lythrum salicaria	Purple loosestrife

Part B: Plant Scientific Names to Common Names

Genus and species name	Common name
Maianthemum canadense	Canada mayflower
Melampyrum lineare	Cow-wheat
Mertensia virginica	Virginia bluebell
Microstegium vimineum	Eulalia grass
Mitchella repens	Partridgeberry
Narthecium americanum	Bog asphodel
Nuphar advena	Spatterdock
Nymphaea odorata	Water lily
Opuntia humifusa	Prickly pear
Panicum amarum	Sea-beach panic-grass
Panicum depauperatum	Starved panic-grass
Panicum lanuginosum	Woolly panic-grass
Panicum virgatum	Switchgrass
Parnassia glauca	Grass-of-Parnassus
Pastinaca sativa	Wild parsnip
Peltandra virginica	Arrow arum
Phragmites australis	Phragmites
Phytolacca americana	Pokeweed
Plantago lanceolata	English plantain
Pluchea odorata	Salt marsh fleabane
Poa compressa	Canada bluegrass
Poa pratensis	Kentucky bluegrass
Podophyllum peltatum	Mayapple
Polygala cruciata	Cross-leaved milkwort
Polygonatum biflorum	Solomon's-seal
Polygonum spp.	Smartweed
Polygonum arifolium	Halberd-leaved tearthumb
Polygonum sagittatum	Arrow-leaved tearthumb
Pontederia cordata	Pickerelweed
Potentilla simplex	Common cinquefoil
Pycnanthemum incanum	Hoary mountain-mint
Pyxidanthera barbulata	Pyxie moss
Ranunculus flabellaris	Yellow water crowfoot
Raphanus raphanistrum	Wild radish
Rhynchospora alba	White beak-rush
Rhynchospora capitellata	Common beak-rush
Rhynchospora kneiskernii	Kneiskern's beak-rush
Rudbeckia hirta	Black-eyed susan
Sabatia difformis	Lance-leaved sabatia
Sabatia stellaris	Sea-pink

Part B: Plant Scientific Names to Common Names

Genus and species name	Common name
Sagittaria latifolia	Arrowhead
Salicornia spp.	Glasswort
Salicornia europaea	Slender glasswort
Salsola kali	Saltwort
Sarracenia purpurea	Pitcher plant
Saururus cernuus	Lizard's-tail
Schizachyrium scoparium	Little bluestem
Scirpus spp.	Bulrush
Scirpus americanus	Olney's three-square
Scirpus cyperinus	Woolgrass
Scirpus robustus	Salt marsh bulrush
Setaria glauca	Yellow foxtail
Smilacina racemosa	False Solomon's-seal
Smilacina trifolia	Three-leaved false Solomon's-seal
Solidago spp.	Goldenrod
Solidago juncea	Early goldenrod
Solidago nemoralis	Gray goldenrod
Solidago odora	Sweet goldenrod
Solidago sempervirens	Seaside goldenrod
Sparganium spp.	Bur-reed
Spartina alterniflora	Salt marsh cordgrass
Spartina cynosuroides	Big cordgrass
Spartina patens	Salt-meadow grass
Spergularia rubra	Sand spurry
Stipa avenacea	Black oatgrass
Stylisma pickeringii	Pickering's morning glory
Suaeda spp.	Sea blite
Symplocarpus foetidus	Skunk cabbage
Taraxacum officinale	Dandelion
Tephrosia virginica	Goat's-rue
Tofieldia racemosa	False asphodel
Triadenum virginicum	Marsh St. Johnswort
Trifolium pratense	Red clover
Trifolium repens	White clover
Trillium erectum	Red trillium
Triplasis purpurea	Sandgrass
Typha angustifolia	Narrow-leaved cattail
Typha latifolia	Broad-leaved cattail
Utricularia spp.	Bladderwort
Verbascum thapsus	Common mullein

Part B: Plant Scientific Names to Common Names

Genus and species name	Common name
Viola primulifolia	Primrose-leaved violet
Wolffia spp.	Water meal
Xanthium strumarium	Cocklebur
Xerophyllum asphodeloides	Turkeybeard
Zizania aquatica	Wild rice

Ferns and fern allies

Dennstaedtia punctilobula	Hay-scented fern
Dryopteris carthusiana	Spinulose woodfern
Lycopodium spp.	Ground pine
Lycopodium obscurum	Tree clubmoss
Onoclea sensibilis	Sensitive fern
Osmunda cinnamomea	Cinnamon fern
Osmunda claytoni	Interrupted fern
Osmunda regalis	Royal fern
Polypodium virginianum	Common polypody
Polystichum acrostichoides	Christmas fern
Pteridium aquilinum	Bracken fern
Schizaea pusilla	Curly-grass fern
Thelypteris noveboracensis	New York fern
Thelypteris palustris	Marsh fern
Thelypteris simulata	Bog fern
Woodwardia areolata	Netted chain fern
Woodwardia virginica	Virginia chain fern

Lichens and mosses

Bryum spp.	Thread moss
Cladina subtenuis	False reindeer lichen
Cladonia rappii	Coastal plain ladder lichen
Cladonia uncialis	Thorn lichen
Dicranum spp.	Rock moss
Dimelaena oreina	Dimelaena
Lasallia papulosa	Blistered rock tripe
Leucobryum glaucum	White moss
Polytrichum spp.	Haircap moss
Polytrichum juniperinum	Juniper haircap moss
Polytrichum ohioense	Ohio haircap moss
Polytrichum piliferum	Awned haircap moss
Sphagnum spp.	Peat moss
Umbilicaria mammulata	Smooth rock tripe
Xanthoparmelia conspersa	Rock lichen

References

Anderson, Karl. 1989. *A Check List of the Plants of New Jersey, 1989.* Franklin Lakes, N.J.: New Jersey Audubon Society.

Bailey, Liberty Hyde. 1963. *How Plants Get Their Names.* New York: Dover.

Fernald, Merritt L. 1950. *Gray's Manual of Botany,* 8th ed. New York: Van Nostrand.

Gleason, Henry A., and Arthur Cronquist. 1991. *Manual of Vascular Plants of Northeastern United States and Adjacent Canada,* 2d ed. New York: New York Botanical Garden.

Index

About the Authors

Beryl Robichaud Collins co-authored, with Murray F. Buell, *Vegetation of New Jersey* (Rutgers University Press, 1973). Karl H. Anderson is director of Rancocas Nature Center in Mount Holly, New Jersey.